The Work We Need

A 21st Century Reimagining

HILARY COTTAM

virago

VIRAGO

First published in Great Britain in 2025 by Virago Press

1 3 5 7 9 10 8 6 4 2

A CIP catalogue record for this book
is available from the British Library.

ISBN 978-0-349-01747-1

Typeset in Bembo by M Rules
Printed and bound in Great Britain by
Clays Ltd, Elcograf S.p.A.

Papers used by Virago are from well-managed forests
and other responsible sources.

FSC
www.fsc.org
MIX
Paper | Supporting
responsible forestry
FSC® C104740

Virago Press
An imprint of
Little, Brown Book Group
Carmelite House
50 Victoria Embankment
London EC4Y 0DZ

The authorised representative
in the EEA is
Hachette Ireland
8 Castlecourt Centre
Dublin 15, D15 XTP3, Ireland
(email: info@hbgi.ie)

An Hachette UK Company
www.hachette.co.uk

www.virago.co.ukk

The Work We Need

ALSO BY HILARY COTTAM

Radical Help

For Mabel,
and for everyone searching
for a new way to work and live

Contents

It is possible that a tempest (long lurking in the clouds) might bring us closer to how we want to be in the world.

DEBORAH LEVY
The Cost of Living

To be truly radical is to make hope possible, rather than despair convincing.

RAYMOND WILLIAMS
Resources of Hope

Preface

None of us can live well without good work. Good work is at the heart of good lives, strong communities and nations that have a shared dignity and sense of destiny. And yet work too often fails to engage our hearts and minds; it gobbles up scarce resources; it takes the time we need to live well and to take care of one another; and, most egregiously, for many millions it fails to provide a basic income. Something has gone wrong – something that traditional economics is powerless to fix.

But we live in revolutionary times. Technology, an ecological crisis and the challenges of deep injustice are upending our world. These forces are changing how we work. They are also prompting us to ask big questions about how we want to live. Could this be a moment to rethink how we work and therefore how we live?

Perhaps such a question sounds idealistic, almost absurd, when so many of us are struggling. But history tells us that it is in the dark times, in the moments of upheaval, that we can – if we are ready – think again.

Five years ago, I set out on a journey seeking the insights of everyday experts: those of us who work. I travelled across Britain and the United States, spending time with people of all ages and from all walks of life; those working long hours for immiserating wages and those whose work offers good pay and interesting prospects. I also spent time with business leaders, academic experts and policymakers.

I asked a simple question: How could we redesign our working lives?

What I have heard in response are rich stories about possible futures. I have heard imaginings which are widely shared and largely hidden. I have learnt that we are exhausted by tips for work–life balance, conversations about whether we should return to the office, or whether the magical promises made about AI will be good or bad for workers. We are yearning for a collective redesign of the values and assumptions that underpin work.

This is a book about ideas that are within our grasp: they are 'do-able', would be good for us, for business, for the natural world and the places where we live. This is a book about hope.

It's also a warning. Silenced or unheard, these ideas can and do wither. Or – as is increasingly happening – they find alternative and sometimes violent outlets: a desire to burn the house down, to make any change, no matter how potentially destructive, in order to break open the social and economic systems that stifle us.

Our challenges are tangled and real, but so are our imaginative answers. This book shows how we can listen and design anew.

Part I

Opening

Who Wants to Reimagine Work?

'Why can't we just rethink it top to bottom?' Heads bowed over a table, a small team of municipal workers – grave-diggers, park gardeners and drivers of gritter lorries sat together. Grabbing the pens in front of them, they started to draw, designing a new and different working life.

'Thing is,' Jonny, one of the grave-diggers, explained, 'I don't want to work until I'm broken. I don't want to take the same weeks of holiday every year, without a chance to travel or really learn. I don't want to try and care for my family in the gaps in between. Aye, why can't we just rethink it top to bottom?'

I had asked what a good working life might look like, and Jonny drew a complex web: an imagined life which does not simply progress from school to work, to retirement and death. Jonny left school at fifteen. Now just turned fifty-five, in a hi-vis jacket and with a pair of horn-rimmed reading glasses perched on his nose, he has the air of someone experienced and happy in his skin. He knows he's lucky to have decent work in Kilmarnock, a town where that's hard to find. But he and his colleagues can also imagine something much bigger: a radically altered life in which patterns of work, life and learning intersect in new ways. Jonny's dream life includes his work, and a chance to do quite different work at various stages; an opportunity to teach others – he particularly cares about young people in the town; and the time for a 'curiosity' project.

On he and his colleagues draw.

Can we reimagine our working lives? That's the question at the heart of this book. Redesigning the way we work would allow us to live differently, to organise our days, our communities and our economies in ways which might suit us very much better, ways that might enable us and the wider systems we are part of to grow and flourish.

This might sound idealistic, but the reality is that millions of us find our working lives no longer seem to fit. For those at the sharp end, work doesn't pay. Most families living in poverty in Britain and the United States have work, but their pay cheque is not enough to cover basic monthly bills. At the other end of an increasingly unequal work spectrum, where salaries are high, conditions are also harsh. Here, the phenomenon of 'greedy jobs' is widespread. Greedy jobs pay large salaries in return for long and inflexible hours. In any work where there is intense competition to make partner, get tenure or gain a significant promotion, success is predicated on putting all other areas of life on hold.

Work draws us too far from the rest of life, but few dare complain. A place at the top of the modern corporation feels precarious; a job in the arts is precious and hard-won: there is the ever-present fear you might fail, fall or be pushed. Wealth brings its own psychological pressures to keep up with peers, with earnings, with looking good.

The intense and competitive cultures of senior positions often cause stress to women in particular. While increasing numbers of men are keen to take on care-giving roles, it is still predominantly women who find themselves the primary care-givers, juggling the demands of work and home to the point of near-madness or, for some, making risky decisions to put off having the children they badly want. Those working at the most senior levels have more options – including incomes that allow them to outsource the work of care and household chores to others – but they suffer from burnout and the wretched guilt of feeling no job is adequately done, and that they are missing out, both at home and at work.

Of course, many of us are fortunate to have work we enjoy, and which offers decent material rewards. This is important because these examples of work offer us clues as to what a good working life can look like.

But the scratchy sense of discomfort that fuels the billion-dollar industry of books on work-life balance, work-coaching and work-based 'wellness' programmes reveal the truth for most of us. We are disenchanted with work, and we are seeking change. It's this disenchantment that lies behind many of the demands to work from home or the subtle protest movements; the so-called quiet quitting, through which young people reputedly find ways to do the least work possible. The Great Resignation made headlines following the Covid-19 pandemic, with workers on both sides of the Atlantic leaving their jobs as they searched for a new rhythm of life. In China the 'lying flat' movement, a protest about overwork and the stress of modern life, became a viral phenomenon through global exposure on TikTok. Young Chinese people posted pictures of themselves horizontal on park benches, in bed or on the office floor as a symbol of their desire to put work second and to step aside from long working hours and broader cultural expectations to compete and exceed at all costs.

We protest, we exchange coping tips with friends and colleagues, and we make small individual adjustments where we can, but we long for changes that are much, much bigger and go much further, for something shared.

I believe this longing is not idle fantasy. Redesigning our

working lives *is* possible. Work has been successively and radically reorganised many times across the centuries as the norms of the good life have shifted according to the ways we have harnessed nature, the possibilities of technology and changing cultural expectations around work. And all the signs are that we are on the cusp of a very big work revolution indeed.

In this century we sit at the confluence of three deep currents which will inevitably change work: a digital technology revolution and the disruptive possibilities of artificial intelligence and quantum computing; an ecological crisis which demands that we alter all our patterns of life, including our work; and a growing disquiet about many of the deeper forces of injustice, the effects of which show up in inequalities of pay, opportunity and working conditions.

What if the dramatic changes required – to direct the technological revolution, to live in a new relationship with our natural ecosystems, to restore balance and justice within communities – offered us the biggest promise imaginable: a chance to rethink who we are, a chance to redesign our working lives? What if, instead of fearing these deep currents, these seismic shifts and the impending changes they bring, we embraced the possibility within them? This possibility – this promise – is what this book is about.

My questions stem, in part, from my own experience. For many decades, my work has focused on the welfare state and on how our social systems might be better organised.

Working with communities, I have re-examined the designs for a social revolution, brought into being by William Beveridge, the man widely regarded as the architect of British postwar welfare systems. A man whose reach extends beyond British shores, since he travelled widely, working with Roosevelt on the design of the US New Deal and meeting with social reformers of all political colours from Spain to Scandinavia.

Beveridge was a labour economist with ideas that challenged prevailing orthodoxies. At the start of the twentieth century there was widespread concern among labour economists and policymakers about problems of unemployment and underemployment. Beveridge's peers – in a consensus that is not that different from much of today's prevailing political wisdom – thought the challenges were wages (too high or inelastic), migration (too many people moving from the countryside to the cities), and weak personal character (too many shirkers).

Beveridge disagreed. He had an alternative thesis: unemployment, he argued, was a result of industrial transition. In a 1909 pamphlet, *Unemployment: A Problem of Industry*, Beveridge argued that a technology revolution in the form of mass production was rapidly changing the structure of work. New social and economic institutions were needed to smooth workers' paths between one work system and another. Beveridge believed the moment required new designs for learning, for health, and for incomes, to support this transition. These ideas were the start of decades of collaborative civic experimentation and invention which would eventually lead to the birth of the welfare state and a social transformation – a revolution – which underpinned the growth of good work and economic productivity in the twentieth century.

Today we live in dramatically different times and Beveridge's blueprint no longer fits our world. In Britain and the United States, as in many other parts of the globe, we have cities, towns and rural areas without work – and, crucially, without good work. I have collaborated with communities in many of these places to create new forms of healthcare, support for families, for young people and for ageing. I'm immensely proud of this work which I believe provides a framework for a twenty-first-century welfare state; the story of my first book, *Radical Help*. But I increasingly realised something was missing: good work. There is no good welfare system which does not have good work at its heart. Without this foundation, everything else is a sticking plaster.

So what happens when this work is in short supply, cannot be accessed by local people or no longer exists? The disappearance of work takes multiple forms, most obvious of which is the disappearance of work which pays well. Today the welfare state spends much more on propping up wages than it spends on unemployment benefits. In a development that would surely shock Beveridge and most twentieth-century social campaigners, the welfare state now provides in-work benefits to eighteen million workers. These benefits are absolutely necessary for family survival. They are a transfer from the state to businesses, who are effectively refusing to adequately compensate their workers.

Work has also taken on new and onerous forms: uncertain contracts, for example, or expectations that we will work ever longer hours, making it impossible to care for one another or fit in basic household tasks. Once again, the welfare state acknowledges the problem, arguing that we need expanded mental health services to deal with the stress and promising more hours of childcare, while all the time trying to force us to take any work available. What is missing is a focus on the root cause of so many of our social and economic problems: the nature of the work on offer.

Observing these shifts in work and the ways in which they are determining individual lives, places and wider happiness has prompted me to ask a set of new questions. I started to ask the politicians who represent places without good work, the labour economists who design regional investment strategies and the policy experts who design national programmes such as Levelling Up what we should do. How should we design work? I found few answers and much despair.

I realised that my work also had to change course, and that something else was needed: new perspectives and new imaginings. I decided to start by talking with workers. I define workers as all of us who, in one way or another, live on wages as opposed to inheritance. I set out to ask people from all walks of life what we should do.*

I had two questions. What would a good working life look like in this century? What new forms of organisation are needed to make that a reality?

Pilgrimage as method

I'd arrived in Kilmarnock, a town towards the western edge of Scotland, where I met Jonny and the team, as a storm closed in. 'Chankin', the locals call it. The sort of weather that bites your bones. That day, we didn't know that the Covid-19 pandemic was about to engulf us. Huddled in a municipal meeting room, we'd been mainly worried about keeping warm.

Kilmarnock was once home to good work: mining, cotton mills and thriving industries of lace making and carpet weaving. The town is also the birthplace of the world-famous Johnnie Walker whisky, founded in 1820, when the eponymous Johnnie was fifteen years old. But in 2012, Diageo, the global corporation who today own the brand, closed the remaining local bottling plant with the loss of the last seven

---

* A worker, in this book and in my enquiry, is anyone who lives on an income paid in exchange for their work activity or while seeking work. It's a category that encompasses those who might be taking a break from this activity, such as to look after children or because they are unwell. It excludes those who live from inheritance or rental income from assets.

hundred (well paid) jobs. Brutally, bulldozers were used to demolish the plant and the street in which it was located. Work histories and cherished memories alike were erased.

It's a familiar story. Technology changes, work moves. Global corporations and their investors play a role, shifting jobs to places where wages can be lowered and protections quietly ignored. Too often the fabric of a place then crumbles and communities hollow out. The loss of mines and factories in a place like Kilmarnock means not only the loss of income within families and local places. It is a loss of belonging, a loss of a place in the world. In the vacuum where industrial work used to be, new forms of shady and illegal activity can grow. Suicide rates in Ayrshire, the county in which Kilmarnock is located, are high and cause particular anguish for Jonny and his colleagues.

These are times when stories can start to turn inwards, to double back on themselves. But there's another story that is entwined with this one. Kilmarnock is a place of strong communities and a place of civic invention. It's surrounded by extraordinary natural beauty. There's a nationally successful football team that everyone supports with rowdy enthusiasm, and there's an everyday kindness that comes from shared history and knowing your neighbours. 'Nobody is coming over the hill to rescue us,' I was told with realistic candour in many places. It's an attitude that in Kilmarnock has created new forms of local farming, good municipal work and more. This is the compost in which rich ideas about our future working lives are lying, dormant but ready to come to life.

Kilmarnock was my first destination. I've travelled to Barrow-in-Furness, where Britain's nuclear submarines are built in the famous 'yards'; to Grimsby, once the home of Britain's fishing industry and now a potential home of green energy; to Barnsley, also a former mining town and now a digital hub and the heart of Britain's warehouse distribution network. I have also worked in my own neighbourhood in Peckham, south London, in Barking in the east and also in the centre of the city, home to finance and the headquarters of global corporations. Later I was invited to work in the United States, and I journeyed east to west, from Baltimore to Detroit, then to the cradle of our current technology revolution: the San Francisco Bay Area. Every place I have been to shares a little of Kilmarnock's story of profound change while also being embroidered with its own unique twists and flourishes.

In asking my questions about work, I wanted to start with those who have already experienced a dramatic transition: with people living in places where good work has moved or morphed in shape. I was particularly interested in voices that are rarely heard. But not exclusively. I also travelled to the boardrooms of London and the tech headquarters of the San Francisco Bay Area because I wanted to find people doing new and different work in places where power is concentrated in Britain and the United States today.

I think of the journeys I made as a sort of pilgrimage – I was seeking stories; I was curious, I wanted to learn and, just as the pilgrim detaches themselves from their everyday world, I was unattached to any institution, wider project or theory.

My only role was to listen.

Pilgrimages rely on the kindness of strangers. I received this in abundance. I was offered places to stay, often in someone's home, and made connections with people and workers – all of whom shared their time with warm and open generosity. And I was taken into people's hearts, in the sharing of stories with deep personal meaning.

I had to 'toss aside' my previous convictions. The Black civil rights activist and author Malcolm X famously wrote of his own pilgrimage to Mecca, describing how he was changed by rubbing shoulders with those he would not usually meet and how the experience led to him 're-arranging' his thought patterns and expanding his ideas of 'brotherhood'. This is part of the joy of the pilgrimage: we travel with an open intent, unsure of what we will find, and, on some days, unsure even of the point of the journey.

Without the usual moorings, we can absorb different things and think new thoughts in community with those around us.

Anthropologists have long held a fascination with the idea of pilgrimage as a research method precisely because it disrupts both thought patterns and structures of power. The pilgrim does not arrive with a business card or a lengthy introduction about their importance or their work. The pilgrim hears both *official stories*, as told by those with formal authority, and the *unofficial stories* which bring alternative, sometimes previously hidden, perspectives on everyday realities. Pilgrimage allows those who are usually the objects of study – and presented as marginal – to be the critical thinkers, offering insight and agency to shape the research and its findings: how, in this case, good working lives should be designed.

I was drawn to this method knowing that research questions about work are usually posed by experts: by labour economists or policymakers who ask questions shaped to test or prove a thesis developed elsewhere. But we are almost all of us workers – we ourselves are therefore experts in the field of work. And so, in my journeys and in this book, I worked in the opposite direction. I started with the creativity and experience of workers, allowing those I met to set the agenda and determine which ideas matter. The six principles of a good working life that form the core of this book were shaped by these encounters. Later, with my journeys completed, I took these ideas into the archives and to meetings with experts, testing the principles and asking how we might form new theories and policy frameworks in order to transition into this good life, reimagined with all the potential this century has to offer.

A collective imagining

I travelled with a small set of tools in my rucksack; props I had designed to provoke imagining and I had my two questions: what could a good working life look like in this century, and what new forms of organisation might be needed to make this good life a reality here and now?

In each place I invited small groups to consider these questions. We met in boardrooms, municipal halls, warehouses, cafés and community centres. Those who joined me and whose stories I tell come from all walks of life: carers, nurses, truck drivers, janitors, craft makers, university professors, digital entrepreneurs, mechanics, weapon makers, gig workers, artists, consultants, bankers, those just starting again after life in prison, after addiction or an escape from domestic violence. I called these gatherings Imaginings. At each Imagining I was attentive to hierarchies and power, for example asking carers to one session and their managers to another. Usually participants were sitting alongside others doing similar work, but whom they did not know.

The Imaginings started by offering everyone a life chart. This was a long piece of paper with an age range printed on the horizontal axis – 1 to 100 – and on the vertical axis a smiling emoji face at the top and a frowning face at the bottom. I asked each participant to draw their life to date, plotting work, relationships and learning. It was an opening exercise. We are all accomplished on the subject of our own life, and I wanted to draw people in, to make them feel comfortable.

At first there was just the sound of pens scratching on paper, but slowly those who came started to talk to one another, to share stories from their charts, to laugh and to commiserate. Critical life points were plotted and then joined together with great swoops of the pen. For everyone the story is the same: life has steep ups and downs. Lines float up with the birth of a child, down with the pain of a divorce, up again with a new home, a promotion, down with the loss of a job. There's an interesting relationship between our personal lives and what happens at school and work. A crisis at home very often provokes a crisis elsewhere. There's a clear pattern of early struggles and poverty setting a trajectory that is hard to escape. There are second chances – hard to come by, but pivotal moments where we can turn our lives around. Those who have navigated a transition frequently spoke of a seren-dipitous connection, an encounter with someone who has been a bridge to the new. These participants also rated their lives at the upper end of the positive axis.

The reality is that none of us live our lives in a steady state.

I marvelled each time at the breadth of life experience and the openness with which participants shared their lives.

Everyone enjoys the exercise and the chance to reflect. The ice is broken, and we can move towards the heart of the Imagining. I offer each group seated around a table a pack of seventy-two cards. Every card has an image and a word. Some clearly relate to work, with words such as reputation, progression, colleagues and pride. Others relate to material need, with cards for rent, food, childcare and holidays; to re-lationships, with cards for friendship, pets, nature; and others to wider life concerns; there are cards for play, hobbies and thinking space. There are blank cards too so that participants can write in any aspect I might have forgotten and which they consider to be important.

Participants shuffle through the cards together, expressing curiosity, surprise, sometimes puzzlement, and they start to talk about what elements make for a good working life. Each small group must decide together which cards to choose. They are then placed on a specially designed chart. Placing cards towards the outer edge of the chart denotes that the chosen element is very important; closer to the centre signifies that the chosen element is part of a good life, but perhaps not the be all and end all. Participants can choose as many or as few cards as they like, and they have just over an hour to decide.

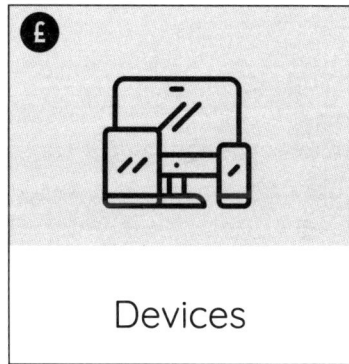

Company mission

Devices

Hobby:

Nature

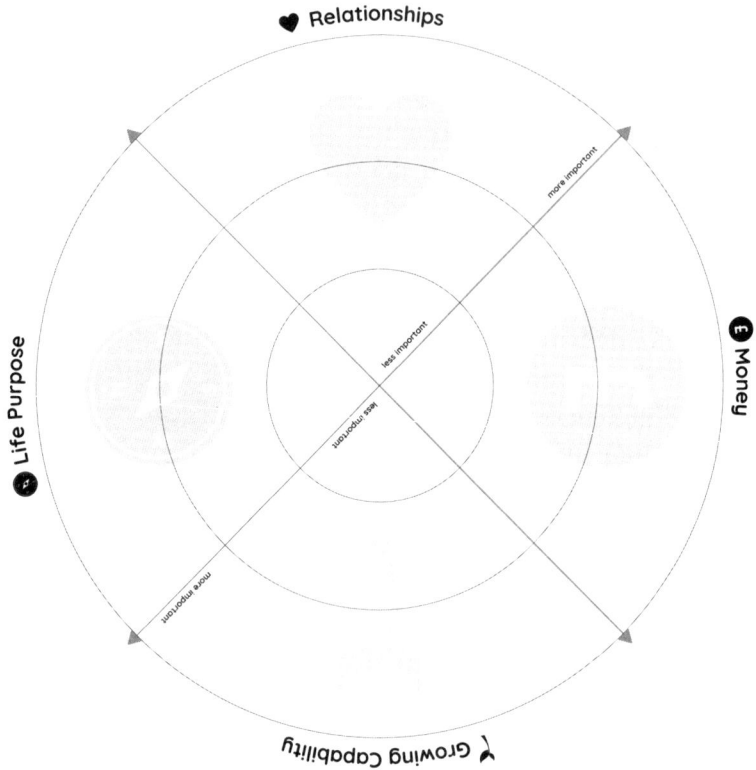

❤ Relationships

Life Purpose

€ Money

Growing Capability

more important

less important

The need to make decisions as a group provoked debate and deep conversation. This was a making process in which ideas were created, remembered, re-formed, perhaps discarded or expanded. It was not an interview process or a focus group in which I was seeking or mining already existing opinions. The collaboration generated new thinking, and the thoughtful development of this thinking.

In the third part of the Imagining I cleared the tables, replacing the cards with a plain paper tablecloth, pens, glue and magazines, and I asked each group to design an organisation or institution that they thought could make their imagined good working life a reality. It was a request that usually provoked nervous laughter. Very few of those who came to the Imaginings had been part of such an exercise before and there was always a moment of doubt. But every time, participants got stuck in and detailed designs emerged on the paper tablecloths.

Dreams: shared, common and rich

I was not prepared for the enthusiasm participants would show for the process. In fact, to begin with I would worry that they might disappear in the tea break. The opposite happened. At the end of three hours together people invariably hung around, enthused and hungry for more. 'We are never asked these questions', 'We have never thought like this before', 'Could we go further?' were some of the common responses.

I knew that there would be an abundance of good ideas, but the extent to which a set of common dreams are shared among us frankly amazed me. When Jonny, for example, started to talk about designing a 'non-linear life', that cold day in Kilmarnock, I was transfixed. His idea of a time revolution was, like many other ideas, echoed and repeated over and over again by participants from all walks of life. Three years, a pandemic and hundreds of conversations later, when I was in the boardroom of a globally renowned consultancy business with a group of mid-career professionals, I heard the challenge once again. 'What does work take away from us that we want back?' 'Our time!' a young woman called Charlotte announced with immense feeling before getting to her feet and starting to draw. 'Our directors and partners have none. Our trajectory is pointing the same way. I'd never want to be a partner because time is so important to me – they have no time. The remuneration is not enough for that. We have to re-value and reinvent time.'

As the journeys progressed, and later as I listened to hundreds of hours of recorded conversations, and pored over life charts, the selected cards and drawings, I heard these repeating strains, like melodies which sang out over the pitch and rhythm of the talking: the hubbub of humour, personal stories, laments and explanations that formed the background hum to every Imagining.

These melodies weave together six elements which emerged from the Imaginings, everywhere and from everyone, as the shared and foundational principles that people want, and I believe make for a good working life in this century. These are the six principles of a good working life, which I summarise as: basics, meaning, time, care, play and place.

The good working life starts with securing a set of material **basics**, without which no one can live a life. Decent pay, predictable working hours, safe working conditions and freedom from surveillance cannot be assumed, but they are necessary. Necessary but not sufficient. For a good working life, the work itself must have **meaning**: it must offer us a sense of purpose, allowing us to shape our lives and to grow. Work with meaning gives us a place in the world. Work with meaning is not always easy to find. (One thing is clear: personal meaning cannot be confused with company values.) Everyone wants to reimagine **time** – this is not simply a desire to work less or to work a four-day week (although both would be welcome), it is a desire to reimagine the pattern of our lives and the place of work within our days. Reimagining time would allow us to **care** and to **play**. Care is a rich concept that encompasses people and place, combining ideas of nurture, service and repair. Play is not simply time off work but the space to live some hours in another dimension, according to different rules and values.

The sixth principle is **place**. Work happens somewhere

and the work available in the places we live shapes us and the place itself. Everywhere I went, I found there is good work, but it frequently cannot be accessed by local people. Those who came to the Imaginings talked about ways to make these connections; they created new thinking about social relationships and education. They also talked extensively about how to create new forms of work and local economy.

Each of the principles of the good working life is connected and on a par. They cannot be separated and ranked in order of importance. Although money is qualitatively different to time, each has value for a good life and we cannot make simple trade-offs. In other words, we can't offer flexibility on time but ignore the basics; or make promises about care that are not connected to place. Each principle must be accorded equal status.

The principles touch on concerns that are already in the public domain – in the burgeoning literature and research on work. But each is taken in a new direction. Like a deft turn of the kaleidoscope, we can see familiar pieces, but they are now rearranged to create something different. New alignments and spaces between familiar elements allow us to see a different shape entirely.

In the chapters that follow, looking at each of these principles in turn, I will suggest how we could make this shared dream of a new working life happen. The answer lies partly in the institutional designs produced on every tablecloth in the third part of the Imaginings in response to the question how to make this new vision a reality now. Designs that offered the creative, collective paths to new ways of working and new ways of growing good work. The answer also lies in the collective thinking that characterised the Imaginings, a conviction that we all have a role to play. In looking at 'place', I look closely at the role of local business leaders, and in the closing chapters I look more widely at how workers, business leaders, intellectuals and those who work for the state (such as politicians and civil servants) can be called on to collaborate in new ways.

I am convinced that we can create new working lives because I have seen in the course of my journeys that two big and important things are happening, and their connections matter. First, because we are growing *shared* common dreams, we can act in new and concerted ways together. As I will show, the changes we want are broadly desired and will benefit everyone. Second, these changes go with the weft of possibility that the combined effects of a technology revolution, an ecological crisis and the hunger for justice create. The opening and the opportunity for the imagined change is already there.

We are living in fast-changing and dramatic times, and the future is ours to shape. If we can understand the ruptures and the opportunities that lie within the bigger paradigm shifts then we can act on our dreams.

In considering why now is the moment to redesign work, and why these paradigm shifts provide the opportunity to make change happen, I also examine what is currently not working in this century, and the demise of twentieth-century work. Today, many of us are suffering. It's not always easy to think about these lived realities, but it is in these complex beginnings that the promise of this book evolves. If you are familiar with the possibilities and realities of the current paradigm shift, you might turn straight to the Imagined Principles. If not, or if you are curious to know more about the context in which both modern and future work sits, you can join me in considering why now?

Why Now? Imagining in Times of Rupture and Opportunity

We are slowly leaving one era – that of twentieth-century industrial work – and entering another, the contours of which are not yet clear. In this fluid moment there is excitement and a growing curiosity. But there is also fear: will work become harder? Might it disappear altogether? Almost everyone at the Imaginings talked about standing on uncertain ground.

Uncertainty can make us long for the things we have left behind: the work we knew. But while we can learn from the past, we cannot nor should not seek to return to it. We should instead pour our energies and imaginations into the very much bigger opportunities ahead.

A technology revolution, an ecological crisis and our shared and growing urge to live in a more just world create radical openings to re-shape work. Each of these connected and deep currents has profoundly altered the pattern of what is possible, sometimes causing impacts which are wretched and difficult, but simultaneously offering immense promise of what could be.

Understanding this can feel both messy and uncomfortable. But if we are seeking to bring about real change, we have to start with raw reality. Understand things as they truly are – not as you wish they were, not as they were written about ten years ago, not as they are presented in 'sacred texts' urged the cultural theorist Stuart Hall. Delving deep into how things truly are can feel difficult and dark but it is the necessary preparation for growing tall, for the possibilities of hope which follows in subsequent chapters; hope we can trust, because it is based on authenticity.

Twentieth-century work: narrow, inflexible and rooted in over-production

'Working nine to five, what a way to make a living,' sang the legendary Dolly Parton. 'It's all takin' and no givin' ... ' she intoned, her nail extensions tapping on an imaginary typewriter. The song, on which Parton is credited for 'lead vocals and nails', was the theme tune for the movie *9 to 5*. Parton topped the charts in Britain and the United States, striking a chord with millions. The film drew large audiences who laughed with empathy at the story of three women who wanted to escape the strictures of their office work, its deathly routines and often pointless tasks, most of which were de-signed to help 'the boss man' climb his ladder.

It was 1980 and this portrayal of nine-to-five work res-onated wherever you worked. The women had left behind the drudgery of housework for the office. Twentieth-century work had improved their lives – but now they wanted more. This is our story too. We can celebrate what improved while also recognising who was left behind and what was left out.

Notions of good work in the twentieth century were narrow. Ideas were predominantly shaped by white Western men for whom the nine to five worked well, as their cares and wider needs were attended to at home by a wife or mother who put her own dreams and ambitions in second place. It was a design rooted in an analogue world of industrial (over-)production. A world in which we were unaware – or uninterested – in the finite nature of our planet's resources, but instead saw everything around us as grist for the mill of progress and modernity. It was a world fascinated by machines, in which we were increasingly encouraged to think of ourselves as simply a part of a necessary industrial system. It was an unbalanced world: economies in the global north grew through the exploitation of people, resources and services provided by the global south.

This design worked very well for some, but for many more it was always onerous: the women left at home; men and women in work that was never unionised or regulated; people who for reasons of class, colour or geography were never able to get their foot on the ladder, let alone rise up it. There was something deeper too – the takin' that Dolly Parton sang about. Twentieth-century work was above all extractive: it took from the worker and from the environments we live in. We were offered something in return: our wages and the support of the postwar social contract but this was a contract already showing signs of fracture.

Today, when for millions the contract has ruptured, we can be tempted to look with nostalgia at a lost world and ask how we can get back those regulated hours, perhaps even the boredom which would come as sweet relief in a world where work in every context seems to carry with it the need to endlessly hustle. This is what much of the current thinking about work does. But it's a mistake to forget the deep flaws in this type of work: we can do so much better. We must understand the bigger shifts which are creating change and shape them in ways that could enable everyone to flourish.

Technology: the end of work as we know it?

Technology revolutions change the course of working lives as successive waves of automation replace and create work. Most of us do work that was unimaginable in 1971, the year the microchip was first commercially produced and the date seen as the start of the digital revolution.

It is not just that new work has been created, most obviously the work of coding and programming, it is that old work can be done in new ways: at home, in the garage or simultaneously with colleagues in different time zones around the globe. Digital automation has changed the way we make everything, from food to cars, music to words. It has changed how we can sell our time and skills, with the explosion of platform-based work driven by algorithms that enable us to share a ride, shop from home or stream culture on demand.

In every technology revolution there are new divisions between good and bad work and emergent fears that technology might end work altogether. One of those currently predicting a dystopian future – a world without work – is the economist Daniel Susskind. The threat he and others see is multiple. It is not only that jobs will disappear but, more importantly, the residual work that is left will deteriorate as tasks are disaggregated and machines (the exponential rise of AI) will encroach on both our capacity as thinkers and on our emotional capabilities.

Others argue that such fears are largely driven by skewed data. David Autor, a leading labour economist, points out that it is much easier to count the demise of work (for example, boxes that are no longer ticked in research surveys) than it is to count the emergence of new work which, in the early decades of a technology revolution, is hard to define and categorise. Autor also argues that new technology largely creates *better* work: jobs are enhanced and often better paid. At Ikea, for example, eight thousand call centre workers have been trained as interior design advisors: they work with AI tools which enhance their basic design skills, while Billy, a new bot, answers the 50 per cent of customer calls which are routine and less interesting for the workers.

It is hard not to be fascinated by these competing theories which pit human against machine. I'm also struck – as someone who is not a labour economist – at what I would call the 'tools first' nature of these stories which focus on the stuff of technology revolutions: the laptop and the iPhone, the algorithms and the astonishing invention of large language models like ChatGPT, which are one day unheard of and seven months later used by over a hundred million workers. These stories position technological tools as an unstoppable force. In the Susskind version of events, this will be to the detriment of workers; in the Autor version, to the benefit of workers.

I think something very important is missing in these 'tools first' stories, something that hides the opportunities in front of us. Technology revolutions are only partly about tools. Who can remember the names of the inventors of the microchip? They have been forgotten for a reason. The shape of technology revolutions (and work) is not ultimately determined by the invention of the hardware and the software but by the evolving and very malleable potential that lies between this stuff and the wider cultural forces that shape what is possible, acceptable and, most importantly, desirable.

It is dreams that determine the direction of technology revolutions and the work that emerges. This is why it matters *who* does the imagining, and this is where I think the opportunities lie.

In the twentieth century, the revolution in mass production

was shaped by a new vision of the good life. We know it as the American Dream: the desire for a car in the drive, a barbecue, a refrigerator (the bigger the better), a washing machine, a television, perhaps a weekend trip to the out-of-town mall. As the century progressed, this idyll of American suburbia grew to define the ideal life across the globe.

The American Dream patterned not only our homes and our domestic lives; it created our work. Mass production is driven by oil, but relatively few people worked in the oil industry. Instead, the work of the twentieth century was in the designing, making, marketing, selling, servicing and cleaning of new consumer goods. It was not simply that we dreamt of new things; we prized constant renewal. New jobs came in design agencies, advertising agencies, in retail, and through an explosion in the administrative work required for the smooth operating of the new corporations.

We can expect a similar pattern in the digital revolution. Our own dreams are still emerging. Some of us are yearning for green lifestyles or to share rather than own. Others are putting a premium on experience or wellbeing, prioritising healthy living. Each of these lifestyles are already generating new work, from the exponential rise in the support econ-omy – personal training, coaching and yoga teachers – to businesses that upcycle clothing, organise the sharing of cars and bicycles or create forms of eco-tourism, and local and organic food production. Some of these early innovations will prove to be fads, but others will be longer lasting and create significant sectors of work. In the early stages the old also continues to jostle alongside the new: we may want a new and large car as well as an electric bike.

Each vision of the good life generates demand for new things and for new work. It also stimulates thinking about what matters, shifting our values and changing what we consider to be good work. In technology revolutions, work can shift in status, becoming more or less highly regarded and better (or worse) paid, something I look at in more detail in Principle Three, when considering the work of care. Previous revolutions have led us to reconsider practices such as slavery, child labour and the prohibition of women from certain sectors of the economy.

This idea, that technology will not only change but will be used and shaped by us to improve our working lives, might sound idealistic or just plain wrong. After all, the immediate and visible impact of digital technology on work has so far often been negative.

Many at the Imaginings had lived through dramatic changes. Former miners and industrial workers rued the loss of work which had carried status and a good salary. Workers experiencing the new divisions of labour that separate the immense wealth that accrues to the owners of work platforms from the misery of those chasing the next delivery and customer rating, told me plainly that they doubted I could fully imagine the stress and awfulness of their work.

The algorithms that drive platform work have led to declining wages and increasingly precarious conditions for millions of workers, in particular those in service, delivery and fulfilment jobs. Growing numbers of skilled workers – train drivers, teachers, accountants – rightly fear the application of the same digital rules and apps, in particular the introduction of on-demand work scheduling, which is starting to erode their hard-won working rights. The extraordinary investments in 'little tech', the surveillance apps that now police work and workers – from the home to the warehouse and the office – have further dehumanised and intensified many forms of work. These are real forces, and they fuel the pessimism and uncertainty with which many regard the current technology revolution. But they are only part of the story.

Taking a longer view of history suggests that we should not assume what will happen based on the experience of these early decades alone. Technology revolutions always have early painful impacts, but, in ensuing decades, each substantive technology innovation has augmented and greatly improved working lives. This is the argument made by Carlota Perez, an economic historian, respected by academics and investors alike, who studies technology revolutions and takes a 250-year view.

Now a British resident in her eighties, Carlota is Venezuelan by birth and had a ringside seat as the oil economy boomed in the middle of the twentieth century. Venezuela was one of the founding members of OPEC, the cartel which controls the price of oil and the number of barrels produced. Carlota watched as complex social, political, spatial and technical currents shaped the oil-based technology revolution. She was left with a set of big questions as to what determines the shape of technology revolutions – it was already clear to her that the direction of travel was not pre-determined, neither was it solely in the hands of the market or those who controlled the primary resource.

Carlota identified five technology revolutions. The first started in the 1770s, with water-powered technology. This is the era most commonly referred to as the Industrial Revolution. Next came the railways in the 1820s (the second technology revolution), followed by steel and heavy engineering in the 1870s (the third); oil and mass production in the first half of the twentieth century (the fourth revolution), followed by the current fifth technology revolution (the digital revolution born in the 1970s).

Each of these revolutions followed a pattern. They start with a period of almost unhinged excitement. There was a mania for canals in the 1770s, a railway boom in the 1840s, and another boom in the 1920s as mass production started to take off. In this digital revolution, the dot–com boom of the 1990s was followed more recently by the hysteria around blockchain technologies including cryptocurrencies and non-fungible tokens.

This excitement creates an investment bubble that is followed by a crash, in which large investments vanish without the promised returns. In the last revolution the roaring 1920s were followed by the desperation, unemployment and hunger of the 1930s. This period of downturn is characterised by growing inequality, poor or no work, recession, political instability and, historically, the rise of populism. This is the period where we sit currently in the fifth revolution, our technology revolution: the divisive, difficult middle period.

In the 1930s, deep poverty and extreme politics went hand in hand. In our own era we have seen the upheavals that led to Brexit and the rise of far-right politics in the United States, in Britain and across Europe.

We are in the doldrums. Difficult times are rooted in a collapse of the twentieth-century work contract and the still-stuttering propagation of the current technology revolution. Alternative futures are growing, but in the turmoil stories of dystopia seem louder, their proponents more visible.

But in every cycle, turbulence has given way. Change comes at what Carlota Perez describes as a 'turning point'; a pivot during which ideas realign, new alliances are formed among workers and between workers and business owners, while a re-making of critical institutions provides the tools required to develop the new technology. This turning point leads to new forms of productivity and widespread flourishing. It creates a golden age, characterised by new forms of shared prosperity and, importantly, a new deal for workers.

The conditions which lead to and enable this turning point are complex and unpredictable. New imaginings about the future and exhaustion with the divisions and devastation caused by extremism both have a role to play. New forms of work organisation, enlightened business leaders and what I will call organic intellectuals – creative thinkers who are rooted in everyday realities – all play a critical role. There can be no turning point without an active state. State actors and institutions alone cannot create the turning point, but at the same time they have within their power the ability to signal a future trajectory. A turning point requires new institutions, new rules that will guide investment and new forms of economic and social development.

In our own story it is not clear what will happen next. And it's important to emphasise – as Carlota Perez does repeatedly – this is not a story of techno-determinism. Each time the future is resolved in a different way, shaped by the ideas, values and imaginations of those who dream of something better. A 250-year view of history shows us that the turbulence will not endure; that we can re-shape our institutions and our economies for a new form of prosperity. We can take hope from the knowledge that in all previous technology revolutions, the conditions of work were changed and dramatically improved. We can also see that positive change is not preordained and that it is down to us: we have urgent work to do.

Ecology: the impulse towards the new?

Nature and work have always been conjoined. From the beginning, work revolved around the harvesting, harnessing and re-fashioning of the natural world, aided by the technology to hand. Since then, from agriculture to mining, the manufacturing of plastics to fashion, we have first used – often with great care – what immediately surrounded us, and then turned to the resources of others, creating systems of colonial plunder to harvest the wood, the minerals, the oil, water and more that successive technology revolutions required.

Today we stand on the brink, entangled in systems of production, still-persistent modernist dreams of more and new things, and the related forms of work that devour natural resources at a rate which threatens our human survival.

The science has long been clear. We are depleting our resources, driving species to extinction, polluting our waters, air and soil. Scientists agree that we have already breached six of the nine planetary boundaries that keep humanity safe on earth.

The impacts of these breaches can be seen in the storms, floods and heatwaves, the so-called once in a hundred years events, which now happen frequently. The impact is also visible in the escalating and increasingly desperate patterns of human migration, one of the biggest social challenges of our century. Families risk their lives to get to the United States or Europe, because they can no longer survive in places they call home. They may not want to leave, but patterns of work and consumption in one part of the globe cause other geographies to become unliveable: sea levels rise, rains make agriculture too precarious and insufferable temperatures close schools, curtailing education for months on end. It is inevitable that millions more will move in search of better work and the good lives that each of us wish for our children, unless we can design new forms of work and living that benefit everyone in all places.

Sustaining our own species now depends on ways of living and working that can restore balance, repairing the planetary boundaries that will keep us from hunger and worse. There is an immediate and urgent need to reduce our consumption of natural resources and our carbon emissions to the globally agreed levels that would limit global heating as closely as possible to 1.5 degrees Celsius. Beyond this point, scientists predict that complex feedback loops will further accelerate change – the melting of ice, warming of seas, release of methane and increase in the sun's reflection – in ways that will rapidly make human life on earth impossible. So far, actions have not been sufficient.

Some put their hopes in technology. But it is increasingly clear that the digital revolution is not helping in its current form. It is insatiably reliant on new materials, modern mining and energy. The carbon cost of the footballer Ronaldo posting a photograph to his 199.2 million Instagram followers is thirty megawatt hours, equivalent to the energy used by three US households over an entire year. Artificial intelligence and the necessary computing power also drive an exponential demand for energy, creating 'algorithmic pollution' on a scale never seen before. 'Green' products have their own intensive requirements. The proposed switch to electric vehicles, for example, will require sixty times more lithium by 2050, but lithium mining is some of the most difficult, exploitative work in the world and is already associated with ecosystem devastation.

Faced with diminishing time horizons and a growing sense of urgency, this temptation to exchange one form of extraction for another is understandable. The material might change – lithium instead of oil or coal, for example – but the systems of work – the extractive bargain – remain the same.

The reality is that we are unlikely to solve our complex current predicaments within these old and narrow ways of thinking. Narrow because the focus is on one metric – carbon – as opposed to the wider ways in which our planetary systems are out of balance. Narrow because this thinking fails to understand how work and ecology are entangled; swapping the extraction of one material for another will simply move the location of unjust and exploitative forms of work. Narrow because this old paradigm keeps out of view the much more complicated and richer ways in which we are connected to one another and to nature, suppressing the emergent dreams of new forms of abundance and flourishing.

Everywhere on my journeys I met people whose work must either cease or be radically redesigned if we are to restore ecological balance and meet our climate goals: from those who pack energy-intensive frozen food in Grimsby to those in London-based consulting firms whose work requires weekly flights. Many of these high carbon workers are well paid, but strikingly few of them like their work: the conditions on the packing line, the increasing sense of ennui and purposelessness endemic in much global consulting, once again the takin' and no givin' trouble almost everyone.

Our ecological crisis offers a chance to rethink what work matters and how we work. It could be our turning point – our pivot – because to meet climate goals, 70 per cent of us need to change where and how we work within a decade. But this is good: a planned transition to new forms of generative work, to differently imagined forms of abundance that would include time with each other, play and care – the principles that form a good working life – would be liberation. We could use the current crisis to galvanise a just transition.

System failure, however painful, invariably reveals possibility. Cataclysms in nature generate renewal just as storms create destruction, opening up spaces of air and light, spaces that are required for growth. This is not to minimise or downplay the devastating effects of extreme weather events, but it is to recognise that dark times create possibility.

Rebecca Solnit writes elegiacally about the ways in which communities continually reinvent with the biggest of hearts, when disaster – from earthquakes to hurricanes – strikes. Each time, something beautiful but hidden is revealed – often the simple human urge to bond despite our differences and make change. The way in which so many communities responded during the Covid-19 pandemic, mobilising to support neighbours, is a recent example.

Both our imaginings of nature and the ecological crisis are already providing us with stories, metaphors and wisdom that can dance us to a different work future.

Think like a forest, urges the novelist and anthropologist Amitav Ghosh in another lyrical meditation on climate crisis. Scientists have discovered that trees 'talk' to each other, sharing nutrients and information to ward off pests, through an immense mycelium fungal network. In the forest, each individual tree stands tall and proud because its roots are entwined with those of others. Humans too, Ghosh is suggesting, need to entwine more deeply with each other and with nature in order to confront the current crisis. At the Imaginings I found again and again that conversations turned to nature, to the balm it provides and to the much-needed new work of maintenance and repair of local places.

Over the course of my journeys, I met those designing new forms of health, farming and food production. In each case they have drawn on ancient traditions and understandings of nature, which they combine with modern technological possibility to grow new and good forms of work for themselves and often thousands of others. They have created new forms of abundance, seeding farms, companies and collaborations that are sustaining and generative for workers, for nature and the local economy alike. These pioneers show us how our ecological emergency can be seized to transform work.

It's no coincidence that these stories of nature and a rich understanding of the way we are entangled with one another and the places we live also animate the justice movements that have grown in strength and energy in the early decades of the twenty-first century. An increasingly widespread desire to address the social and economic chasms between us is the third force urging us and enabling us to think again about work.

(In)justice: the hidden seam

Much work, as it is currently designed, is killing us, the workers. This is the conclusion of the World Health Organization and its sister institution, the International Labour Organization. These are sober, some might say staid, global organisations. They are not known for fiery rhetoric or for ideas which shake the status quo. But in 2021, both identified something deeply shocking: work is the cause of our modern ailments. Work is causing new forms of sickness, disease and death.

Death from work is indiscriminate. Long working hours and the work-related stress that causes many illnesses, from depression to heart attacks, affects workers both in the board-room and on the factory floor. But while the CEO who, newly enlightened by their own health diagnosis, takes time with their family and urges their employees to work less, is an important figure, they are not the norm (nor are their concessions a legal right for all). It is the steady thrum of poverty and stress endemic to low-paid work that is driving the epidemics of physical and mental illness, and, in the most desperate cases, early death.

Too much modern work is characterised by tenuous contracts, wages that have fallen precipitously in value, workplaces that are pitiless and often unsafe, and work cultures that deny us our dignity. This is unjust work with effects that are profoundly affecting our social lives.

In Britain today, most families that fall below the poverty line have at least one adult in full-time work. Millions of households do not earn enough to feed their families or heat their homes. In the US, the statistics are yet more shocking: millions who are in work are below the poverty line and cannot afford basics such as health insurance or housing. The homeless worker is a new and terrible phenomenon; in Britain, one in every two hundred families is homeless. In both Britain and the US this financial poverty is compounded by the withdrawal of welfare services and shared infrastructure. Those in low-paid work and poverty are concentrated in places where public transport is limited, schools are underfunded, health services are overwhelmed and childcare is scarce and too often unaffordable.

Insecure work takes a physical toll: we don't have the time or money to eat well; we can't sleep; our immune systems and often our limbs are exhausted; our lives are shortened. Manual workers and the low paid live on average ten years less than their better paid office-working peers; it's one reason why Jonny, the grave-digger I met in Kilmarnock, has thought so hard about redesigning his life. The anxieties creep home – how to afford school shoes, a birthday present, a bus fare or fuel for the car that gets us to work – and these worries make us mentally unwell. In Britain, 17 per cent of working age adults take antidepressants to cope with troubles that often start at work.

Work injustice can take the form of prejudice against those who are differently abled, LGBTQ+, or simply seen as the wrong age. 'Please don't invite anyone over forty to the interviews' is the continual request made to one managing partner in a senior British headhunting firm. Another had a candidate rejected by a client who explained that while the applicant was perfect in every other way, 'fifty-three is just too old'. Research from Europe and the United States reveals that prejudice against older workers is remarkably prevalent. In the US, businesses used the Covid-19 pandemic to push out 3.8 million workers aged between fifty-five and seventy-four. In Britain, politicians urge older people to go back to work, apparently unaware that many would love to do so, if only someone would employ them. More than a quarter of a million workers over fifty who left the workforce during the Covid-19 pandemic to care for another family member have not been able to find work. Astonishingly, only one in three workers are still working at the current state pension age of sixty-six.

Young workers have a different set of barriers and concerns. Often loaded with student debt, they report that they find work unbearably stressful, living pay cheque to pay cheque, struggling to find work-life balance while nurturing deep-seated fears that a generational injustice in housing costs means that, no matter how hard they work, their job will never bring security or a home of their own. Younger generations are also more concerned with issues of justice in general, unwilling to take work that conflicts with their values and their concern about climate change in particular.

It is the injustices of gender, race, place and class that run deepest and are knotted most closely together. In Britain, where we live determines our income above all other factors, with an enduring impact on every aspect of life. Most low paid, insecure work is found in the post-industrial north of the country. In the United States, the depths of despair found in post-industrial places, where a lack of work or poor work creates ill health, addiction and deep hopelessness, have been graphically documented by the economists Anne Case and Angus Deaton. Within and beyond these geographies, work injustice falls disproportionately on women and on Black and brown people, who are over-represented in low-paid sectors of care, and in service work. In Britain, twice as many Black families as white families cannot feed their children, a result of being trapped in low-paid, bad work. The effects are not only economic: stigma spreads its tentacles through cultural mockery of certain places and classes, while Black workers are forced in subtle ways to prove again and again that they are competent.

The effects of low-paid work become structural as they are passed from one generation to another. You cannot study at school if you are hungry or constantly moving from one temporary home to another – the experience of one third of London's primary school pupils. You cannot do your homework if you are cold at home, there is no space or if the local library has been closed. You cannot take on an internship in a big city if you don't have friends and family who can offer you a place to stay.

Without explicit attention and design, one seam of injustice is again stitched to the next as generations and work revolutions evolve. The danger is particularly acute in technology revolutions – eras in which generational wealth can be transferred and entrenched. Historical maps show how the sites where the British Industrial Revolution was born were the places where slave traders lived. Slaves were fungible. They could be easily sold for liquid cash, enabling those who had made fortunes through violent exploitation in one economy to be winners in the next. When, in the 1940s, the historian and Trinidadian independence leader Eric Williams attempted to publish his groundbreaking academic research, tracing these connections between slavery and industrialisation, his work was dismissed as an 'interpretation'. Today few question the analysis, but the patterns through which technological innovation too often simply transfers wealth while shifting exploitation elsewhere continues.

Many of us feel a deep dis-ease. We don't want to live lives that depend on the exploitation of others. We want to understand how we can make different choices. This curiosity is perhaps why a most unlikely book, dense with data and complex economic equations, shot to the top of international bestseller lists in 2014. The French academic Thomas Piketty became an overnight sensation with *Capital in the Twenty-First Century*, which, like the work of Carlota Perez, took a 250-year view of history in order to plot in meticulous detail how wealth is created and then transferred. Piketty's research shows how wealth, rooted in property, rents and inheritance, is outstripping any income that can be made from work, creating and entrenching intergenerational injustice. Piketty coined the term 'patrimonial capitalism' to describe this growing concentration of inherited wealth in societies where birth matters more than any talent.

Wealth disparities are difficult to talk about. In Britain, to mention income inequality or the pay of CEOs is to elicit an eyeroll and perhaps a rebuke. In the 1970s, as the digital revolution started to unfold, an average company CEO in Britain was paid twenty-one times the *median* wage. By the 2020s this multiple had risen to over one hundred. Or put another way, in the US where the trend is identical, pay at the top end has risen 1,400 per cent over this period while the pay of the average worker has risen by 18 per cent. There is often a misplaced assumption that questions about the ethics of these arrangements come from a position of envy. In fact, the data shows that these disparities are harmful to everyone, even those at the top of the income scale. There appears to be a close relationship between inequality, low economic productivity and a general decline in population wellbeing. In other words, when disparities become too great, as the epidemiologists Richard Wilkinson and Kate Pickett demonstrated in their book *The Spirit Level*, we all live poorer lives.

When disparities become too great our social and political institutions also decline. A broken economic relationship at work connects directly to a decline in trust and participation in democracy. We can see the distortions most overtly in the United States, where those with immense wealth are able to openly influence political parties and the course of politics. But it is the more insidious connections between bad work and democratic decline that should also worry us. When there is a widespread feeling that things are rigged: that our children will never have chances, that we are being taken for a ride – our bosses preaching values while signing off increasing disparities in pay – there is a deeper hollowing out of civic trust. In Britain and in the United States a decline in living standards and economic certainty has been accompanied by a simultaneous burgeoning of political rhetoric that speaks of 'opportunity for all'. The promise of equality and justice is loudly and continually made, just as meaningful opportunities are vanishing. Unjust work makes us ill and stifles our dreams. It also fuels populism and sabotages our democratic institutions.

And yet, Piketty's research tells a story of possibility. First, the international comparisons on which he draws clearly show that there are many different ways of organising property, political systems and education within countries that have similar economies and levels of technological development: patrimonial capitalism is a choice, not the only way.

Second, we can constantly re-order and restructure how we divide up wealth and organise work. Choices are *reversible*. Sweden, for example, is a country that many consider to be an exemplar of equality and work justice, characterised by strong worker representation on boards and by progressive taxation, both of which have wide cultural acceptance. These arrangements are, however, as Piketty shows, remarkably recent and the result of hard-won struggles. Piketty urges us to get involved; questions of economics and the organisation of work, he writes, are too important to be left to others.

When, in the summer of 2020, British Black Lives Matter protestors toppled the statue of a slave owner, Edward Colston, into Bristol's harbour, they were getting involved. These activists were exposing the line that runs from slavery through to the institutional racism that affects the work of so many today, and they were reacting with frustration to repeated promises of technocratic progress that fail to change everyday social and economic injustices.

Black Lives Matter, like many of the other social justice movements that have flourished in the early decades of the twenty-first century – Me Too, Occupy, Just Stop Oil, Extinction Rebellion and others – is an expression of a loss of faith in existing social and economic arrangements and a collective demand for justice. Those who are organising don't want to manage things differently; they don't want the sort of change that will preserve existing ways of living; they want to repair these long-running tears and to create something else. Their questions are part of a wider imaginative opening. Their tactics, ideas and energy create part of the context, specific to our moment, in which a work revolution might take root. One thing, they tell us, is clear: work as usual is not an option.

On revolution

Revolutions happen when the meaning of life as we once understood it has ebbed away. They are successful when a new story interprets the past and gives a shape to already existent ideas and hopes. This is how the welfare revolution happened in the twentieth century. When William Beveridge travelled across Britain, he found that people everywhere had already imagined a new safety net – they had visions of health services, of schools, of support for those who had work accidents or who had lost their jobs. Beveridge gave form to dreams and in turn, when his plans met the critique and often ire of civil servants, the people held the dream, making it impossible to backtrack.

This welfare revolution is the template I have in mind when I imagine the work revolution we will create in this century. A new social contract requires struggle and complex realignments of power, but it is not a violent revolution, in part because the consensus has been forged. The imaginings exist – these new ideas need to move into the light, to become the principles for a new work system.

The word 'revolution' has long been associated with restoration, just as the word 'radical' originally meant a return to the roots. Today we think of revolution and restoration as opposites, but throughout history revolutions have been as much about restoring a lost spirit – of equality, of care, of freedom, of time – as they have been about invention. In her famous study of revolution, the historian and philosopher Hannah Arendt writes, 'The modern concept of revolution [is] inextricably bound up with the notion that the course of history suddenly begins anew, that an entirely new story, a story never known or told before, is about to unfold.' But, as Arendt is at pains to point out, revolutions do not work in this way; they look back without nostalgia, 'in a practice of thinking together and combining things meaningfully' to create the new. As we will see, participants at the Imaginings did exactly this, thinking forwards and backwards, combining the old and the new, the close at hand and the dreamed of, in their creation of the six principles of a good working life.

History is a story of labour revolutions: the abolition of slavery, the regulation of working hours and working ages, the invention of the paid weekend and the introduction of equal pay for equal work. Each of these things seemed, up to the moment that victory was secured, almost impossible to imagine. It's a history which is not linear. Things change. Others stay the same, left over, perhaps to be resolved in a future revolution. Sometimes things move backwards; gains like the paid weekend seem to move out of reach.

This lack of historical linearity is one reason it is so hard to tell what is happening to work at any point in time. Another is that we tend to consider work from a very personal perspective: have I won the right to work from home; can I finally find the skilled workers I need for my business/team; will my son/daughter ever find work that enables them to afford a home of their own?

Work is like the elephant in the Indian parable in which six blind men try to understand what an elephant looks like. Each man can only touch one part of this enormous animal: one the tusk, one the legs, the belly, the ear, the trunk and the tail. The blind man who feels a leg says the elephant is like a pillar; the one who feels the tail says the elephant is like a rope; the one who feels the trunk says the elephant is like a tree branch and so on. Comparing notes, the men find that they disagree completely about what the elephant is like. They start to quarrel bitterly among themselves, and then a sighted man walks by. He sees the whole elephant and

immediately exclaims at its size and shape, and tells the men,
'All of you are right', but 'you are each telling a different story
because you have touched a different part of the elephant
which has all of the features you have mentioned'.

Our understanding of work is often like this. Each of us
rightly feels something is happening, but it is very hard –
partly because our own work is so consuming – to see the
whole picture. We are also 'blind' in another way. We tend
to accept the common sense that governs the work of our era.
We implicitly assume that certain things are beyond question.
We are rarely invited or given the time to think otherwise –
to have the bolder conversations we need.

'Are we just dreaming?' Jonny and his colleagues asked me,
suddenly looking up from their design of a good working life.
At the Imaginings I was often asked this question as people
ran with their ideas and then suddenly halted, seeing the gap
between the current reality and their dreams. 'Are we mad?'
Imagineers, as I came to call them, would ask, laughing and
then continuing to imagine regardless. This is how it is: we
must continue to imagine regardless, because the revolution
is ours to shape.

Part II

The Six Principles of a Good Working Life

Principle One: Securing the Basics

Where shall we start? Each small team coming to the Imaginings shuffles through the seventy-two cards, and invariably decides they should start with 'the basics'; we need money, to know when we will work (and when we won't), we want to feel safe, we don't want to be spied on. The basics define a compact: the minimum we might ask from work and from wider society in order to live decently.

Few want to spend long on the subject. There are more interesting things to discuss: things that feel less raw and more worthy of the imagination, things that everyone is impatient to get to. But many who come to the Imaginings have lived through periods when money was tight; others are currently feeling the sharp edge of precarity. Everyone knows the basics can no longer be assumed and some feel a visceral, scarcely containable anger about a broken contract.

Workers or slaves?

'They are playing with us, we are slaves. Look ... there's no pattern, it's not predictable. It's very shit money. Fridays, Saturdays, Sundays – before, you could earn £7 an hour. Before, it was better – now it's £2.62 ... I've got bills, council tax, kids, a wife – it's not enough ... I can't live, I can't sleep.' Jeetu looks wretched as he bends his head into long and slender hands.

I'm in Barking, on London's eastern edge. Barking, with its more famous neighbour Dagenham, has a proud place in Britain's industrial history: the home of the Ford car plant, and before that of smaller industries that made use of the level, low-lying land – close to the docks and markets of London. It's a place with a strong working-class history and a pattern of continual migration. One third of Barking's current residents are of Asian heritage and many have found work in the gig economy, delivering food and parcels for companies such as Uber, Amazon and Deliveroo.

Barking is not an out of the way place. It's nestled next to the landmark skyscrapers of London's financial district in Canary Wharf, and public transport connections are good. I can get there from my home in about half an hour. But walking from the station under gun metal skies, I feel I'm far from anywhere. A mean and gritty wind slices across the arterial roads I have to cross, while traffic thunders past. I had arranged to meet Jeetu and seven of his colleagues, all gig workers for Uber Eats, at a community warehouse, a space we have been lent.

The men arrived early, to allow time for a smoke outside. Huddled by their scooters and talking in Bangla, they are friendly, curious about what we will do together, perhaps relieved that for a few hours at least they will be safe, warm and earning a living wage. There's an edginess too. I feel the men might leave at any moment (they don't). But as Jeetu and his colleagues come in and sit at the tables, accepting the tea I pour, they don't remove their puffer coats or woolly hats.

'Are we working as slaves, or normal staff? That's the main thing I would like to say.' Palash, in his forties, picks up Jeetu's theme. Ahmed grabs a pen. Jabbing right through the paper tablecloth, he starts to make increasingly frenzied calculations. Each line shows a job, the time it takes, the tiny margins and the real possibility that a day's earnings might be wiped out by touching the app and starting the wrong delivery. He lists his possible earnings and then, alongside, the cost of his rent, his children's clothes, the phone he needs to run the app. 'I do two shifts, I do night shifts – I'm spending my sleep on delivery, I'm spending my family time on delivery.' He jabs down more sums in front of me. 'I am sucked out. This thing,' he tells me angrily, 'you can't understand it, if you're not inside, you really can't get the problems we are facing. I was twenty-two when I came here. It's no good – but you can't even think to leave, you can only be a slave.' Ahmed jams the lid back on the Sharpie and flings it down.

These men, like everyone else who comes to the Imaginings, want to move on and talk about other things, but their anger and upset spills over.

'Why don't government enforce the wage?' Palash asks. 'The council, government – why don't they keep their eye on this? This company is operating here, and the government has raised the minimum wage – but they are ignoring it, they have cut the wage by half. Why? Why is the government not helping with this issue?'

'Maybe the government will engage,' Jeetu responds, 'but government comes to everything late. Right now they are being played by these people.'

The week before we meet in Barking, Uber's CEO Dara Khosrowshahi had visited London in an effort to publicise the company, mollify a not altogether supportive mayor and recruit more drivers. 'It's a corporate thing,' Palash says, 'they push the mayor, government, everyone.'

'And you know it's not even 1 per cent secure. I tell you, you turn up, there's no work. Or you turn up and you find twenty-three litres of water in sixty-four bottles, plus food – how you can move that on your bike? There's a law – maximum safe weight you can handle on your bike is 12.5 kg – but what happens? You take it or the restaurant complains and that's it, they close your app – no more work. I tell you, all the newspapers are full of simple things – what has happened to Kim Kardashian, today [Prince] William's daughter has a lovely new smile – but these things, what's happening to us, these things are never there.'

Gig work is not a twenty-first-century phenomenon. The term originated in the world of 1920s jazz, where a gig was slang for a short-term engagement to perform, but the concept of the gig economy went mainstream following the 2008/09 financial crash, referring to those who had to take on multiple jobs to ad hoc schedules as the economy and wages shrank. The release of the iPhone in 2007 and the explosion in app development had provided the conditions in which a new technologically driven form of gig could proliferate.

Gig work, we are often told by the same government officials that Palash rails against, is liked because people can work flexibly. In my experience this is rarely true. In fact, it's notable that everyone I meet who feels acute precarity describes themselves as a gig worker as a shorthand for the unwelcome instability that defines the work they are doing. Strictly speaking, gig work in this century is defined as work that is managed by an algorithm. But many freelancers – writers, designers, artists, journalists and others – have adopted the term to describe their vulnerability. The World Bank estimates that 47 per cent of the world's workforce are now freelancers, workers that in their words 'are particularly vulnerable to having their rights eroded'.

Everyone would like *predictable* flexibility, but the harsh

reality of gig work (like much freelance work) is unpredictable flexibility. Not knowing where your next paid hour is
coming from, or if you will earn enough to survive on any
given day is not a tenable way to live. Jeetu and Palash have to
be continually available to earn enough to pay the rent and to
feed themselves and their families. (Uber drivers are of higher
status and earn better than Uber riders, although the churn in
Uber drivers is very high: 95 per cent of drivers stay only six
months, hardly a marker of good work.) For all gig workers,
the constant on-call status means that they can't use the hours
that they are not working: they can't promise to be available
to parent, they can't take on any other part-time work, they
can't sleep or relax. The resulting physical and mental stress
ran like a loud static frequency through our shared space in
Barking that day. I found the tension hard to bear.

A minimum basic lifestyle

How much is enough? Participants at the Imaginings discuss
what they need: the financial security to pay the rent or
mortgage, to eat well and afford heating, a decent broadband
connection, electricity and to have a holiday – 'We don't need
to fly.' Little extras would be nice, but being able to afford
the right things for the kids is essential. Putting something
by for a rainy day is also considered to be very important, but
usually out of reach. This tallies with the data, which shows
that the average British worker is more likely to be in debt
than to have savings. Half of the population are unable to
save, given their low income, and one in six workers has no
security in any form to fall back on.

The material things considered necessary for a good working life are relatively modest and uncontested. You must of
course have enough to eat, clean air and water, a warm and

secure home. Whether you can rely on strong public services is also a critical factor: if you are not worried about transport, education, care or health costs, then you think differently about your earnings and feel more secure. At the Imaginings everyone was worried about these costs, feeling that public services (another form of wealth and security) can no longer be relied on. You need access to affordable digital infrastructure, which cannot be assumed. You must also be able to interact with your neighbours and peers without shame: your children must have the right football kit, your home must have enough space to invite people round, and when there's a birthday party you must feel you can afford to go, and to take a gift.

During the course of the twentieth century, the philosopher and Nobel Prize-winning economist Amartya Sen shifted our understanding of material wellbeing. Sen's research shows that neither poverty – which was the focus of his work – nor wealth can be measured by an arbitrary income line. Whether you feel materially secure is contextual: it depends on the cost of housing in the place you live, for example, and what is required for wider social participation – to join the school teams and clubs, or to take a dish to a neighbour's pot luck supper.

At the Imaginings, those working for corporates in London and San Francisco were more financially oriented, quick to choose the cards that related to money, in part because the location and cultures of their work compel them to earn more both to pay the rent and to keep up with their peers. Young professionals talked about the high cost of living in each city and their anxiety about being locked into financial contracts which made them feel precarious. The loss of their jobs would bring everything crashing down.

Many others talk about their experience of gut-wrenching

poverty, 'the constant sums in the head, the worry, the lying to the kids', as they chew over the basics. Palash had no work for a year. He had a young child, and the worry and desperation ended his marriage, his wife leaving with their small son. He is working now. Decent work should by rights mean that you have enough to live without worry. There's a consensus: 'if you can't provide these things, what you are offering can't really be called work'.

Jeetu, Palash and their colleagues, like many others, railed against being paid below the minimum wage.* This experience is not uncommon. One third of the lowest paid British workers receive less than the legal requirement. Almost a million workers have no paid holiday, despite this also being a legal entitlement, and 1.8 million workers do not get a payslip (a lack of formality which makes it hard for them to pursue their rights).

'We are not unwell, we need the basics,' Palash told me in reference to the widespread political misperception that workers refuse work because they are unwell, rather than because intolerable work is making them unwell and the contract is broken.

For Jeetu and Palash a lack of wage enforcement is accompanied by a lack of adherence to safety standards: they must carry dangerous loads on their bikes or risk the closure of their apps which is effective dismissal. Enforcement of safety at work legislation is often flimsy for many workers. The international requirement is that there should be one labour standards enforcement officer per ten thousand workers. Britain has one for every thirty-five thousand workers. On average in Britain there has been less than one criminal prosecution a year for not paying the legal minimum wage and attention to safety standards is even weaker.

* At the time of my journey, the UK minimum wage was £10.40 an hour and the London living wage £13.15 an hour.

The picture is similar in the United States. In Detroit, a group of construction workers who joined me at an Imagining talked with similar vigour and desperation about the danger of their work, while their life journey charts detailed frequent accidents and the hardship that follows without wages or benefits of any kind. 'I was left alone in a flooded water main until after ten at night,' Lucho told me. 'That water rose six foot in two minutes, I can't swim but I also know I can't lose my job – my family will starve and I've been told so many times by the higher ups that I'm replaceable.' 'OSHA?' he said with a derogatory snort, referring to the US Government Occupational Safety and Health Administration. 'They don't care – the inspections are organised – everyone knows who is coming and when – it's a stitch-up.'

Erosion of the basics has become more widespread with the growth of both the freelance and the gig economy, but workers started to lose ground much earlier, and the effects are spreading even to those who until very recently could count on traditional work contracts.

In the 1980s, deindustrialisation led to the loss of well-paid jobs in whole geographies as work that was once regulated moved to places where workers could be paid less. In turn workers in those countries, including Bangladesh and Mexico (Lucho's former home), felt compelled to leave a low-wage economy in search of work that would not be immiserating. Millions have instead found themselves in unregulated work which is either physically or psychologically unsafe. Palash has a political science degree from Dhaka University. Jeetu is a trained chef. Their qualifications are rarely recognised in their new home country, and so instead they worked as security guards, in kitchens, in low-paid administration roles, 'but we felt pressure. The problem is, you know, there is so much racism; I'm a Muslim.' Palash shook his head sadly, acknowledging that, even with British citizenship and twenty years' residence in Barking, he can still feel like an outsider.

In Barking the tenor of the conversation was angry but its content and the definition of the basics were no different from any other place I went to. The 'minimum basic lifestyle' that Jeetu wryly suggested was his due is expected by everyone, even as the basics start to slip out of reach for workers who never imagined they might be vulnerable: those such as teachers, health workers and other public servants who used to count on modest but decent salaries, secure contracts and a pension.

It is said that 80 per cent of workers in Britain feel precarious. They are not, like Palash and Jeetu, in danger of losing their homes or, like Lucho, fearing for their physical safety, but they are unsettled by a wider undoing of the work contract. Technology has pushed the boundaries of work, and the effects are being felt by increasing numbers of workers, including skilled professionals. Even those with good jobs don't feel their jobs or salaries will last, while older workers and women in particular are often the most vulnerable to being eased out and newly dependent on finding freelance work. Younger workers, as already discussed, are frequently in debt from their studies and feel a widespread despair that they will never find work that brings them an equilibrium.

As I made my journeys, a period of strikes rolled across Britain and the United States: doctors, academics, train drivers and many more started to protest not just the declining value of their wages, but the encroaching culture of 'gigification'. These workers were being forced to accept new contracts which demanded they be available for any shifts necessary while no longer guaranteeing core work. 'We want our Daddy time back' ran an ingenious campaign organised by engineers at British Gas. These skilled workers, mainly men, posted images of their children on social media in an attempt to show what was at stake in the new contracts being offered by Centrica, the multinational owner of British Gas: their ability to control their working hours and thus the basic right to a family life. They did not win.

Freedom from surveillance

There's an uneasy elision which starts with technology. More and more workers are always 'on' – an expectation that calls will be taken, emails answered, Slack and Teams threads actively monitored and shifts accepted – which all too easily becomes a form of spying. 'They watch you. They are not supposed to, but we know they do,' I was told by many workers who distrust the use of cameras installed at their workplaces and who resent the requirement to download companies' apps on their personal phones.

Billions are being invested into surveillance, with applications monitoring everything from call handling times to body temperatures. Work from food prep kitchens to call centres, Amazon fulfilment lines to delivering home care is increasingly monitored and driven by surveillance algorithms. In the care industry, for example, My EVV is just one example of the reach of this new technology. The app is marketed as a management tool 'to make real-time decisions that benefit your organisation', implying that workers who make home visits will be able to more efficiently update themselves on a person's needs as they move through their working day. But in the United States, care workers whose companies use the app liken it to being under house arrest, such is the minute (and punitive) tracking of their movements.

Surveillance algorithms are used by thousands of

companies and are attracting billions of dollars of investment. Apps such as FlexiSPY, developed by Thomson Reuters, or InterGuard, which boasts it can read WhatsApp messages, are deployed by giants such as Walmart and smaller shops such as Sunglass Hut. The technology increasingly governs who gets hired and monitors how workers communicate with each other – detecting and punishing, for example, worker sarcasm and attempts to organise. Surveillance is largely unregulated and often reaches beyond the workplace as workers who are forced to download apps onto their mobile phones find that everything from their location data to their informal messages can be monitored. Those in hospitality and service sector jobs have been particularly vulnerable, with reports surfacing in the media alleging that companies such as McDonald's are spying on their employees.

In her alarming and groundbreaking book documenting the rise of 'surveillance capitalism', the Harvard Business School professor Shoshana Zuboff drew comparisons between nineteenth-century industries which ravaged nature and twenty-first-century industry which is ravaging human nature.

These technologies impact most on the lives of the low paid and therefore disproportionately on women and workers of colour, further intensifying work injustice. But their use is more widespread. In the summer of 2024, employees were fired from the Wells Fargo bank for 'simulation of keyboard activity'. They had used devices which activated their computer keyboards, allegedly creating the impression that they were actively working when they were not. The discovery of these devices confirmed long-held suspicions that surveillance technology is being routinely deployed to monitor 'white-collar' workers who opt to work from home. Campaigners point out that this technology not only infringes rights; it also comes with a huge ecological price tag, with research showing the accompanying intensification of energy use.

Surveillance has always been present at work, although in the last century our bosses found it much harder to monitor exactly what we were doing most of the time. When I worked at the World Bank in the 1990s it was standard practice to leave your jacket on your desk chair as you slipped out to catch an early movie. A colleague or a boss glancing into your office would simply assume you were in a meeting elsewhere in the building. In this century, surveillance has intensified in part because technology makes our whereabouts and work activity easy to monitor, but also because trust has disappeared with the fracturing of the social contract. Workers no longer trust that they will have predictable work or be justly rewarded for their time (the basics) while bosses – from Uber to Goldman Sachs – are adamant that if they can't see their workers working, they don't believe they are. When trust disappears, surveillance takes its place, and a negative cycle is reinforced as surveillance in turn further deepens distrust.

Surveillance matters, not just because no worker should be spied on and because none of us can do good work when we feel we are being constantly watched and monitored, but because surveillance data is used to further drive down wages, a process which in the digital age can be ruthlessly efficient.

Surveillance provides real-time observations and data of working patterns that can be used to increase the work required in any shift. In the short term, workers immediately suffer, but interestingly it seems that in the medium term surveillance may also damage the company. Workers find being overtly monitored intolerable and tend to leave. Documents leaked from Amazon, for example, appear to show that the company loses $8 billion annually in attrition costs related to surveillance practices underpinning work routines that are so intense few workers can stand them for very long. Securing the basics and thus the loyalty of workers is a more sustainable route for workers and their companies.

New technology initially transforms systems according to existing priorities and values. It's like water that finds a groove and deepens it. At the start of this century most – but critically not all – businesses are designed to reduce costs as far as possible in order to make greater short-term profits for their owners and shareholders. For workers, reducing costs means low pay, unpredictable work, a disregard for safety regulations and the introduction of surveillance.

Increasingly we protest, we imagine and then we design something new. Workers who come together around new imaginings, in new organisations, are critical in bringing about an inflection point – the turning point that Perez describes in every technology revolution, in which new forms of technological deployment lead to a 'golden age'.

This cycle is something Palash, Jeetu and Ahmed – like many others I meet as I journey – instinctively understand.

'We have become slaves because of the technology,' Jeetu told me. 'But this is just the beginning of this game. It takes time to come together, to raise our voice. It took decades last time,' he said, referencing the Industrial Revolution and the initial squeeze on workers which eventually gave way to union-ensured basics and good working lives for many.

Jeetu and his colleagues flipped their paper tablecloth and started to design an organisation that they thought could redress the balance, an organisation they called The Raiders.

The Raiders' mission would be to secure the basics for everyone in the community, providing a physical space, 'a place where everyone can gather', and ownership of the technology platform itself: 'We would own the technology, changing the rules of this game.' As the men developed their ideas the mood shifted. They started to tease one another and their propositions for the future grew bolder. The Raiders would have guaranteed wages and working hours; they would have new forms of training and education, enabling them to grow into new roles or convert the skills and certificates they had brought with them from Bangladesh to qualifications recognised in Britain. 'We would have a seat at the table.' The Raiders would be able to talk with government and create new relationships with customers and neighbours.

A vision of hope and good work was drawn on the table, one of a series of propositions that I will return to later in this book. As I headed home from Barking, I pondered whether the spelling of this new organisation's name was a mistake on the part of the Uber riders, or a declaration of intent, signalling that The Raiders would come together to take back what was rightfully theirs, basics which in their eyes have been almost magically vanished by the algorithm and its invisible and far-away masters.

Discussing the basics was always the most difficult part of the Imaginings. It was not a topic that brought out the creativity and joy found in the principles to follow. And yet the subject could not be avoided. There is no good working life without the basics – it's the first principle of a good working life. At the same time, the basics alone are not sufficient. The gig riders that morning were also looking for a space to dream, and one of the things they dream about is work with meaning.

Principle Two: Meaning

'What do you want to do?' we ask young people. And the question repeats again within us, at different ages and stages, when we feel dissatisfied or have an urge to change course. What do you want to do? It's not an easy question to answer because what we do is a question of who we will be. Work is the chrysalis; an exoskeleton within which we hope to form ourselves. It's why having no work is so painful – our development is blocked – and it's why work that does not fit us is almost worse – we cannot grow. Work is a search for meaning, something everyone at the Imaginings wanted to talk about.

Practising, failing and trying again is a path to meaning. It's something that Laura, shy, ethereal and much younger than me, has already worked out. Laura is a welder at the BAE Systems nuclear submarine base in Barrow-in-Furness. I meet her at the Yard, as the base is known. It's a sprawling place of immense sheds which are visible from every part of town, looming, sinister, above the warm brick of Barrow's streets. Carrying my rucksack of materials, I cross a narrow pedestrian bridge, below which I can just make out the dark hulk of an almost completed submarine – a malevolent killing machine, submerged in waters dappled by early spring light. Waters barely a mile from a local primary school.

Arriving, I am shown to the place where I will work. It's a training room built to the exact and narrow footprint of an Astute submarine. But here, unlike on the submarine, one wall is made of glass and the morning sun floods the room. Laura is already there. With blond hair, a steady blue-eyed gaze and a fox, life-like and almost twitching, inked on her left arm, she isn't the person I imagine when I think of a welder. I've been told there are only a few skilled women welders at the Yard, and while we wait for her colleagues to join us, I ask how Laura got here.

It turns out, it's a family line of work. Laura opens her left palm to show me the number 36 tattooed in dark blue. 1936 is the year of her grandfather's birth; he was an electrician in the Yard. Her two brothers are also electricians at the base and an older brother is a submariner. But still, it wasn't something that seemed an option for Laura. She describes how she felt lost in her late teens; her parents divorced and her life felt muddled. 'At school, I sat and did my work, so they focused me on university and it took me a while to work out for myself I needed something more craft based.' Laura had thought she would be a vet, but the course 'was awful, I hated it. I'm very quiet and I just felt too isolated. I couldn't hack the classes on my own, so I left and followed my friends.' She took a job at Morrisons, where she worked on the checkout. 'That was even more of a waste of time . . . ' Laura shakes her head.

Salvation came through a friend, who had a welding set in his back garden. Laura was intrigued. 'BAE wasn't even in my mind – it just looked so big, so scary, but the welding felt really natural – I thought, I just want to do that, and he persuaded me to do a college course. When I completed my course, BAE were pushing for women so . . . It's coming up ten years now and I love it.'

For Laura, it's a good life; 'Perfect,' she tells me. Her work is intense but there's respect, good pay and scheduled down-time allows for climbing and hiking in the vast and beautiful expanses that surround the town. Laura has her home, her beloved dog Chester and her partner who works in the Lake District National Park. She's a skilled climber and a fell runner. Her face lights up when she describes the landscape, the elation of running down the fells' steep tracks. I feel her deep connection to the hills and the lakes.

We're interrupted by the arrival of Laura's colleagues. Mike is an electrician and Rob an electrical apprentice. Matt is another welder, who I can't help but notice is missing an ear. The men pull out their chairs, all loud scrapes on the floor and cheerful banter, teasing each other with an easy familiarity. Once seated, the tone changes and they immediately start to grumble about their work: a small to-do on the latest shift, about the safety gear, the pace and content of new training and the rigid work patterns. Mike has young children and the lack of flexibility is starting to take a toll. 'We wouldn't do it if we didn't have to,' they say, but the pride and camaraderie with which they describe their work belies this declaration.

Laura describes the rhythm of her days. She's a TIG welder – this is the most skilled and complex form of in-dustrial welding, and the work requires deep concentration and acute dexterity with the torch in one hand, the button and wire in the other, each moving in synchronicity. Every joint must be perfect and invisible, like the work of the haute couture seamstress. 'It's close and loud – I'm often working upside down and there's so much stuff already in there – it's really tight.' Laura is slight and agile: she can squeeze into the hot nose of the submarine to do the work that others can't. What I hear as she talks is her satisfaction and sense of fulfilment. Laura trusts her hands and she knows that lives will depend on every seam. Rob puts it plainly: 'Your work really matters. If you get it wrong, the team down there [in the submarine] will die.'

'Do you ever make a mistake?' I ask the team.

'Yeah, sometimes,' Laura tells me, 'if the angle is too awkward. When I started, I had such dread that it might go wrong but now it's like I'm in the zone, the focus can be relaxing.'

The Astute class submarines that Laura and her colleagues are building are the backbone of Britain's security. Their controversial purpose and their expense (each one costs in the region of £1.6 billion) is regarded by many as obscene. In Barrow, however, a job in the Yard is prized. The pay is good, your skills matter and there's an important sense of mission, being part of a national project. 'It's really important,' Laura tells me, 'with other countries doing what they're doing.'

Most of the teams work on one submarine from start to finish. No Astute is exactly alike, given that the technology moves on over the six-year construction period, making their assembly one of the most complex engineering projects in the world. Making end to end with the ability to see the final result is an inherent part of the team's pride and satisfaction. So is the approbation their work receives from the town.

What is made in a place runs deep, and it gives meaning to a community too. When each submarine is completed, the whole town turns out to see it leave the dock. There is a festival atmosphere, and the team stand tall. It's also something of a secret – the day and the time are spread by word of mouth to prevent the arrival of protestors. Somehow everyone gets the message and, young and old, they line the sides of the dock to wave and cheer. The completed submarines will never return to Barrow: they are maintained and repaired over two hundred miles up the coast in Scotland.

Laura and her colleagues have work with meaning. The work is absorbing, requiring skilled hands, mental focus and commitment. The work has purpose: they are making something that they believe matters, and others will depend on their skills. And Laura and her colleagues see themselves as part of a bigger project: they have a place in their town and in the world.

The way in which this team talk about their work – even their grumbles are active and engaged – contrasts painfully with the lassitude I encounter among those whose work is to simply move something made elsewhere along the global supply chain. A sense of ennui pervades the workers who toil in Barnsley's fulfilment centres. Moving a garment just one step in its long journey from a far-off factory to the customer and then often a landfill site feels meaningless. For those on the lower rungs of the ladder in large corporations, the sense of tedium is similar. 'It's all rinse and repeat,' management consultants tell me in a London boardroom, describing the process of putting together the slide decks which drive the business of global consultancy work. These well-paid professionals might, if they are lucky, be invited to the final client presentation, but they have little control over their work as it is edited and used in its passage up the chain of command. They describe their work as 'pointless'.

Illness often results when we feel that we have little control over work which has been chopped into small, repetitive bits. Particularly toxic is work which is at once high pressure and in which the tasks have been atomised; we do repetitive work, often alone. (This is the work of the London junior management consultants and the Barnsley warehouse packers.) Health professionals have a term for this: they call it 'isostrain'. Isostrain is a significant cause of mental illness because work that feels pointless infects our sense of self: we start to feel adrift and disjointed, that life itself is meaningless.

This splitting of work into tasks which no longer require end-to-end making and which call on only one part of our bodies – either our brains or our hands (hearts and souls are already discounted) – is not new to this century. The invention of the industrial production line introduced a culture of efficiency predicated on each worker focusing on a discrete task. The violent human effects were described by Karl Marx in his historical accounts of the Industrial Revolution. 'It is not only the labour that is divided, subdivided, and portioned out betwixt divers men: it is the man himself who is cut up,' he wrote, graphically describing the human impact of this work revolution that separated head and hands.

In this century, the innovations in logistics and communications, powered by the digital revolution, has created exponential growth in extenuated global supply chains, further subdividing tasks and creating work with characteristics that are the very opposite of those which give Laura and her colleagues purpose and meaning. Increasing numbers of us have been socially and spatially distanced from what we make and who we work with. The result is too often a profound sense of detachment and alienation.

Even people aren't made here any more, a Hartlepool parish priest explained to the author Stephen Armstrong when he visited the once-thriving steel town on the North Sea. As industrial work has left, the community has felt its identity being stripped away. A tipping point for the anger and despair was the decision to move the hospital to nearby Stockton-on-Tees. The move included the relocation of Hartlepool's maternity unit, with the result that babies would no longer be recorded as being born in the town. 'It's almost irrational, but it's a feeling that the town's identity is being wiped out,' the priest explained. In *The New Poverty*, Armstrong stresses the spirit and 'fight' that remains in Hartlepool, but the connection between the decline of meaning and the decline of making – from steel to babies – is sharply drawn.

But force always creates counterforce. And so we should not be surprised that the accelerating specialisation of work tasks and the unmooring of work from place has been met with an energetic response: a simultaneous surge in place-based making.

Everywhere I journey, from London to Baltimore, I meet those who have seized the possibilities of the digital revolution to make things end to end and often close to home. These makers can use sophisticated, digitised (often low-cost or shared) machinery and they can reach global markets through no-cost online marketing. Interestingly, they are often responding not only to the urge to find work with meaning but also to the bigger questions of ecology, which ask how and what we should make in cultures where cheap and throwaway goods are pervasive.

Making that matters

Elena Deminska's vegetable ferments sit jewel-like in their jars, stacked on shelves in a reclaimed nineteenth-century railway arch in Bermondsey, south London. Fermentation is an organic, chemical making process akin to alchemy. With the simple addition of salt, plants start to break down; water is released, and humble pale vegetables are transformed into brilliant reds, oranges, pinks and purples. It's not only colours that are enhanced, so too is taste and nutritional value. I could describe fermentation as a form of pickling, but this does not do justice to the complexity of the flavours that result, or to the 'smart' nature of the process. A plant which has been heavily sprayed or polluted in another way will not ferment and so has to be discarded.

'It's the colours that first drew our customers,' Elena tells me. Beneath the railway arches, she is pioneering a food revolution. She takes the food waste left over from vegetable trading and turns it into delicious highly nutritious ferments.

Born in Murmansk, the former headquarters of the Soviet Union's submarine fleet, Elena was nine months old when her father, a submariner, was transferred to Latvia. She grew up in Riga and spent summers with her grandmothers in Russia and Belarus. It was a childhood everyone should have, she says: swimming in rivers, picking berries and wild mushrooms, running free.

The collapse of the Soviet Union and Latvia's proud and newly won independence brought trouble for Elena and anyone else perceived to be ethnically Russian. Latvia was her home but in the heady early days of independence she felt unwelcome and trapped. Elena, like many people from the former Soviet Union, has manifold family roots: part Russian, part Polish, part Ukrainian, with Jewish heritage on her mother's side. When her husband Andrei was offered a building contract in London through a friend, they jumped at the chance to move to a diverse and (they hoped) more welcoming city. It would be a tough transition for Andrei, who would have to abandon his work as a chef, but a better future for their five-year-old son.

Elena spoke no English but found work at Tony Booth's, a legendary wholesale vegetable seller in London's Borough Market. On a Saturday Tony sold veg to Londoners interested in food, but his main business was the restaurant trade. Every top chef bought from Tony. For Elena it was a stressful, rapid-fire education: learning to speak English, learning about the vegetables and about the work of elite British restaurants:

'How different it is behind the scenes, behind the celebrity chef. I've seen how the chefs were suffering, and it was everywhere, the stress, the addiction.'

Tony also suffered from stress and the pressures of working with the high-end food industry, where payments are notoriously late and hard to chase down. When he retired, Elena took over, but she didn't want to keep the restaurant side of the business. It had high financial returns, but she had seen the personal cost. She would need to find another way to generate sufficient income. Meanwhile, something else bothered her too: the waste endemic in vegetable trading. The Department for Environment, Food and Rural Affairs calculates that 7 per cent of the vegetables we grow – 3.6 million tonnes per year – are thrown out, uneaten – an enormous challenge to any ecologically sustainable food system. Elena could see her unsold vegetables were part of the problem. 'Follow your grandmothers,' Andrei urged. 'Ferment.'

'I wasn't sure,' Elena told me. 'English people have different tastebuds, and those cabbage ferments got us through harsh winters but I thought of it as poverty food.' But, since she had some plastic tubs lying, around she thought, Why not try? Three months later she needed new shelves, equipment, storage and workers. Elena had become fascinated by the flavours and possibilities and so had her customers.

'This is creative food,' Elena explains. 'There are no rules, it's free, because you are using food that would otherwise be wasted, and you don't need a recipe.' She's being exceptionally modest, because to produce the quality and quantity of ferments that are now the work of the London Fermentary requires a team, knowledge, skills and craftmanship. Ensuring jars don't explode in transit is just one of the challenges.

If the frozen pea is the enemy – delivered to our homes through the long energy-intensive cold chain links that characterise our high-carbon food industry, to sit silently in every home freezer, consuming energy while it waits to be eaten – the ferment is the future. Ferments not only take waste and turn it into food, they provide vegetables that are high in nutrients and flavour without the need for refrigeration or for imports, even in winter.

Elena has taken an industrial site and a pre-industrial technique and turned it into a very modern business. Demand continually outstrips supply and Elena has taken on significant investment to grow the business. Her knowledge is sought from Newlyn in Cornwall to Oaxaca in Mexico, places where Elena has trained others, and her products are now widely available.

'Without technology, this would not have happened. It's as simple as that,' Elena explains as the trains rumble overhead. The London Fermentary has no marketing department. Social media drew customers – individuals and retailers alike – transforming something that might have been a niche hobby into a business. Software drives smart ordering and stock systems, ensuring there is no waste at any point in the process. Modern machinery plays a role too. 'When everyone is chopping cabbage by hand, well, it's a shithole,' Elena says with disarming frankness. 'I've been stunned by this emphasis on "home-made". In food, it usually means people are doing horrible work for low wages in disgusting facilities. Chopping, jarring, bottling, labelling – this is repetitive and boring work.' There is manual work at the London Fermentary, paid at the London living wage, but as little as possible and people are promoted as fast as possible. Fermentation is about bubbling – and the work needs to be creative too.

Elena is a modern maker: tying digital technology to an ancient craft, she is disrupting food systems built on overproduction and waste. She has also found a life and work with meaning, bringing together a childhood love of plants, skills learnt from an earlier generation and a mission to transform our health through the way we eat.

When I am invited to take the Imaginings to the United States, my journey starts in Baltimore, a city where I also find a new abundance of making. April Lewis is the director of Open Works, a makerspace where residents share skills and tools. 'Things were made here before,' April tells me. 'It's all gone away and now we are rebuilding it from the grass roots.' We are standing together on the steps of Open Works, at the intersection of Greenmount Avenue, a city artery that traditionally separated affluent white residents from their poorer Black neighbours.

Makerspaces are collaborative work places: physical spaces where workshops, tools, materials, knowledge and very often projects are shared for common use, and sometimes in common ownership. Makerspaces are growing in popularity around the globe, responding to the resurgence in making and to a belief that this is important for the future of national economies. In China, for example, the national innovation strategy prioritises local maker movements, while in Paris mayor Annie Hidalgo has made subsidising neighbourhood makerspaces part of her socioeconomic strategy, vital for the city's economy and cultural mix. In places like Paris, London or Baltimore, where land prices rise rapidly and rents are high, it can be a challenge to keep makerspaces in business and affordable to all. When I met members of the Baltimore makerspace at an Imagining hosted nearby, I had been curious to hear about the space and I had asked if I could visit.

With bold orange lettering, Open Works announces itself from some distance. Standing on a patch of desolate ground between railway tracks and an abandoned industrial site, the building exudes a promise and an invitation with its wide steps, glass frontage and awnings that create a shady outside space. April knows that teenagers might not – at first – want to come inside, but they need somewhere with free Wi-Fi to do their homework and to hang together.

April's formal title – director – barely begins to describe what she does: part host, part manager, part anthropologist, investigator and artist. Her mission is to make sure Open Works includes everyone, while not morphing into a gentrified white space. 'I'm myself Baltimore-made in those neighbourhoods,' she tells me proudly, indicating the historically Black neighbourhoods that surround us.

Anthony and Nicole are from those same neighbourhoods, and both are based at Open Works. When I met them at the Imagining the day before, they had plotted previous corporate roles on their life charts and talked about how they had tried to marry their art with jobs that offered stability, respectability, a place on the ladder. But both had struggled in work which turned out to be neither creative nor meaningful. Nicole took the leap to leave her job with an in-house graphic design team to establish an art studio. Anthony, who had been an in-house photographer, told me he had found it hard to screw up the courage to make change, but after being fired from three jobs, it was time. He recounted the stories of his dismissals, prompted in part by his inability to fit the corporate culture, with a wry smile. It felt shaming, but it was also galvanising. He has re-trained as a project manager – a role he combines part time with his photography studio. This works, Anthony explained, because 'in each role I have integrity'.

The Detroit social activist Grace Lee Boggs has been scathing about the exploitation behind the fashionable idea that we can or should all DWYL (Do What You Love). Parents often encourage their children to find work that they love. But this same mantra, Boggs argues, is used by business as a form of 'brainwashing', in an attempt to dress up jobs which in reality are not creative, and to intensify work and exploit workers. DWYL creates another form of splitting, particularly in corporates and the service industry, where everyone is encouraged to don a personality, forced to pretend in front of customers and colleagues alike that they are warm and creative, and that they love what they do. If everyone really is a movie maker, as Pixar famously claims for its thousand-plus employees, that's fine. But if the work is actually something else – you are making the tea for the design team, or shadowing the CEO to take their portrait – it's better and less damaging to the worker's sense of self-esteem to say so.

The French sociologist Jacques Donzelot has gone a step further, arguing that the very idea we might find meaning in any work is a lie inculcated in us by the state in its efforts to make sure we are reared to be good cogs in the economic machine. The lie of meaning, as Donzelot sees it, is an attempt to persuade us to be fully available to the labour market and to work ever harder in our (misguided) attempts to find both purpose and work we love.

I think that attempts by the welfare state, in particular to force citizens to take any work, no matter how demeaning or badly paid, because it will in some way be 'better' for us, are clearly wrong and a performance of this lie. I also, as I will come to below, do not believe that all work has meaning or that work is all of life's meaning. But like everyone who came to the Imaginings, I think that good work is critical to the sense of a life path with purpose. It's why we must wrestle honestly with the questions of what work has meaning for us personally, what work enhances the places we are from and what work can sustain our planet.

At the Imaginings, many like Anthony and Nicole had tried working in roles that promised creativity or for companies where values were touted as a reason to join. The way in which many businesses commission costly and time-intensive corporate value exercises in an attempt to create cultural cohesion and meaning is a source of both mockery and ire. Workers came to the Imaginings from green companies, from campaigning charities and from corporates professing ethical values and principles of justice and anti-racism. When these espoused values are not lived within the internal culture of an organisation – when a charity, for example, professes to be helping others but not does treat its own people kindly, when policies of equality are reduced to an acronym adhered to by lip service only, or a corporate preaches 'integrity' and 'service' but outsources its cleaning to workers paid less than the minimum wage – the discomfort and dissonance are painful. Many, like Anthony, talk about how they first underperform through a lack of motivation and then, if they can, they leave.

Tanisha, who shared a table with Anthony and Nicole, and is also based at Open Works, has swapped work as one of America's few women firefighters for knitting. Imani, also at the table, left her job as an accountant to train in metalwork. 'We are off the beaten path, but we are not lost,' Tanisha said to me as she pulled out her phone to swipe through pictures of her knitwear – her latest collection included sweaters with exquisitely produced portraits of Black activists. Here was a group of people who had decided to find a new accommodation with money in order to sustain a creative life. 'We will be sitting at home with the dishes dirty and we don't have much, but life is meaningful, because we have this work,' explained Imani, ironically dressed in a *Real Housewives of Baltimore* hoodie.

From the outside, the lives of these makers did look precarious, but strikingly this was one of the few groups who joined me at the Imaginings who did not talk about precarity. They felt themselves to be grounded, partly through a conscious reckoning and realignment of material needs, but also because, in a digital economy, they have found ways to live good lives and meet the basics. 'Our currency is our skills,' Tanisha remarked as she shuffled cards related to money and other material matters. 'We've got flexibility and autonomy,' she added, before explaining that in addition to her knitwear business, she runs a podcast and is a part-time carer for her son who has autism. Caring responsibilities are another reason for seeking the autonomy that making in particular offers, which I consider in more depth in the next chapter. Tanisha has the balance she wants and has created for herself.

The surge in making which Elena, Anthony and Tanisha are part of is a response to our search for work with meaning. It's made possible by a connected growth in the appreciation of craft. The ability of digital design processes, harnessed to global mass production, to produce so called 'hand-made' objects – from food to fashion, furniture to art – at an almost unimaginable scale and low price has created an unexpected interest in the real thing. There are now many who are starting to reappraise the worth of objects that are made in a way which is sustainable for the maker and for ecological systems.

The design critic Alice Rawsthorn has described a turn to craft in the design industry: 'Initially it was widely assumed that as more and more aspects of our lives were digitised, our appetite for artisanal culture would wane. Instead, the reverse has happened, and it has heightened our appetite and interest in the intimacy, singularity, tactility and sensitivity of craft and making in general.' Tanisha's bespoke and beautiful knitwear sells for considerable sums to collectors and fashionistas alike, within and beyond the United States. Her customers understand the value embodied in the work. They find Tanisha through social media, meaning that, like Elena, she has no marketing costs and can make a living from her craft in a way that would have been unimaginable thirty years ago.

Technology can take old practices and bring them alive at scale in new ways. It could also, if we choose this direction, significantly reduce if not eliminate meaningless work, work the anthropologist David Graeber memorably called 'bullshit jobs'. 'Bullshit' work includes, in Graeber's words, 'the box tickers, the flunkies, the task masters' – and, Elena might add, the veg chopper. Graeber argued that more than half of the work done in modern economies is pointless, defining a pointless job as one that could disappear tomorrow and make no difference, work that is 'a scar across our collective soul'.

Graeber, echoing Donzelot, stressed that bullshit jobs exist to keep us under control. 'It's as if someone were out there making up pointless jobs just for the sake of keeping us all working,' he wrote, pointing out that in capitalism this is not meant to happen. The search for economic efficiency in capitalist systems should eliminate pointless work. The answer to this conundrum must be moral and political: a fear of what citizens would do if they had too much time on their hands.

It is, however, hard to decide what work is meaningful. Graeber concluded that only a worker would ultimately know if a job was 'shitty', pointing out that many jobs which feel most 'shit-like', because of the conditions, are in fact the most important forms of work: caring and cleaning, for example – work on which we all depend. A decade on, the Imaginings reveal that questions of meaning are growing in complexity. Today, ecological concerns are raising new questions about what work matters and should be sustained. At the same time, technology is allowing us to expand our horizons, changing the possibilities open to us and offering us potential – if we choose it – to automate some of the least loved work. Entwined within these concerns is a deeper question: what work will enable us to grow as humans?

Head, hands and heart

'Even though I was born and brought up and my documents all said *human*, there was something about his behaviour that made me think he didn't consider me to be an equal, and for a few brief and terrifying seconds I felt I was artificial, made, nothing but a humanoid machine.' In her dystopian novel of work in the twenty-second century, *The Employees*, the Danish novelist Olga Ravn viscerally describes a future of work in which every human is seen simply as a set of body parts. They are useful to the extent that they can be commanded to perform a given task.

This is the feared future of work that emerges at the Imaginings. A fear that is not directed at technology or machines *per se*, but rather at the structures and cultures of work that will force us, the humans, to become more machine-like. This is a future in which we are yet further atomised, in our distance from each other, from the work we do and from our inner selves.

Many of us have already experienced this type of work. As the twentieth century progressed, the splitting of tasks and the associated separation of human heads from human hands extended from the factory floor into the office, and then into the classroom and the clinic. At the Imaginings it was not only warehouse packers and management consultants who talked about how they must leave a part of themselves at the door in order to do their work. Teachers spoke of numbing their minds, discussing an unhealthy dependence on antidepressants and sometimes alcohol, to cope with the pressures of teaching often hungry children in schools without resources, where 'teaching to the test' to achieve exam results and pass inspection thresholds are the only things that count. A doctor told a similar story: 'I have to cut off,' she told me with a vehement swipe to the body, signalling the impossibility of providing human care with insufficient time and resources, and therefore the need not to think too much about the job in hand or the person in front of her, in order to survive.

Work in education and medicine once implicitly denoted work with meaning, in large part because professionals had autonomy, controlling both the resources available and the way they did their work. But as these professions have become routinised, with patterns of work largely dictated by those managing resources who are located elsewhere, so disenchantment has set in. What will happen next? Many predict that AI and in particular the profusion and exponential development of large language models means that technology will start to codify and therefore atomise professional work which until now has been out of reach: that of lawyers, consultants and accountants.

AI is just warming up, Richard Susskind, an expert advisor to the legal profession, warns. His advice to the newly threatened professionals is to seek transformation. The medic or lawyer should not imagine they will do enhanced work managing the robots that do surgery or routine case law, for example. They should instead reimagine what preventative medicine or preventative law might look like, becoming trusted again because they are creating societies and systems of work that will be more humane.

This is the alternative possibility that, partly enabled by technology and motivated by our concern for each other and for our natural systems, we become more human. This countervailing path is one with heart. It depends upon putting back into our narratives of work that part of us which is so often silently passed over.

The industrial work revolution and the splitting of head and hands – as first told by Marx – has become so familiar that we tend to follow its grooves and patterns without noticing what is missing. In America, I went to see another version of this famous story, the enormous and beautiful Detroit Industry Murals made by Diego Rivera in the early 1930s. The frescos unfold over the Institute of Art's walls, depicting hundreds of muscled workers beneath the fiery heat of machinery whose scale and solidity seems to threaten that the workhands might be pulverised at any moment. In one corner there is a brain, a portrait of the car maker Edsel Ford (son of Henry and president of the Ford Motor Company) neat in suit and tie. Almost at the ceiling is a baby, curled within the root structures of a womb: another worker waiting to be born.

Rivera's worker – usually white, male and in his overalls, almost collapsing under the weight of the physical task – is the image that comes to mind when we think of the Industrial Revolution and its work. Astonishingly, however, as late as the 1940s there were more domestic servants in the United States than workers on the railways, in mines or on production lines combined. These workers, mostly women and predominantly Black, are almost invisible in all forms of work history.

Those who tell the stories of work, labour historians and labour economists, are almost all men and usually white. Domestic labour is not close to their interests. It was not the work of their forefathers, even as those men were dependent on women in the home for their washing, their meals, their loving and their offspring. This lack of personal experience is one reason the work of the heart is missing in the familiar stories.

There is also, I think, another reason. The heart intrudes; it's disruptive and sometimes unruly. Matters of the heart stop us working – they interrupt any machine-like tendencies with the tug of love and our need to tend to children, parents and each other, which I look at in the next chapter. The heart provokes us to imagine and search for something more, and feminist scholars including the economist Nancy Folbre and the sociologist Hilary Rose have long emphasised the need to make the heart visible if we are to transform work. Rose studied the often-destructive patterns of work she found at the centre of the British industrial-military-scientific complex, arguing that bringing the (invisible) heart into focus would not only transform the conditions of work, it would raise important questions about meaning, tilting techno-science in more productive directions. The heart is creative, it makes us ask why: why must work be designed this way?

Every worker, from Laura to Elena, Anthony to Tanisha, women and men, had found a path with meaning by following their heart, not in a synthetic Do What You Love way, but through listening to something deeper within. The work they found brought meaning, which in turn brought their heads, hands and hearts together.

This is the work Bren Smith was searching for. 'I was a pillager,' he told me when we first met. It's an arresting introduction. Bren was a fisherman, or a pirate of the high seas, depending on the way you look at it. He dropped out of high school to chase cod on industrial trawlers. To feed the world's ravenous appetite for fish, the trawlers ripped up entire ecosystems, and to make up financial shortfalls in a supply chain that squeezes those who fish, drug-running was part of the economy. It was gruelling work: '[My] body is beat to hell,' he says, and a chemical splash in Alaska means he has lost half the vision in his right eye. 'I've been in prison, addicted to drugs, almost killed at sea, but every shiver of pain was worth it.'

Bren loved his ocean-going life. But when the cod stocks crashed in his home of Newfoundland, he had to face reality. 'We lost our work, and we lost our meaning. We spent our time standing in line to buy Russian cod for our fish and chips. People came promising so many dreams – like we could work in a seatbelt factory for pets, as if one job can be swapped for another just like that ... Lots of people left to work the tar sands in Alberta.' Bren describes how there had always been a community-based 'working-class environmentalism', a deep connection and love of the surrounding land and seas, but times were desperate and people had to find work where they could – not the promise of the next big idea in the form of a factory making seat belts for pets which never materialised, but actual existing work mining the tar sands.

Something different tugged at Bren. He said, 'There will be no jobs on a dead planet.' He wanted to somehow find or create ocean work that was not a form of eco-robbery or, as he puts it more poetically, 'I wanted a working life I could sing about.' 'Blue-collar workers have all the songs,' he tells me. 'Songs about mind, body and solidarity. Lawyers and Facebook employees, they don't write songs about their work. There's something wrong there.'

A second voyage led Bren to ocean farming. He started with oysters, farming successfully for almost a decade before successive 'once in a lifetime' storms hit. In 2012, Hurricane Sandy destroyed his livelihood altogether. Bren had to reimagine once again, and this time he turned to more ancient wisdom. Learning from methods that are centuries old, he started to farm kelp, sargassum, sea lettuce and other edibles. His farm was now vertical, growing on nets tethered to the sea bed, and his produce delighted foodies and famous chefs alike. It was also restoring the sea bed, filtering water, pulling out the nitrogen that had been killing the fish and regenerating a complex ecosystem.

When I next spoke to Bren, I asked him about the relationship between technology and ocean farming. Working in 'soil' that turns over a thousand times a day, technology could augment ocean farming by signalling some conditions, but currently the relationship works in the other direction. The health of the kelp provides critical information for ocean scientists, which feeds mathematical models on ocean conditions. Robotics that could help with harvesting are not anywhere near the horizon, given the delicacy of the product and the constantly shifting conditions. 'Technology! I barely have freakin' internet,' Bren concluded as our internet connection momentarily froze.

He had just finished a harvest, exhausted but also elated by the physical labour he loves. His other work is at GreenWave, the non-profit he co-founded with Emily Stengel, to support others to join him in creating new work and a new ocean economy. More than eight thousand prospective farmers from every coastal state in the United States and a hundred countries around the globe have requested support, and GreenWave is scaling to meet the need for good work and for an ocean farming model that can breathe life back into our oceans.

You need a boat and to lease your patch of water; it's affordable and you have agency and a livelihood, Bren explains, describing why the work is popular and within reach of his own people – the 'blue-collar' workers he cares about. 'Very soft inside, very gettable,' he says. I think for a moment he is describing the ocean's crustaceans, but Bren is talking about his peers, who like him want to be tethered again to the places they love.

Work with heart is work in which we have an affinity with what we are making, growing and inventing with our hands and minds. It's work where we see ourselves as part of a collective project linking our individual efforts to a bigger economy we can be proud of. It's work with meaning, and for some of us it stitches us back into the places we are from.

Working our purpose out

Can all work be meaningful? It's a question which scarcely detained our grandparents, who worked to fulfil their basic needs. 'Become like me': this was the path of early modern times. The son of a bricklayer became a bricklayer, the son of a printer, a printer. Even if you did not go into your parent's profession, you almost certainly did what they decided for you, and once established in an occupation you were expected to stay there. If you were lucky, you might find enjoyment and meaning in the life chosen for you. Lucky and probably male, given the very narrow opportunities open to women.

Today this model is broken. It is not mourned. We want our work to offer us meaning and to have purpose. 'I'm not Gen Z . . .' people tell me, smiling, before they make a serious point. Gen Z (those born roughly between the mid-1990s and 2010) are a generation shaped by digital technology, climate anxiety and financial insecurity. They are perceived to *only* want work with purpose and meaning. When workers from other generations make the comparison, they are telling me that purpose and meaning matter to them too. There is a sense of gratitude that Gen Z – or at least the public portrayal of Gen Z – has liberated all of us to articulate our own desires for meaning.

But finding this meaning is not easy. Laura, Elena,

Anthony, Tanisha, Bren: each have a story to tell of the twists and wrong turns that were part of finding their meaningful work. The difficulty of coming by a second chance is something much discussed at the Imaginings, and as I noted earlier, those who have found second chances and more rate their working lives and their happiness highly.

To make change we need connections, income, care for our children, emotional support and often retraining. This challenge of finding the right path (and the fear of a wrong turn) is why young people in particular often feel paralysed by the question 'What do you want to do?' 'It's the idea that you should find a life purpose that *is* the stress,' a young graduate vented in Grimsby. He was not alone in his despair. The competition, to not only find a good job but one where you feel fulfilled, follows – for today's young people – years in the highly pressured sorting machine that is industrialised education. Gen Z have rich visions of the future of work, but these young adults are also suffering an epidemic of mental illness, much of which is related to this competitive struggle, laced with psychological pressures born of the expectation that you must not only do well by external benchmarks, but you must also love what you do.

Have we now freighted work with so much expectation of meaning that we find ourselves depressed and frustrated?

Work cannot offer meaning all the time. All work has humdrum days, when we do the things which interest us less. 'Button-making days', as the modernist potter Lucie Rie called them: the days she made buttons which sold for a good commercial fee, allowing her the time to make the exquisite pots which in her lifetime did not earn her a living.

We can accept a measure of humdrum. We can learn that work with meaning is something we make over time and are unlikely just to fall into. We can also see that we have an opportunity. Work which no one finds meaningful should be the target for automation. The rest of work can and should be redesigned around what motivates and sustains us.

Designing twenty-first-century work: a new template

Humans design work, so we could design it differently. To do this we would have to change the template that has guided policies and thinking about work for over a hundred years. Just as the dress or suit is modelled on a human form, so our work is cut out too. The dress pattern has in fact changed: we are no longer the same size or shape we were a century ago. But work has remained stubbornly unchanged despite being similarly out of shape.

The human template around which work is designed is not immediately visible to those of us who are not economists or labour historians. But he is there all the same, the man economists call *Homo economicus*.

Homo economicus is a child of early industrial technology and the Industrial Revolution, a nineteenth-century invention based in part on the works of economists Adam Smith and David Ricardo, then sharpened by the writings of the philosopher John Stuart Mill and elevated to his current status by the twentieth-century economist Milton Friedman. *Homo economicus* is a ruthless individual, single-minded in his competitive drive and, most importantly, he is motivated solely by rational calculations as to how he can maximise his personal material circumstances. *Homo economicus* is the boss; he wants money and power. He is in many ways more machine than man, and he spends little if any time on questions of meaning.

Homo economicus is of course a caricature, but like all good caricatures he is drawn with a modicum of truth – just enough to draw us in.

We recognise *Homo economicus* because he is everywhere in the official stories of work. We see him in job adverts that tell us what we will earn and promise a prestigious title, but almost never tell us anything about why the work will matter. We see him in the media coverage of strikes which focus almost exclusively on workers' wages to the exclusion of wider issues such as the gigification of workers' time and the threat to family lives discussed in the previous chapter. We see him in the politicians' speeches which promise more jobs, regardless of quality or purpose. And we see him in national policies for productivity in which more work and more profit are prized no matter the consequences. *Homo economicus* is a man particularly admired and mimicked by populist politicians hungry for power. But he is also at the heart of our eco-destruction, overproduction, unbalanced economies and unbalanced lives.

As I journeyed, I met hundreds of workers, but I never met *Homo economicus*.

Instead, conversations about work were deeply entangled with concepts about the meaning of being human. Workers and those who run businesses alike wanted to think differently, sharing ideas about the complexity that makes for a rich life: our hearts, our minds, our bodies, our relationships with one another, with nature and the places we are part of. We need money – securing the basics is the first principle of good working lives – and many of us like the thrill of competition, but this is just a *part* of who we are. We certainly don't want to live constantly pitting ourselves against one another, and we can't thrive on money alone.

And, interestingly, recent scholarship across a wide range of disciplines has made some striking new discoveries about our human make-up. Anthropological observation, breakthroughs in physics, social psychology and biology have all revealed that human beings are both rational and deeply emotional. We are driven and formed by a deep desire to bond with and care for one another, a desire that frequently compels us to act in the common good, even when such actions may not align with individual self-interest. The selfish gene – that wicked cousin of *Homo economicus* – is another fictional model, recently debunked by leading biologists and psychologists. Our communities, our families, our shared cultures and values – those elements that contribute to what social psychologist Cecilia Heyes calls 'our collective mind' – play a stronger role than genes in determining who we are and what we value.

We should pay our respects to *Homo economicus* and then give him a decent burial. His death can give way to the birth of something much better.

A good working life requires a new pattern, a new human model to inform the design. I'm going to call this person *Sapiens integra*, an integrated, whole being. *Sapiens integra* is a template I conceived jointly with the lawyer and political scientist Anne-Marie Slaughter, and is someone I met over and over again at the Imaginings. Laura and her colleagues, Elena, Anthony and Tanisha, Bren: they are complex humans with mixed and rich motivations. Each of them wants to make themselves through meaningful work and they want to shift a set of normative ideas that no longer serve us. One of these is the solitary gravitational pull of work. *Sapiens integra* wants meaningful work and to ensure that the pull of that work is not so extreme that it distorts other parts of us or the nature we are entwined with. *Sapiens integra* places meaningful work on a par with time to care for one another, to play and to tend to the places we live.

Principle Three: Care and Repair – Tending to What Sustains Us

Care is what we do to maintain and repair our world, ourselves, the places we live and the natural systems on which we depend. Without care, our lives do not work. At the Imaginings, the deep unmet need for care – at work, within the community and from professional services – was talked about by men and women, the young and the old. The absence of care is making work difficult, while hampering the possibility of good lives.

'We shift jobs, we shift again, nothing quite seems to work out.' Julie, Covid mask tucked beneath her chin and a much-needed cuppa in hand, has just finished her shift. She shrugs off her hi-vis vest as she describes to me what she calls 'the juggle, juggle': her constant struggle to get work and life to fit together.

We're in Barnsley in South Yorkshire. It's a spread-out place, a collection of former mining towns which have undergone a reinvention in the face of the devastation left by the closure of the mines. Barnsley's local government have invested in a successful tech hub and low property prices have drawn a small, flourishing community of artists and musicians. But work for most people is found in assembly and distribution, which is where I meet Julie.

This new warehouse economy is one solution for a place with abundant land and motorway connections. Municipal leaders have worked hard to establish Barnsley's reputation as a place where you can invest and get things done. They are proud to have persuaded Asos and Hermes (now Evri), among others, to locate their flagship distribution centres in the metropolitan area.

The company Julie works for is part of Britain's emerging green economy, producing affordable insulated windows. It is estimated that 14 per cent of our national carbon emissions come from leaky homes; the insulated windows Julie helps assemble are changing the carbon footprint of homes where they are installed. Julie tells me she's been in her job for two weeks and I am curious to know why she had made the change. Was she seeking a different purpose?

Julie arches a slender eyebrow before frankly stating that what the company does matters very little to her. She changed her job, accepting a demotion, because she needed work that would allow her time to organise her life, and most of all to care for her family.

'I were a store manager,' she tells me in broad and beautiful Barnsley cadence. 'Why did I come here? Stress! When I clock out here that's me done. In me other job I had the area manager messaging me, emailing me – I could never switch off. Until last year I cared for me mum – she lived with me and she had dementia – and me brother: I do his medication, I help him, clean, whatever – he's got epilepsy. But I wouldn't want it full time. D'you know, I could pack in me job, but I wouldn't want to because he's very needy. Here I can work and take the time to care: that's revolutionary.'

Julie has spent years feeling frayed and scattered, while continuing to work. She's not alone. One in four British adults – eleven million people – are caring for someone, fitting it in around their paid work. A further five million working age adults have given up work altogether in order to care for a family member. They have found the tensions between their desire and need to care and the demands of paid work impossible to manage.

Martin is one of Julie's colleagues. A burly man and breathing heavily, a legacy from his years in the coal mines, he joins us at the table where we are about to start the Imagining. Like Julie, Martin is juggling work and care. 'It's me mum. She has Alzheimer's. She's all right, but she wanders – I just have to hope I'm not at work when it happens.' Martin is also ambivalent about the work. 'Just clipping things together' feels empty compared to his 'twenty good years' in the mines. 'We went through all that pain and heartache and not eating properly,' he told me, referring to the miners' strikes of the 1980s, 'for what? Just this warehouse work. It's all gone,' he wheezed, shaking his head in disappointment.

Martin can at least take care of his mother, and for now this keeps him at the window plant: like Julie, he can work and care. But how much longer can they hold out? That depends in part on whether they also can get help from Barnsley's social services. Martin's mum is getting to a stage where he can't cope very well. 'I had a terrible period out of work, after the mine closed. I was proper depressed and me wife left me.' Living alone makes juggling his mother's needs and his work that much harder.

Julie is desperate to get some counselling for her teenage daughter. Kaitlyn has become very depressed since Julie's mum died. She dearly loved her grandmother, and the loss was made more painful because it coincided with the isolation of Covid-19 lockdowns. Kaitlyn is now very thin and slipping out of reach. Julie feels alone with the problem, and helpless. 'She's on a long waiting list . . . ' Julie trails off, unable to mask her emotion and worry.

In Barnsley an estimated one in five residents are now on a waiting list for either health or care services. These long waiting lists are part of a bigger national emergency. The Covid-19 pandemic has left many chronically unwell and others still waiting for procedures which were postponed. Those who have since become unwell must join the back of this lengthening queue. A third factor is work itself. Millions feel that they cannot continue, mentally or physically, in work that does not provide the basics, and they turn to health services as they seek to find a remedy for stress and pain. Demographic shifts add to the predicament: we are living longer but our bodies and our minds can wear out. The result is a chronic mismatch between need and capacity in all areas of health and care, which in turn creates acute strain on overworked professionals. Retention of staff is one of the biggest challenges facing health systems as nurses, midwives, carers and many more look for a way out. In Barnsley, the new warehouse economy has given some just the escape route they were looking for.

The work is punishing – the hours are long, the work is repetitive, often surveilled and isolating – but it pays more than minimum wage and employers offer 'sweeteners' in an effort to attract the workforce they need. Many of the town's core workers have decided to give it a go, creating an unanticipated and problematic churn in the low-paid but essential workforce across the wider area. Those making a change include taxi and bus drivers. As one former taxi driver who joined the Imaginings put it, 'If you are going to work for shit pay, you might as well not have to deal with the public as well.' Care workers might not talk about the public in such terms, but they too, like many health workers, have taken the opportunity to at least try something different. As a result, Barnsley have haemorrhaged health and care workers.

At the time I visited, local leaders were in the process of 'importing' seven hundred health and care workers from India, in an attempt to stem the bleeding. This is a not a strategy unique to Barnsley. Many places in Britain are currently bringing in a similar workforce from countries in Asia and Africa. It's a complex transaction, extracting very scarce professionals from nations that can ill afford to train and then lose their people. Each of these professional carers must also pass the care of their own homes and families, now far away, on to someone else, often an older daughter who should be in school. Patched-up solutions in one place open up wounds in another.

At the Imaginings, I am struck by quite how painfully stretched everyone feels – without time, resources or support to deal with the small things (a doctor's appointment, for example) and the big (the challenges that face Julie, Martin and so many others). I am also struck by the ways that care is framed.

Official stories about care – those told by politicians and policymakers – are narrow and focus on care services: how to organise and provide professional support, and who should pay. Official stories are rooted in the *Homo economicus* template. They demand (and assume we wish for) as much outsourcing of care as possible, from the cleaning of our homes to the tending of our children, friends and parents, so we are free to pursue what officials regard as our primary role: paid work.

In contrast, the Imaginings, and what I think of as unofficial stories, grapple with a more complex understanding of what it means to care and be cared for, and how these things are entwined with our desire for paid work. No one really wants to outsource all of the things that enable us to tend to and love one another. Caring is part of what makes us human, it is part of our *Sapiens integra* dreams. But we also don't want to struggle and juggle alone, to be *only* caring.

In the difference between these two very different stories lies not just despair and denial, but hope and possibility.

From Barnsley to Baltimore, Grimsby to Detroit, the elements of a new design for caring emerge in the Imaginings, a new design that brings together care and repair at three interlocking levels. It was created by people at the sharp end of experience.

First, this proposed new system includes employers who are encouraged to care for us as workers and in turn allow us the predictable flexibility we need to care. Second, attention and resources are focused on the informal community networks which pick us up when we fall through the gaps and, connected together as nodes within a new system, could do so much more. Third, professional care – whether provided in a clinic, a care home or our own home – must become good work. Only well cared for professional carers can fulfil their vocation and, in turn, care for us.

Today we misgovern this critical area of life, but at the Imaginings, the rearranging of thought patterns and the expansion of ideas – the stuff that every pilgrimage provokes – created not only the elements of a new design, but a necessary widening of the story in which care for one another was joined to the need to repair and mend natural systems and places. In these new connections lie the seeds of a different way of arranging work and life.

Taking care of the crew

The fact is, quite small adjustments on the part of employers can allow us to care. Julie changed jobs to find work where the hours are predictable and the boundaries respected. She calls this revolutionary, although she's had to take work that is lower paid and of lower status in order to fit in everything else she needs to do. A real revolution would be the introduction of the adjustments that would allow her to retain good work, to care and feel cared for.

Sometimes these changes are hiding in plain sight, perhaps unseen by a manager who does not themselves have care responsibilities. In Baltimore I visited a factory very similar to the one where Julie works in Barnsley. The manager who showed me around talked about his struggle to hire and retain workers, even though salaries are decent ($22 an hour, the equivalent of three times minimum wage). He explained that a significant investment in smart machinery had lessened the physical load and management had therefore hoped to attract women workers, but this was without success. I asked whether workers are allowed to keep their phones with them at work. 'Oh no,' he responded. 'Phones must be left in the lockers you saw on the way in.' 'There's your problem,' I suggested.

Men as well as women want to care – it is one of the reasons we are talking about it more – but the reality is that women are still responsible for most family matters: making sure there is something to eat, the washing is done, the school shoes have been found. The mother needs to know she can be rung if a child is ill and that she can check if a school pick-up went smoothly. The same woman is most likely in charge of elderly parents and their needs. A job where you can keep your mobile phone at your side is prized – an important thing that is continually overlooked. If every employer could assume that every worker also has a caring role, this small imaginative step would not only attract more workers, it would make for better work.

Lisa Smith understands the need for these changes and how

to care for her 'crew'. She runs a community-based service supporting families who live on the East Marsh in Grimsby. Families who live on the East Marsh have their children removed by social services at an estimated fourteen times the national average rate, a tragic outcome of the entrenched poverty which has followed the decimation of the fishing industry. Resources are scarce and the work of support is not easy. As Lisa explains, the starting point has to be a strong and stable team, and that means first taking care of her employees, many of whom come from the community and face challenges of their own.

Taking care of the crew is a principle Lisa learnt from her father, who was a skipper on one of the boats that used to form the backbone of the Grimsby economy. One night, on a fishing trip that started out like any other, he found himself adrift in a storm. His boat was taking in water and the engine was down. In the ensuing panic, Lisa's father calculated the time it would take for the boat to be rescued, and in that time, he fed his crew. He knew his men would need energy to survive in the cold until rescue came. The crew ate and then took to their lifeboats. Every person survived. Lisa applies the same anticipatory thought and care to her own team.

If you work in a place where you do not feel cared for, or valued, there can be devastating consequences. 'It can tear your mind,' Regina Campbell told me, referring not just to employees but to business leaders who also need to have space and support to attend to their own wellbeing. When I met Regina she was leading the Build Institute, which provides support to the growing ecosystem of two thousand small businesses that are thriving in Detroit. On offer is financial investment and professional advice for the hiccups and challenges that face new and growing enterprises. But for Regina, the most important thing the Build Institute offers is advice on health and wellness. 'It's human first,' she says. Her long experience has taught her that small businesses burn out, not because the business plans are weak, but because founders and leaders are not sufficiently cared for.

There is abundant evidence that caring for workers and understanding their needs creates committed and stable teams and better work. The Build Institute shows that attention to care can foster stronger economies by nurturing the smaller businesses that in the US and in the UK are the source of most work and new jobs. Sharing what works and bringing business leaders who know how to care into the conversation is the first step in redesigning care.

No longer alone: resourcing communities

The second step is to make sure that the places in which we live and work offer a rich infrastructure of support; support that helps us create new and fluid borders between our work and our care.

Most communities have somewhere we can go in a moment of crisis: a place of worship, Citizens Advice, perhaps a café where we know we will find our neighbours. In Barrow, there has been a concerted effort to stitch this social infrastructure together in a way that responds to our deeper longings to feel cared for. Those involved call it the Barrow Way.

'You know you can come here when you're at rock bottom,' Georgie told me, tilting her head to indicate the room we are sitting in, at an Imagining hosted by Women Community Matters. WCM is a local organisation that supports women who walk through their door in whatever way feels most appropriate. Women come seeking advice, support when facing abuse, or a safe space to simply sit and be.

Georgie grew up in care; her father was violent and abusive, and her mother was unable to cope. She's had an ongoing struggle with her own mental health and a series of abusive relationships. Tilly, who is with us, has a similar life story. She's proud that, with the help of WCM, she has completed an apprenticeship as a football steward. She's back on her feet with good work and is volunteering at WCM to help others: 'They've repaired me,' she tells us. Marta is older, ebullient in a red checked shirt – she's just returned to Barrow from Spain, where, in her words, her life went off the rails. Kelly used to work at the Yard, but after an injury she's struggling with her physical and mental health, unable to return.

Georgie, with her dark hair scraped back and deep brown eyes, seems much younger than her thirty-seven years. She has the names of her children proudly tattooed within a heart on her upper arm. Listening to her I detect both vulnerability and a quiet determination. Georgie recounts how, after hating the hotel work she found when she left school at sixteen, she took night classes. Her dream was to become a professional carer. It took time but she stuck with the course, qualified and found work she loved.

Georgie's affection for the older people she cared for is evident as she talks. For a good stretch, things were working out, but slowly the long hours, the stress and the low pay endemic in all care work began to bite. As Georgie's children grew older, she found that supervising homework, monitoring teen whereabouts, doing the laundry, saving enough money for bills – all the small things necessary to maintain family life – became increasingly difficult. Then came the bombshell. In debt and exhausted, Georgie discovered that her adored fifteen-year-old daughter was pregnant and had been playing truant from school for months. 'I wanted something better for Harper,' Georgie told me sadly, 'but I just wasn't there to be a parent, and it didn't work out.' She could no longer cope and needed someone to take care of her and Harper. She turned to Women Community Matters. 'I'm looked after here with enormous kindness,' she tells us all.

WCM is one of the organisations, including Love Barrow Families and the Well, which are part of the Barrow Way. Care is offered to mothers seeking help for teenagers in crisis; those who have suffered due to the pace of work in the submarine sheds at the Yard or the punishments of repetitive work, whether in the care home or on the distribution line; others who have experienced domestic violence, addiction, the slights that can sometimes happen in a town; people of all ages who simply need a place of kindness. The Barrow Way prefigures what a community care infrastructure could look like: a firm commitment to all and any of the town's citizens, who can come through a door at any time and find respite, care and help. The vision is robust and the approach affordable, but the constant need to fundraise absorbs precious time and creates uncertainty.

The work at the Well, founded and pioneered by Dave Higham, has been recognised as outstanding by others in the same field across Europe. When I first met Dave, he suggested I sit in on a community meeting. It was a deeply moving experience as those in different stages of recovery from addiction welcomed me and Liam, a painfully shy teenager. I had already met Liam's distraught mother in reception, before she was scooped up by Lynette, another Well worker. The newcomers, Liam and I sat together as stories of desperation and redemption were told with brutal honesty. From somewhere Liam found the courage to speak up. Bullied at school, he had been chuffed at first to find some different friends, but so began the slow luring into a county lines gang and his own addiction.

Later, full of warmth and humour, Dave came to find me and told me his own story. 'I used to come here [to Barrow] and steal. When I finally got clean, I wanted to give something back.' Dave grew up in a family home he describes as 'chaotic and, at times, intensely frightening'. In trouble with the law from his early teens, he spent twenty-one years in and out of prison, stealing anything he could get his hands on, to support his habit. 'Ged's the same,' he told me.

Sitting with the group, I had failed to realise that Ged – who'd shared his own story of years on the streets, surviving on buns dug out of bins – was in charge of the building and the meetings. At the Well, just as at Women Community Matters, it's not always clear who needs care and who is offering it. At the Imaginings, Georgie had shared her story of her need for help with frank honesty, but the next day, dropping in to WCM, I found her on the front desk, helping others coming through the door. 'It's done right', many who are part of the Barrow Way told me, explaining that they feel they can come and be open precisely because of this absence of hierarchy.

'It's more than flexible, it's fluid.' Sitting between the support a friend might offer and a formal service that assesses your needs before offering something on their menu, this work contains within it the principles of a twenty-first-century care system. Caring is about something shared: it's nearby, you can pop in, and you are not alone. It is relational: you don't need to have a list of needs; it's about human connection. There are no boundaries, no thresholds, no complicated entry requirements: if you need help then you are in the right place. Finally, and critically, the crew is cared for. Care within the Barrow Way is as much about tending to those who work for the organisation as to those who seek support: there is no distinction in a culture that instinctively takes care of everyone.

Things that are tended in common tend to flourish. This was the finding of Elinor Ostrom, the first woman to win the Nobel Prize for economics. Prior to her research, the opposite was widely believed: that systems of common ownership would incvitably lead to disrepair at best (since no one would feel personal responsibility) and plunder at worst. Without the rules and oversight of either the state or, better still, market-oriented businesses, it was argued that individuals are hardwired to take as much as they can – money, water, firewood, time off. While stocks lasted and no one was looking, people would cheat. This was what ecologist Garrett Hardin called the 'tragedy of the commons' in the late 1960s, and for years his poetic summation went unquestioned. It was assumed the only way to govern resources of any kind was through a price mechanism and hierarchical, preferably private, systems of policing and ownership.

Ostrom suggested that, instead of assuming, economists might actually study what was happening, and she set about this work. Moving from California, where she had done doctoral research on water management, Ostrom set up a research workshop in 1973. For a decade, Ostrom and her team made detailed, data-rich studies across three continents, of forests, irrigation systems and fisheries that were owned in common. This meticulous, closely observed research produced findings that defied widely held assumptions. Ostrom showed how people across very different cultures and settings are able to self-organise and steward resources through mutually agreed forms of governance that are equitable and generative. Resources in commonly held systems were shared and sustained in ways not found within state- or market-managed systems. In fact, common ownership was leading not to plunder but to thriving ecosystems that seemed to grow stronger as they moved from one generation to the next.

Ostrom's work has implications for how we think about human nature and how we might design the community infrastructure that will enable us to thrive. Her studies show how cooperation, as opposed to ruthless competition, is part of human instinct which can be enhanced and deepened (or repressed) by the systems we live within. Institutions designed with an understanding of this *Sapiens integra* wiring can enable a greater flourishing of the individuals involved and of the enterprise itself – whether a forest, a water system, a window factory, or an organisation of community care. Allowing us time to tend to one another rarely results in a cheating of the system. Instead, in coming together to share the work we can repair ourselves and the way we live. We are also better workers.

Good care work

Sometimes we do need a little more. We need expert help. When this happens, we want the professional care service to feel human, cooperative and flexible. Unfortunately, when we finally make our way to the top of the waiting list, we are more likely to be greeted by a very different culture, one which is closed, inflexible and unresponsive.

One in ten of the world's workers work in care – sometimes in formal settings such as care homes or within a domestic setting. They work in a global sector that in both the US and the UK is run much like any other industrialised system with a logic rooted in twentieth-century mass production. This logic prizes routines, numerical targets and financial metrics. Hours worked and tasks completed count for more than human connection and the amorphous, hard to measure components of human flourishing.

Efficiency is the ultimate goal within these care systems

which seek to continually lower the costs of production (squeezing wages, the number of staff and the time allocated to care tasks) in order to lower costs. For adults requiring care, all tasks have been allocated a portion of time: fifteen minutes for bathing and dressing, for example, regardless of a person's own capacities or the time required to chat, which makes all the difference to the quality of care. In the case of small children – and against the advice of childcare experts – up to eight preschool children can be left with one adult carer. Policymakers assure us that the carers are increasingly well trained. But no single adult, however well qualified, can allow eight very small children to run free in a park or make something with so many tiny hands at once. The activities at the core of our human development and wellbeing are inevitably curtailed.

'Capitalism is a guzzler of care,' writes the American political theorist Nancy Fraser in an excoriating attack on the corporate world taking more and more of our time and emotion, plundering both our natural systems and people. She calls this 'cannibal capitalism'. The feeling that more and more is being asked of us (or taken) at work is why the juggle, juggle has intensified.

But capitalism is guzzling care in another way too. Global investment firms have moved into owning care businesses. Relentlessly seeking new forms of extraction and requiring high levels of profit in order to pay shareholder dividends, the production model is further intensified. Academic research shows these new forms of ownership (often invisible to the care home resident, whose 'home' may well still carry the logo of the NHS or another trusted name), is increasingly compromising safety and care while further driving down wages. At the same time precious public resources are being leached. One pound in every five of public money invested in care in Britain ends up siphoned off as private sector profit. Care is big business and fortunes are made by owners and investors, many of whom reside offshore and do not pay taxes.

But care is not like any other business. The 'units' at its heart are humans who need love and tending, not efficient processing. Providing this human care is only possible if workers feel they have the space, time, resources and respect to fulfil their vocation. 'I had a one-hour break on a thirteen-hour shift,' Georgie tells those seated beside her at the Imagining, 'then it was reduced to two thirty-minute breaks and only one was paid. They squeeze and squeeze and squeeze you, but you can't care or do good work like that, can you?'

In *Labours of Love*, her moving and magisterial study of the crisis in care in Britain, Madeleine Bunting has documented the devastating impact of current arrangements on carers and the cared for alike. Describing her own experience of shadowing care workers, she describes how nothing could have prepared her for the intensity of the work: 'grief, anger, fear, shame, frustration' was 'the raw stuff' of the working day. In a hospital setting she watches as nurses become, in their own words, 'hunter gatherers' searching for the equipment they need to do their work but which is hard to find in underfunded institutions. Later, volunteering in a well-run care home, the emptiness and the sense that so many humans have been simply cast adrift becomes too much to bear. Bunting writes how she 'retreated, overwhelmed by the sheer scale of human need bursting out of that neat building.'

Trying to provide human care within inhuman systems, on low wages, without resources and where surveillance and abuse are not uncommon, requires heroic effort that few can sustain for very long. It is no wonder that the English adult care workforce has over a hundred thousand vacancies; one position in ten is vacant. The choice facing care workers is extreme: numb out or burn out.

There can be no good care without good care work but in Britain, despite the continual generation of policy proposals designed to tackle the problem (twelve government papers, five independent reviews and one royal commission in the last twenty-five years: a review almost every eight months), there has been a fatalistic acceptance that care is an intractable problem and it has continued to be unjust work, mostly done by women and people of colour.

Georgie is not alone in feeling that things have gone severely wrong. A national helpline for victims of modern slavery reports that one in five of the calls they receive is made by an overseas worker who has been brought to Britain to fill gaps in the care workforce and whose rights are being abused. Carers tell of their experiences of injustice and racism. 'I am just a number,' a Black British nurse tells a film maker in *Exposed*, a film made by Black and brown British nurses, re-counting her experience of nursing care during the pandemic and the ways in which she was made to feel expendable. 'Racial outsourcing' is the term used by the sociologist Adia Harvey Wingfield to describe the way health and care or-ganisations in the US abdicate the responsibility for creating diverse and stable institutions. Her research shows how Black professionals are continually undermined and overburdened by their peers, but also that Black professionals routinely go the extra mile to make sure their services are accessible to mi-nority communities, something that is known and frequently tacitly exploited by managers who organise care shifts.

The official story is one of an insoluble equation: pay more to workers and the already creaking system will simply go bankrupt. But the answers to our need for care can be found outside the official story: drawing in employers who understand and care, and directing public resources towards community infrastructure such as the Barrow Way are part of the solution. Reconnecting generations within wider movements calling for justice for carers has also been effective in the US, as demonstrated by the pathbreaking work of the care advocate Ai-Jen Poo.* But even within professional care systems an alternative – good care and good care work – is possible, as a small team of nurses in the Netherlands set out to show the world.

In the early 2000s, Jos de Blok watched in dismay as a series of reforms were introduced into the Dutch health and care system, designed to replicate the market principles common in Britain and the United States. Where once there had been professional autonomy – the ability to call in on those who needed help, to decide how to spend this time and to discuss with a patient or cared for person what might be best – now there were time sheets, risk registers, managers and a 'menu' of services that could be offered. Consultant-driven efficiency programmes, a ruthless focus on cost cutting and the introduction of technology to micromanage frontline workers was fast becoming the norm.

Jos was convinced that this was not the way forward. He believed that good care relied on a sustained relationship with an individual and their family, and on jointly agreeing what a cared for person might require to live well. And as a care professional himself, he knew that sustaining this work required taking care of the crew: good working conditions and decent pay, both of which were being hollowed out by consultant recommendations.

---

* Poo, a movement-maker and labour activist, has successfully campaigned for guaranteed work conditions for US domestic care workers while also expanding the language of care, focusing on love and inter-generational work. She writes about some of this work in her book *The Age of Dignity*.

Jos left his job and with four like-minded nurses started to experiment. They believed that good care is built on two principles. First, a close and continuous relationship with the person needing support, and with their friends and family. Second, that care is about fostering autonomy at every stage of life. This means not doing things *to* a person but finding out what would create capacity and flourishing. This in turn often means supporting primary carers within families as much as the individuals requiring care.

Buurtzorg is the organisation that grew out of this experiment. It employs fifteen thousand nurses and carers, providing 25 per cent of care in the Netherlands. Small autonomous neighbourhood teams make joint decisions and cooperatively share the work, just as Jos first started to do over twenty years ago. Technology is used to support administrative tasks in a deft way and support is at hand if problems are encountered, but each team is trusted to make its own decisions and plan work. Buurtzorg's headquarters are in a modest and nondescript building. There are only forty-five people working in this back office, a mark of the commitment to keeping every possible resource in the hands of workers themselves.

Care work at Buurtzorg is not just about a list of tasks: administering an injection, bathing and dressing. It is about taking time to talk, to facilitate connections with existing friends, which might for example mean a bit of tidying for a house-proud older person who otherwise will not receive visitors, or making sure a young adult has the support they need to travel and get home safely at night. The approach might sound expensive but in fact this way of working saves time and money. A Buurtzorg client requires almost 40 per cent fewer hours of care than a similar person within the more traditional systems, and there is a two thirds reduction in the need for expensive hospitalisations.

This is the beauty of the model. Buurtzorg attends to and honours those who need care and the workforce are in turn looked after. Very early on Jos and his colleagues discovered that there was no need for low wages in their sector. Without middle management, costly consultants or a lavish back office, there was more than enough to go around. Good pay supports stable teams, making the principle of a close and continuous relationship within the community and with families a reality. Jos de Blok describes the relationship between the workers and the organisation as a 'psychological contract'. All systems are transparent – including the financial systems – so workers know what is available. Rather like one of the systems studied by Elinor Ostrom, Buurtzorg workers steward resources which they understand are held by them in common.

Technology and care work: a revolution?

Buurtzorg is a deeply human response to the need to weave support through our families and communities, to ensure we can live the best life possible. It is a large-scale model of good care and good work which has now been implemented in twenty-four countries. Some still ask, is it enough? Steeped in the data which shows that ageing populations in particular will require an exponential growth in care workers, while longer lives mean that one in four of us will live with a disability and a care need for at least part of our adult lives, many argue that what we really need is a technical fix.

Can technology underpin a care revolution? Inspired by the Imaginings, I think it can, but just not quite in the way that official stories imagine.

Technology in the form of tools – hardware and software – will not solve the problem. Neither robots nor the predicted advances in AI will fill yawning staff vacancies and prize-winning apps can only help us chase already existing and insufficient resources. Robotics may, in time, prove useful, enabling, for example, the safe and comfortable lifting of older patients, or helpful 'hands' for some less able younger adults. AI may – and often already does – alert family members or staff teams to falls or other accidents, albeit only once they have happened. Technology might therefore enhance human care, but it cannot replace it or achieve a care revolution.

The technology revolution, however, does provide a significant opening for a profound re-valuing of care work. This is because technology revolutions are, as we have seen, revolutions of possibility and imagination that can, through their effect on culture, dreams and economics, lead to a re-evaluation of what matters. In technology revolutions jobs can change status.

Engineers elevated themselves as a profession in the period Carlota Perez labels the third technology revolution – the age of steel and construction that began in the 1870s. A small group of workers in the United States – about fifty in number – understood both the laws of physics and the craft of construction. With the invention of steel, they were able to use these skills to erect new structures – visible, distinct and very large – and their work was universally marvelled at. These engineers seized the moment to draw a professional distinction between their work and that of builders with whom they had previously been categorised. They were rewarded with high wages and social status; thousands started to study new courses and dream of a future in engineering work.

Something similar had happened to artists. At the start of the Renaissance artists were rarely known or rewarded as individuals. By the end of the sixteenth century, many were wealthy and personally famous. Various factors contributed to this transformation: technological advances in paints, canvases and scaffolding; new sources of trade wealth (technology enhanced shipping and maps) producing benefactors; and new cultural norms that made it acceptable for the newly wealthy to display their opulent lifestyles in the commissioned artworks. At the close of the century, artists were no longer classed with carpenters and house decorators.

Jobs are not high or low income by nature, they are culturally and politically defined, Carlota Perez argues, citing the significant rise in the wages of middle-income manufacturing jobs in the twentieth century. Western governments made an expedient decision; supporting unionised wages would ensure salaries sufficient to drive demand for consumer goods, which in turn would drive national economies. This same manufacturing work, Perez points out, has been relocated to Asia and is now low paid. Work changes status when a new element enters the equation.

Could the complex elements of today's technology revolution provide us with the context to re-value care? Could governments make a new expedient choice supporting good and high-status work in care and repair, in recognition that this will drive human flourishing and new green economies? I asked Jos de Blok for his thoughts.

When we meet for the first time, Jos for no apparent reason serenaded me loudly, much to the bemusement of passing conference delegates. We were both speaking at the World Economic Forum in Davos, a place where the care crisis is frequently on the agenda because central bankers and global chief executives alike have come to realise a lack of care means a lack of workers, and therefore lost productivity.

Jos moved seamlessly from his song to a story about eyesight and disability. I have terrible eyesight so, although this was not the response I was expecting, I was listening hard. Both my eyes are impaired, I told Jos; I have early onset cataracts and my right eye borders on clinical blindness. I often think about my luck to have been born in the twentieth century. In earlier times I would have been confined to home, dependent on my family and handouts from whatever rudimentary welfare system might have existed. 'Exactly!' Jos exclaims. 'Short sight was a cost and a problem. But not now. Today we assume that everyone's eyesight can be corrected, and eyewear alone is a $170 billion industry in the US.' Since the nineteenth century short sight has been reimagined with the creation of a new economy which includes new professions and new machinery for testing and connecting vision.

Care, for Jos, is something which today is misdiagnosed as a problem and a cost, as opposed to an opportunity for good work, technological advance and a reconsidering of what we mean by a just flourishing for all. Jos wants to widen our vision.

Widening the lens: start with a murmur

How to widen the lens and re-value care? Driving home one evening from a Barrow Imagining, I was ruminating with a new friend, a local doctor, on both the beauty of the landscape and on this problem of care – a problem that so many have tried to resolve and which for so long has defied great minds and scholarship.

Barrow sits on the Furness estuary at the tip of Morecambe Bay. It's a vast area of mud flats and shifting tidal bays where waters from the Lake District drain into the sea. The skies are wide with racing light and the bog land is home to (increasingly rare) meadow pipits and short-eared owls. Morecambe Bay supports a third of the birds that winter in England and many thousands more stop here on their migratory passage. On my first visit I was billeted in a family home further down the estuary. 'We are a sort of modern friary,' my wonderful and fascinating hosts joked, unaware that I saw my own journeys as a form of pilgrimage.

As we drove that evening in the fading light, a murmuration of starlings formed above us. Startled first by the noise of wings and then by its immense size, we stopped the car and ran, childlike with excitement, to the edge of a field, craning our necks. Thick like iron filings drawn to a magnet, thousands of birds swooped above us. They darkened corners of the sky as they formed and re-formed their patterns. Experts still don't know how this extraordinary collective choreography works but as I watched I thought about the love of nature that had been discussed once again that day. 'It's why we live here,' I'm told in Barrow, and also in Grimsby, Kilmarnock and many places where extraordinary beauty is on the doorstep. Is the balm found in nature the start of a different way of thinking about and organising care?

When I listen to recordings of the Imaginings, I find the idea is already there. Loved people and places are constantly woven together in conversations that connect care for each other – in small ways and big – with ideas of maintenance and repair, for humans with all our mental and physical needs and then for nature and the local fabric. I realise that people are already *seeing* care differently. Care is not invisible, sidelined or in any way denigrated within the Imaginings. It is *seen*. It is as if the cataclysm that was the loss of industrial work and ways of life has allowed something else to break through. Care and repair have become essential. Only with the loss of things once taken for granted has the need to think again and organise differently become obvious and key.

'It's all gone,' Martin had told me when we sat together at

the Barnsley window factory Imagining. He was referring not just to the work of the mines, but to a deeper loss: the places that attached people to one another and underpinned what he and many others remember as a more caring way of life.

Martin urged me to visit the boarded-up former home of the National Union of Miners and the Miner's Welfare Hall in Goldthorpe, one of the former mining towns that make up Barnsley, and where Martin was born. Later I visit both places, admiring their grandeur – the hall complete with pillared entrance and broad steps, and the imposing NUM building which is known locally as Arthur's Castle, a reference to the crenelated architecture and to Arthur Scargill, long-time Barnsley resident and president of the NUM during the miners' strikes of the 1980s. Standing in front of these buildings, I too feel infected by what has been undone. I know why people speak of 'sore hearts'. These were centres of community culture – the home of famed brass bands, bowling and cricket clubs, places of celebration and protest – of care and belonging which underpinned social relations and value systems.

Root shock is the term used by the American social psychiatrist Mindy Thompson Fullilove to describe the kind of traumatic experience of displacement Martin refers to. Root shock comes with the bulldozing or closure of treasured local landmarks which accompanies the demise of local industry, often provoking in turn evictions, displacement of neighbours and the disintegration of the bonds of care.

Root shock creates community-wide tremors and may be the reason that younger people who come to the Imaginings focus on care. In Grimsby, a group of recent graduates, not yet parents themselves or of an age that their own parents need care, talked with heat and passion about the subject.

'Who is going to care about us and how will we care about each other?' one demanded. 'There is a hole in our society . . . There is "care", but no one feels cared for,' another responded with visible distress. A need to be taken care of is deeply wired within our beings. When that care is missing, we feel unattached, anxious and unsure, with a wider sense that we are standing on unstable ground, alone and searching for a more caring way of life.

When the political scientists Berenice Fisher and Joan Tronto describe care as 'everything we do to maintain and repair our world', they are drawing on a deep understanding of this human wiring. They argue that care is not simply work which needs to be better recognised and paid, but something more fundamental, a 'species' activity – work which must be valued because it connects us to who we are (*Sapiens integra*) and to the wider living systems we are part of.

This is a new paradigm of care: one which places all living systems on a par, tending human, plant and place alike. In it we can perhaps see the first glimmers, ways in which we could widen the work and re-shape the economy in which the work takes place.

The work of repair

The work of repair is all around us. In Belfast, as in an increasing number of places in Britain, people come together to meet once a month at the Repair Café. They bring things in need of mending: clothing, household appliances, bicycles and much else besides that might otherwise have been thrown away. The Repair Café celebrates practical skills that exist within the city and it brings people together: everyone shares a cup of tea and something to eat while the repairs take place.

In the midst of the local troubles that still beset Belfast

and the macro challenges of a global climate emergency, the Repair Café might seem a small act, almost tragic in the face of the enormous waste generated by a modern city. But it is something quite different. As the founder Lee Robb explains, few of us want to live in a throwaway society – it hurts us, but we feel powerless to act. And many of us are lonely, isolated with skills that are immensely valuable but we don't know how to share or use. Lee is in the business of repairing this heartache. The café – which is not actually a place but a group of people – moves each time to a different corner of the city to include everyone and to mend people and things.

Another person who understands the potential of repair work is the labour organiser Saket Soni. Floods, fires and other climate-related disasters have rapidly created a vast (if largely unseen) economy of climate repair. In the United States the size of this publicly funded economy is estimated to be $200 billion as, in the wake of disaster, government awards contracts to large private contractors to repair the damage. This is the economy that Saket literally stumbled upon when he tripped over Alicia sleeping in a New Orleans car park in the wake of Hurricane Katrina. Alicia is a so-called storm chaser – part of a vast climate disaster workforce.

Workers arrive from the Dominican Republic and Bolivia, where rains and therefore harvests are no longer dependable, or Ecuador, where shrimp waters have been decimated by a combination of warming seas and industrial fishing. They accept the dangerous work of climate repair because they are economically desperate and their status is usually illegal. They also understand what it is to no longer be able to come home and they feel empathy for the displaced families. Exhausted storm chasers are often to be found on a Sunday (their day off) voluntarily helping Americans who are uninsured and will get no help rebuilding their homes.

Saket encountered Alicia because she had chosen to sleep out. Storm chasers work by day without protective clothing and by night often choose to sleep rough rather than face the crowded and unsanitary conditions of the housing provided. Worse, Saket was to discover, workers are frequently not paid at the end of the job. When company operatives turn up to check that the work is done, they sometimes pay but just as often they threaten a call to immigration officers, knowing the workers cannot fight their corner and will simply move on, unpaid.

Saket's stumble was the start of a long journey to build a new work organisation. Resilience Force has successfully negotiated rights for the storm chasers, an almost unimaginable victory for workers who feared public organising, the might of corporate interests and the cold violence of US immigration officials. Saket's success is rooted in no small part in the close attention he gives to cultivating the bonds of care and connection between those who live in the affected communities and have been dispossessed and the newcomers who are seeking a better life. But this is just the start: Saket sees possibility in this new and vast economy, for good work and for reimagined places in which communities are rebuilt with collectively owned assets and places of safe belonging.

He has in mind a co-design project that will use the public money already being spent to create new economies of repair, with good working lives and asset-rich communities at the centre. The model he proposes has strong parallels with the work of both Jos de Blok and Elinor Ostrom, and shows how we might reimagine a current threat in such a way that places are repaired and good work is created.

Such thinking encourages us to focus not on scarcity, but on the considerable resources available that could be repurposed. It widens whose work is included.

Carers who came to the Imaginings often pointed out that skills in different settings have different value. Those, for example, who look after the needs of CEOs may have various job titles, from executive coach to personal assistant, but they are in effect caring for a busy person whose high status transfers to those doing the caring work. Anne-Marie Slaughter and I call this the 'care-plus' economy, and Anne-Marie argues that those who coach athletes and opera singers, as well as those with wider learning roles – anyone who does human-to-human tending – are all part of this economy. In my own work I have created circles of care and belonging for those over fifty, and I have seen how a different offering and organisation attracts wider interest for what is considered to be good work. London Circle attracted a former tech entrepreneur – a warm and charismatic leader – in its early incarnation, while Rochdale Circle thrives under the leadership of a former welder. Neither of these individuals would have been previously attracted to caring roles.

Some years ago, I was lucky enough to study conflict resolution at the Harvard Kennedy School. I learnt (but until my pilgrimage had forgotten) that two principles are central for the successful negotiation to repair any deep and lasting conflict. First, the subject of negotiation must be expanded – nothing changes when we quarrel over scarce resources and fear that any gain will be a loss for someone else. Successful negotiation always requires widening the scope and bringing more possibility into the conversation. Second, participation in the conversation – who is invited to the table – must be expanded. This is a just process that enables moving from one set of arrangements to another. It offers the potential for everyone to gain and grow from the negotiation. The alternative is always a scrabble to the bottom and a continuing conflict.

In positioning the 'juggle juggle' as a conflict of care and repair, of people and of place, the Imagineers were instinctively expanding what might be possible and thereby drawing more people and more resources into the conversation. They were also placing care, alongside repair, as future work. This is the work we need to emphasise and grow for a successful and just ecological transition. Resolution is not yet at hand, but this is a new and promising path. It would force us to face squarely the contradictions of our current work systems and to think again.

At the Imaginings the contradictions between the loud demands of paid work and the insistent but silenced demands of care are widely experienced as an intolerable tension, one which cannot be addressed by either individuals or the policies of solitary firms alone. The desire is to reorganise the economy and the work of care and repair.

Principle Four: Time –
Rethinking it Top to Bottom

Everyone I meet wants to work. Many of us love what we do. But we don't want to feel consumed by our work: most of us want to work less and we want to work differently. This requires a reimagining of time.

Jonny, at fifty-five, has forty years of work experience behind him and a good few working years to go. But he's starting to imagine his retirement. His eyes smile behind his glasses, a glinting gold bangle on his left arm. 'I love life and I love learning,' he told me by way of introduction. 'I left school at fifteen – I learnt to be a bricklayer. At seventeen I was in a sawmill and then I learnt grave-digging. I've learnt to be a parent too.'

Jonny is the grave-digger I met on my first wintry journey to Kilmarnock. 'Why can't we just rethink it top to bottom?' he asked that day. His question was partly about the possibility of redefining the hours of a working week or a working day. But he also had in mind a much bigger idea about the ebb and flow of work within a life; about whether it would be possible to disrupt and stretch linear notions of what he disparagingly called the 'learn, work, retire' life.

As Jonny started to sketch ideas on the tablecloth in front of him – vigorous arrows creating new circles of time, projects and learning; stick figures standing in for new relationships, work practices and structures, his colleagues – Marion, the first woman to be trained by the municipality as a horti-culturist, Robbie, a grass cutter and George, also in the grave-digging department, nodded along. Because Jonny's enthusiasm was contagious, they also picked up pens and added detail to the emerging picture. They were absorbed in their work, carried along by their imaginings until, like characters in a cartoon that suddenly notice the ground is no longer beneath their feet, they paused. 'Are we just dream-ing?' Jonny murmured. Could it really be possible to reinvent our working time?

Re-drawings of working time, once deemed un-imaginable, have happened. A totemic example is the introduction of the paid weekend. If you had told the ex-hausted and impoverished workers who first crowded into cities at the start of the Industrial Revolution that they would be given money to rest on Saturdays and Sundays, you would have probably been dismissed as a fantasist. And yet it hap-pened. Boots the Chemist was one of the first companies to introduce the paid weekend, experimenting with the idea in its Nottingham factories in the early 1930s and introducing a company policy in 1934. The idea – long campaigned for by the trade unions – spread rapidly, becoming common practice across the US and the UK in the same year.

Shifting time

Working time is not immutable. It was once organised ac-cording to patterns of prayer and the agrarian calendar, to the ebb and flow of tides, natural light and warmth, but the factory owners of the Industrial Revolution discovered they had a major problem. Reaping the dividends of their large and risky investments in new machinery depended above all on workers turning up on time for their shifts. Any gap in the new production lines rendered everyone's time and the machinery less productive.

The challenge faced by these early industrialists was both technological and cultural. Mechanical ticking clocks are a fourteenth-century technology. They were wildly popular almost from the moment of their invention, but the early prototypes were rarely accurate. Well into the nineteenth century it was common to reset clocks by consulting a sundial and most clocks were one-handed, measuring hours but not minutes. Such timepieces might be useful to orientate oneself within the day, but they could not be counted on to guide a new idea of punctual arrival for shift work.

Accurate municipal clocks, financed by industrialists, began to appear in town squares in an effort to get workers to the factory gates on time. In America, Henry Ford went further. In his drive for efficiency at the Ford car plant, he established a Sociological Department. Fifty investigators were hired to assess workers' home conditions. The five-dollar wage (and a regulated eight-hour day) was linked to the investigators' judgement as to whether a worker was neat and would be punctual. This was a unique form of surveillance, but as the Italian Marxist philosopher and union organiser Antonio Gramsci famously noted, the aim of Fordism was not only to create a new type of worker, but 'a new type of man'. One of the core characteristics of this new man would be an internal metronome, ticking at all times and in all places to the rhythm of the factory.

The ancient Greeks recognised two types of time, one being *chronos*, time measured by the clock, the other being *kairos*. *Kairos* is the time we spend immersed in activity, almost unaware of external factors including the passing of hours: time on the yoga mat, time spent caring and loving, making and playing. Before the Industrial Revolution, *kairos* was the dominant measure of time. Work, whether the hoeing of a garden, harvesting of a field or the making of a garment, took as long as it took. But today, *chronos* is the law of time and the clock we have come to believe we cannot escape. It rules us and almost every type of work.

A history of twentieth-century work could be told as a story of *chronos'* progress. Standardised tasks which can be measured by the clock moved as the century wore on, from the factory floor to the office where time sheets and clocking on and off became the norm. This was the nine-to-five culture that Dolly Parton and so many others wanted to rebel against many decades later. Next *chronos* moved into the social sphere: a secondary school lesson is averaged at fifty minutes regardless of attention spans or the time it takes to learn; doctor's appointments are strictly limited to ten minutes regardless of the presenting condition; care appointments are limited to fifteen minutes, again regardless of a person's needs.

Teachers, doctors, nurses and carers at the Imaginings talked about the exhaustion that follows in *chronos'* wake: the sense that the meaning of work is squeezed out by an arbiter – the clock – which does not understand the task at hand. In modern policing, the pressures are severe. 'Our human instincts tell us this is not right,' Barrow's superintendent explained to me. 'I head up policing for the south of the county. Centrally estimated time slots predict (based on crime figures) how many people we have to deploy. Of course, it's essential to have a system to determine how and where we deploy staff, but it's not right that our interactions can be limited to a certain number of minutes, because everybody's different. Everybody that we deal with has different backgrounds and they need different types of support . . . Where's our human connection, where's our compassion, where's spending more time with people who need it? That gets lost. We need to reimagine how we share our time, in a kind way, in the right way.'

How could we share time in the right way? Unbeknown to most of us, there are a remarkable number of experiments that demonstrate we can in fact rethink time. That even factories do not need to run on 'factory time' and that most of us are more productive, wherever we are working, when we are not ruled by *chronos*. These experiments show that reducing the number of hours we work and increasing our control over how we use these hours not only makes us happier, it makes us better workers. Rethinking time also turns out to be one of the most important things we can do to repair our communities and our planet's fragile ecosystems.

A lesson from history

Ninety years before I meet Jonny, in equally wintry weather, a time experiment started in Battle Creek, Michigan. Kellogg's, the largest manufacturer of breakfast cereals in the world, announced that they would pay their employees the same wage to work less. Fifteen hundred workers were offered six-hour shifts, in place of their former eight-hour day.

The six-hour day was primarily designed to create more work in the context of the Great Depression and the severe unemployment of the 1930s. A national campaign to 'share the work' chimed with William Kellogg's personal belief that work is a common good, something collective that should be shared, even when there does not seem to be enough to go around. Changing the shifts gave work to three hundred more Battle Creek families.

But Kellogg also expected his business to benefit, and the results were to prove impressive. By 1935 – five years into the experiment – profits had risen and business had grown. This increased productivity had been achieved not through a cut in wages or a cut in workers but through a 40 per cent reduction in accidents and a more than 50 per cent reduction in absenteeism. It turned out that rested, happy workers were better workers.

Journalists and rival business leaders flocked to the Battle Creek plant to see the experiment for themselves. The economist John Maynard Keynes had just predicted that the future would be an even further reduced fifteen-hour week. Most people – workers and observers alike – believed that modernity in the form of new technology and mass production would mean that everyone would eventually work less and there was an excitement and intense interest in seeing future work in action. President Hoover dispatched his economic advisors and the Women's Bureau, a national investigative research body, started a process of detailed household surveys.

Workers told journalists and researchers that they felt 'free' and that they had 'more life'. Through interviews and research diaries they shared the ways they could use their new time. Men and women emphasised that they were now able to share household duties and to care for others. They reported that they were less fatigued and less reliant on professional help and services. The six-hour rotation was popular because, unlike an eight-hour pattern which offers only one daylight shift, the six-hour division reduces the night-time work which is so punishing for the body and for family relationships.

'We are better parents, we have the energy, how could

you ever put a price on such a thing?' Myrtle Ostrander told the researchers. Joy Blanchard, another worker, eloquently described how the new leisure 'was not just for resting in order to do more work' but enabled her to 'craft' the best life, with her family, in the community and as a citizen. Donna Holser described the social part of working for Kellogg's – the picnics, the dances, the way she could do her housework before her shift and how she had time in the evenings for trips into Kalamazoo (the local town) and to play ping-pong in the local team.

Donna, like many interviewees, breaks off to apologise to her visitors, for talking about 'unimportant things'. But what's interesting is how these unimportant things, the gaps in between that are 'nothing special', create good lives. Participating in team sports and later 'chewing the fat', making jam together – there seems to have been a particular value placed on gifting and exchanging homemade goods – going for walks, playing games. The household surveys convey a powerful feeling of a good life that can flow at a rhythm of ease and in which all things can be accommodated.

Time, for the workers, was not fetishised – there is no sense of scarcity or specialness; time does not have to be useful, it can be passed, not spent. Kellogg called his model 'liberation capitalism'. Much influenced by the Lancastrian soap magnate Lord Leverhulme, who believed that work should 'bring a sufficiency in wages . . . and such a sufficiency it leaves leisure for things of the soul', Kellogg saw his model as the antithesis of welfare capitalism and its emphasis on 'jobs, jobs, jobs'.

Making time

At the Imaginings, every conversation circled round and back to the need to make more time. There's a longing for meaningful work in which *kairos* is restored and for days within which the ebbs and flows of work are differently patterned.

The future is already here – it's just not evenly distributed, runs the famous adage. When I set out to learn how we might put into practice the ideas of the Imaginings, this is just what I found too. We are living through a rich period of time experimentation.

Working less: the thirty-two-hour week

What about a four-day week? When Jeremy Corbyn, as leader of the Labour Party, suggested a four-day working week in 2019, there was laughter from the live audience in the TV studio where he was being filmed in an election debate. His political opponent, the Conservative prime minister Boris Johnson, called the idea 'crackpot'. But almost every participant at the Imaginings suggested that a shorter working week would be part of a good working life, and in a mark of how fast things can change, in June 2022 seventy UK companies began to pilot a four-day working week. More than three thousand workers were involved, from a small chippy in Norfolk to a Sheffield robotics company and London based corporates. These British companies were followed a month later by sixty US companies who committed to sharing their learning in a joint scheme.

'What's the catch?' one of those working at the chippy asked, so countercultural is the idea of working fewer hours for the same pay. There was no catch. The companies taking part expressed a range of motivations: some wanted to be good employers; others hoped it would give them an edge in a competitive search for skills. Company leaders also had personal reasons, acknowledging for example that 'time is precious' or that they did not want to reach retirement and think, What next? because they had worked so hard to the exclusion of everything else. Every business leader was also convinced that productivity would not suffer and would probably improve.

They were not disappointed. An evaluation led in Britain by Cambridge University and in the US by Boston College found that revenues in all companies were protected and in some rose markedly. Participating companies experienced a 57 per cent drop in turnover (during the post-pandemic period that later became known as the Great Resignation) and a 65 per cent drop in absenteeism and sick days. Workers reported that they had a greater sense of purpose, they were sleeping better, they were happier at home, in their friendships and in their relationships. Reported stress levels dropped by 71 per cent and parents in particular felt the benefits, better able to share childcare and to find time for themselves. Ninety-two per cent of participating companies continued the four-day week beyond the experimental period. As the authors of the evaluation conclude, the four-day week has moved from 'desirable to achievable'.

Working less is good for workers and for business. This is something Karen Mattison has known for some time. Karen and her partner Emma Stewart founded the consultancy TimeWise in Britain in 2005. Their premise is simple: they believe that well-paid, predictable and flexible work will attract a talented, loyal and highly motivated workforce. In the beginning, many TimeWise clients were new mothers seeking ways to balance the care of their very small children with the continuing love of their professions. More recently the gender balance has shifted somewhat – after all, fathers want to care too – and millions of us (TimeWise has placed over 1.7 million people) simply want more time. Karen and Emma have persuaded leaders in national banks, energy companies, blue-chip consultancies and GCHQ – the UK's intelligence agency – that the majority of jobs, including the most senior roles, can be shared or done in new and flexible ways. High-calibre candidates are attracted to companies thinking in new ways about time.

Experiments in other parts of the world have produced the same results and they've shown it's possible to shorten working hours even for those who it is assumed must always be on call. The US military has won awards for its flexible work policies while the Pentagon has pioneered generous policies for those looking after injured family members. In Sweden, nurses in Gothenburg have been offered the same pay for six-hour working days with a corresponding increase in retention and health outcomes. In Iceland, between 2015 and 2019 a similar deal was offered by Reykjavik's city council to a range of workers including those in schools and hospitals. Researchers described this experiment as an 'overwhelming success'; productivity remained the same or improved, while workers reported better health and wellbeing. Eighty-eight per cent of all workers in Iceland now work shorter working weeks.

Most women at the Imaginings were keen to rethink working patterns. Instead of a four-day week, however, they frequently suggested spreading the same thirty-two hours a little differently. One of those was Emma, director of a Barnsley-based digital agency specialising in health sciences. The company offers employees the choice to allocate their hours as they wish. 'I lied,' she told me at the Imagining.

'When my daughters were small, I felt I couldn't mention to anyone that I had a family. They couldn't know that I couldn't take a call at all hours and now I've got girls who have grown up, but I've hugely missed the growing up because I had to choose a work life – being there at any moment for a client – that I now think was really ridiculous.' Emma and her peers talked at length about burnout in the digital sector: 'What we hear from our people is that they don't want more money, they want time: at 3 p.m. on a Tuesday, they want to be there, picking up their child from nursery.'

Working less offers something else, which is of much greater collective importance. Reduced work hours are of significant ecological benefit. Working fewer days, we reduce our carbon footprint, particularly in the US where most work commutes are done by car. The data also shows that when we are time poor, we make carbon-heavy decisions. We eat on the go out of disposable containers, we hurriedly buy clothes we often never wear, and we send gifts to apologise for being late or not showing up. If we are rich and really busy, we take the private jet, telling ourselves we just haven't got time to travel in any other way. Shorter working weeks – more time – offer a triple dividend: the arrangement is better for workers, companies and our ecosystems.

At the Imaginings, working less is almost always tied to bigger ideas about how we want to live – it is not simply about wanting to work less, but to live differently. 'I think the four-day working week thing is really interesting but it's only a stopping-off point, isn't it, because we are trying to get somewhere else,' Jonny proposed. 'Yeah, it's a tactic, isn't it,' his colleague Robbie agreed. Participants across the Imaginings constantly showed a beautiful ability to think big and marry their dreams with pragmatism. A four-day working week – or, much better, a thirty-two-hour working week – would be a step in the right direction, normalising less work for the same pay. But for most people the real dream was to stretch time in more far-reaching ways, starting with Jonny's first suggestion: a design for the non-linear life.

Working differently: the non-linear life

Jonny wanted to disrupt the pattern by which we progress from school, to work to retirement. He wanted to accumulate time in different ways; 'not always the same weeks of holiday a year', for example, in order to rest or pursue an alternative project before returning to work. Like almost everyone (and as discussed in Principle Two: Meaning) Jonny talked about 'second chances'; about how to find time to 'really learn' beyond school. He doesn't want to defer his plans until retirement: he would rather take lengthy chunks of time – for family, for learning and for other projects – throughout his life.

Many of Jonny's ideas are already available for some and show what is possible. Sabbaticals are an accepted way for those in academia and in senior professions to take extended time out of work, often on full pay. In Nova Scotia in Canada, school teachers are also offered periodic 'years out', again on full pay and with pension contributions maintained. This policy recognises that teaching is tough but important work. Nova Scotia, rural and relatively remote, has a teacher shortage but instead of doubling down on those they do have, increasing stress and workload, the state offers a form of sabbatical, ensuring that they retain experienced teachers, lowering the costs of churn and raising educational outcomes.

Paid parental leave (although poorly supported in the US and under pressure in the UK) is another example of how it is demonstrably feasible for people to take paid breaks of up to a year and to then resume their careers where they left off. In theory, gig work, like freelance work, could also give freedom, although for gig workers in particular grindingly low pay means ever longer hours. 'I am my own holiday maker,' Palash had told me with a wry smile when we met in Barking. In reality his low income means a holiday is an impossibility. Time off would lead to immediate eviction without money to pay the rent. More time must always be linked with the basics, starting with good pay.

In Britain we work very long hours but even so, leisure time has risen by 58 per cent since Keynes made his famous prediction of a fifteen-hour week in 1930. Some academics argue that Keynes's prediction has come right, just not in the way he imagined. But the problem – from Jonny's perspective – is that this leisure has been accumulated at the end of our lives. For everyone whose work entails deep physical or mental stress, the promise of rest in the form of retirement is an empty one. These workers know they will rarely live long enough, in good enough health, to enjoy the accumulated and deferred leisure.

'I will put down that mop and I will die,' Philip told me. He was one of a group of janitors and cleaners who joined me for an Imagining in Baltimore. 'We over-work, we over-work, but we men, we don't talk about it,' he continued, being open about the macho culture that still prevails in many forms of male-dominated physical work. A former felon, Philip had already had time forcibly taken from him, as he languished for several years in prison, missing out on education. In Baltimore, more than half of the city's young Black men have been or are incarcerated, an experience that showed up frequently and painfully on their life charts. This gentle man would like to somehow recover what he has lost in order to train and work in care. After the Imagining he quizzed me on good care projects I had seen in the world. 'Can you write?' he asked Dwayne, the colleague and former felon he was seated beside. 'Let's get it down.' Philip wanted to google all the examples I gave him – to find a way to carve out time and money to get this second chance.

Jonny's life experience has not been so brutal, but like the construction workers I met in Detroit he too fears that 'overload' could be followed by a heart attack, curtailing any promise of a retirement. One answer to this problem would be to adjust retirement ages according to data which shows variations in life expectancy by profession.

In East Ayrshire, where Jonny lives, local government has another idea.

Katie Kelly, the former deputy chief executive of East Ayrshire Council is a force of nature. She's small, but easily spotted in any room, dressed in a trademark vibrant pink jacket. Katie assumed her leadership position just at the time that the loss of industrial work was compounded by swinge-ing cuts in public funding. In East Ayrshire, budgets would be immediately reduced by 25 per cent, with more to come, while at the same time Katie was tasked with public sector 'transformation'.

'So, are we going to keep slicing out our public budgets and just die a little sooner or are we going to think differ-ently?' Katie challenged her peers, in the full knowledge that residents in East Ayrshire already had a staggering twenty-year gap in healthy life expectancy compared to the UK norm. Katie was born in the community. She started to work for her local council as a teenager. 'I knew the community would know how to go about this,' Katie told me, 'but we were so far from the community.' She had the humility, born of lived experience, to know that it would be really hard from her position of power to win trust so that the community

would honestly share their ideas with her. The starting point
had to be showing she cared about her workers.

Katie called an open meeting of council workers and asked
who was happy with their work. No hands went up. It confirmed her hunch that burnout and exhaustion needed to be
tackled first and any credible plan for transformation should
start with those whose work was to look after Kilmarnock:
the parks, the town centre, the graveyards. 'You've got to be
able to love your place,' she told me. It might seem obvious
that a community strategy for transformation should start
with the ideas and talents of local workers who are in turn
in charge of caring for local people and places, but the idea is
exceptional in its originality.

Katie called her plan Vibrant Communities: the mission
was to ensure everyone in East Ayrshire could lead a vibrant
life, starting with municipal workers. The first experiment
was beautiful in its simplicity. Instead of hiring council workers for a specific job – grave-digging, for example – a generic
position would be offered in environment and housing, and
the work would evolve over time. Reserving the less ardu-
ous tasks for older workers, Katie conceived of a new pattern
where you might start on the bins or digging graves (heavy
lifting), progress to training as an HGV driver on a council
gritter lorry (medium intensity) and then become a housing
caretaker (*kairos* work, paced to allow for doorstep chatting
and to foster community relationships – something trusted
older workers are very good at). It's a powerful way of re-
weaving life and working time.

Where we have control of our working lives, we tend instinctively to alternate between intense activity and periods
of idleness and reflection. Being able to blend *chronos* and
kairos time creates a feeling of space and freedom. We see
this in small ways: the popularity of working from home, for

example, which allows us the possibility of being absorbed differently in our work – a day for writing and thinking, others for busy meetings and collaboration with colleagues. History suggests these patterns are ancient and coded deeply within us. Centuries of pre-industrial work followed the rhythm of the seasons. All living beings need patterns of work, rest and restoration.

Factory work – a new arrangement of sustained, repetitive work intensity which came with industrial and technological innovation – was a deep shock to the human system. In 1913, the year the assembly line was introduced at Ford, there was a 370 per cent turnover in the workforce. Workers began to refer to a new illness they called 'Forditis'. Today many of us have adapted to factory time through necessity. 'We are overwhelmed, but we are taught to be always on the go,' a modern Detroit car worker told me, explaining how he feels conditioned from early life to keep going. Others feel guilty if they can't keep up.

Vibrant Communities is a creative attempt to rethink work in a place which for a long time has felt like it is not keeping up. A first step is rethinking the way workers can move within and between work. The next step for Katie and her colleague Suzanne Clarke, who now leads the project, was to think about re-purposing community and care roles in ways which would fit better into community days. A budget from the Scottish government to provide truancy officers, for example, was repurposed to create what they called a Home Link team. Arriving at homes with tea bags and a loaf of bread under their arm, these workers don't castigate harassed parents but instead put the kettle on and start to help in any way they are asked. Small acts of practical support combined with a strong sense for parents that someone is on their side proves – unlike fines and other traditional reprimands – to be an effective anti-truancy policy. The Home Link team have consciously introduced a *kairos* culture, going with the flow of families' lives, and they love their work.

Next, Vibrant Communities considered how reduced but still existing resources could be used to stimulate stronger social connections and local economic activity. Sixty-five assets were transferred from municipal ownership into community hands: land, gardens, buildings, swimming pools (the last with budgets to run them in different, community-led ways). Public budgets, such as the £3 million spent annually on school and hospital meal contracts, were redirected towards buying locally. This strategy ensured that funds would circulate within a nascent farming system generating some new work (new organic egg production, for example) and supporting already existing pioneers such as Mossgiel Organic Farm (famous across Scotland for the quality of their milk).

A strategy which started with rethinking worker time has created new economic activity and stronger community bonds. 'This is about my children's future,' Suzanne tells me before adding, 'We've come a long way, but we've still got far to go.' This intergenerational thinking and the recognition that substantively changing work patterns is a project that needs attention over a sustained period of time are markers of a serious depth of commitment.

Universal basic time

Towards the close of the twentieth century, the Austro-French philosopher André Gorz picked up and reinvented the pronouncements on working time made almost fifty years earlier by John Maynard Keynes: new technology could and should reduce working time. Gorz advocated a four-hour working day. He was convinced that advanced technologies were creating more meaningless work, and could instead be used to create what he called a 'multi-activity' life. The 'multi-activity life' would not only restrict work to four paid daily hours, it would introduce a social income paid to every citizen by the state. Gorz was a pioneer in suggesting that work, time and income should no longer be conflated or directly linked to each other.

In the intervening decades the idea of a universal basic income (UBI) paid to every citizen has gained attention and found support on the left and the right of the political spectrum. On the left, UBI is seen as a potential way to combat poverty without stigma, ensuring that every citizen will receive a secure wage, regardless of their working status. On the right, the idea has gained traction with Silicon Valley plutocrats in particular, who hope the policy would leave them free to determine the direction of technological advance without concerns for human welfare. Despite this unusual political consensus UBI is a proposal that seems impossible to implement: a scheme which truly affords a liveable income would be immensely expensive and unpalatable to current electorates, while more affordable schemes achieve little more than the cash transfers already received by low-income workers.

At the Imaginings, few people mentioned UBI. More were interested in the possibility of an income that would fund retraining and second chances, an idea that I call a transition income because it could support the transition into good ecological work in particular. A transition income could meet our particular moment – the need to shift to work which supports our wider ecosystems and, because it would not be universal and could be time limited, it would be affordable, making good working transitions a possibility for millions of workers. At the Imaginings, another perhaps more radical proposal also unfolded: the idea of universal basic time.

Universal basic time (UBT) would reduce the time we spend at work and start the planning of our days and lives from an alternative axis. UBT might, for example, suggest an allocation of four hours to playing, two hours to dreaming, four to caring and, after an allocation for sleeping, the remaining six hours would be for paid work.

UBT is about creating time for all areas of life, 'time that is not tainted' as a Grimsby participant described it, conveying a frustration with the way we often have time but feel guilty if we use it to play or just to sit and think. 'Disposable time', Jonny's colleague Marion called it; time that we can allocate just as we wish, she explained, also drawing a parallel with a commonly understood description of (disposable) income. At the Imaginings, a particular premium was put on 'time to be': the time we need to dream or simply let our minds wander. Just as we commonly understand that we should get eight hours' sleep, so participants develop an idea of universal basic time to allocate norms to other parts of life that are currently squeezed. If factory time enabled us to be efficient industrial workers, then UBT would give us time in such a way that we can develop across the multiple dimensions of our *Sapiens integra* identity: as workers, friends, creators, carers and guardians of nature.

UBT is a tangible reimagining of time and, importantly, it goes with the grain of possibility embedded within the DNA of current technologies. Digital technology is asynchronous, so in theory we no longer need to work at the same speed or at the same time. This was the argument made by the group of technology pioneers who joined me from the Barnsley tech hub. Digital technology might so far have been used to intensify the extraction of worker time (Little tech surveillance and the predictive algorithms that mean gig workers must be always 'on'), but its real potential, this group argued, lies in the opposite direction.

Digital agencies sit in the crosshairs of time. On the one hand, like any service business they feel a commercial need to respond to their clients, who regularly expect real-time responses from one individual in charge of an account. On the other, the founder entrepreneurs, like their creative workers, value a sense of autonomy that, as Emma, advocate for her company's thirty-two-hour week, put it, 'leaves us in control of our wider destiny'. Each of these tech leaders was thinking hard about how to reimagine time. Craig, founder of Genius Division, a digital branding agency, is another who has introduced a strict thirty-two-hour week. 'It wasn't always like that,' he tells me, 'but as I got older [he is in his mid thirties] I wanted time for different things – to be with my partner, to practice ju-jitsu – and I could also see how inefficient the long-hours agency culture is – tasks expand to fill the time at hand.'

Craig, genial in a lumberjack shirt accessorised that day with impressively oversized headphones, is restless to push things further. Asynchronous digital technologies, he reasons, should offer liberation to live and work in very different ways. He qualifies at once that this doesn't mean workers being always 'on', nor does it mean endless Slack threads, although technology can be smartly deployed to help to manage work-load and allow people to work at a different pace. (Part of the success of the four-day week pilots referred to above was found to be the digital overhaul that all participating companies decided to undertake before starting.) It's also about allowing people to work in the way that suits them best. We have 'the brilliant Sue', he tells me – she's semi-retired and she can work as and when she wants, and it works perfectly for maintaining the websites the agency builds.

Craig reaches for a pen and writes 'Barnsley Time Machine' in bold letters across the paper tablecloth. 'Let's work backwards from this biggest problem,' he says to his colleagues at the table: 'How to redesign time.' This group know each other well and there is an easy camaraderie. Laughing, they draw a Tardis – the time-travelling machine from the long-running TV series *Doctor Who* – and their ideas start to tumble over each other.

A small blue police telephone box on the outside, the Tardis has infinite space inside. In the same way, Barnsley's Time Machine is 'a place where once you enter your belonging and your time is expanded'. In the machine there are different cultural norms and high trust, which means all forms of work surveillance and time management can be put to one side. Being part of something larger helps manage client expectations: many also belong, collectively expanding the sense of what's possible. And there's time for care and for creativity. The digital leaders refer to what they call 'the modern mines', the local warehouse economy: 'In those boxes there is time compression and you are treated as less than human, and there's so much anxiety and mental illness.' These pioneers want to include everyone within the Time Machine, distributing time as a form of public good equally across the town.

Craig and his colleague Steve, who is also at the table, work in schools. Like others at the hub who I meet later, they are upbeat about the talent of younger people in Barnsley. 'We go to colleges and the young people don't stick up their hands, but we hang around afterwards and they come up and have a chat. It's incredible what they're doing – this is the next generation, and they are using all the [digital] tools in their bedrooms and they are making serious money.' Craig's concern is that adults don't understand the emerging patterns.

'Their teachers are telling them to focus on university – but a lot of them aren't interested and it's not the only path. These are kids with huge talent and equally big aspirations, and we need to get behind them in a different way.'

'We're a digital cooperative,' the group tells me when I return from sitting at another table to look at their now very detailed drawing. The Time Machine is designed as a DAO,* a digital cooperative that works with an alternative digital currency – the Barnsley coin. This, the group explains, will ensure that wealth generated by local businesses will circulate within the town. (This lack of money circulating within a local economy is much discussed; Barrow and Grimsby face similar challenges, with the good, well-paid work done by those who do not live in the town and who spend their wages elsewhere, a challenge I consider further in my Sixth Principle: Place.) The Time Machine will reset the economic norms within the town through trading time, through using money to secure the basics for everyone and through sharing the surplus in new ways, such as the learning projects, that can grow the town. 'It's the Barnsley Dividend,' Emma says. 'It increases the value of the place you are from and your own humanity.'

The Barnsley Time Machine brings together international practices ('in Scandinavia everyone leaves to pick up their children – it's normal'; 'in Estonia the government thinks about time and how to organise online services to give time back to citizens') with ideas about sharing work that would have been familiar to William Kellogg, new thinking about

---

* DAO stands for decentralised autonomous organisation. Interest in DAOs has been strongest in crypto communities but more recently there has been a growing interest in exploring the potential of this form of organisation – based around a common purpose, with decentralised governance and a local currency – for local economic development.

technology and perhaps a dash of science fiction found stored in the Tardis.

'We've not explained it very well,' Craig tells another group who come over to take a look at the ideas on the table-cloth. The Time Machine is still a work in progress, but it's clear that the central idea is to use time to stimulate a good economy. The Time Machine is an expression of the desire to bend time in a just and more creative way.

Time-bending

When white settlers arrived in the North American Great Lakes, they were amazed by the abundance of the wild rice harvests. They were equally surprised that, as they noted in their journals, 'the savages stopped gathering long before all the rice was harvested'. The Native peoples were following their ancient practices of a harvest which started with a ceremony of thanksgiving and continued for four days, leaving most of the rice to re-seed and support the wildlife which they revered and on which they also depended. The Europeans were aghast at this waste and the lack of productivity. They did not understand how these indigenous land-care practices were creating the abundance they encountered, and they concluded instead that 'the heathens' were, in the words of that familiar trope of the master/invaders, 'lazy'.

Robin Wall Kimmerer, who tells this story, draws on her work as a scientist and on her Potawatomi heritage to show how both people and the plant world are interconnected and how we can attune to the seasons to learn how much work – metaphorically, how much harvesting and hunting – is enough for our own wellbeing and for the continued flourishing of the natural systems we are part of. Kimmerer's stories are about understanding the impact of our work in very long-run time horizons and about only taking enough: what we need and not too much. These are ideas that closely connect to Elinor Ostrom's work on the commons in their emphasis on the collective tending of whole systems.

But so successful has been our ingestion of the *chronos* metronome, we can find it hard to relate these ancient stories or the experiments and imaginings of others to our own worlds. Another way to think about it is to see that work is like a drug – we should be told how much to take, just as a packet of paracetamol provides us with directions for use. This is the conclusion of two business school professors, Lynda Gratton and Andrew Scott, who have investigated how to live a good long life. Like the workers at Battle Creek, the business leaders who have piloted a four-day week and everyone I have met on my journeys, they are convinced that too much time spent 'in the tunnel of work' blunts other capacities, including our knowledge of how to live well and relate to one another.

Gratton and Scott propose the use of thanatological time. Thanatological time would measure our age not by how long it is since we were born (as chronological time would do – birthday parties are also a modern, *chronos* invention) but rather by how long we have left to live. Such a calculation – as Gratton and Scott admit – is complex, because none of us really knows how long we have left. Population statistics can help with the calculation, but what is more important is the *idea*: focusing on the time in front of us changes our opinions about what's important and how we should allocate our time. This is how Jonny and many others think instinctively.

The success of work–time experiments – some of which have collected data at significant scale – demonstrates that rethinking time would be better for everyone. Working less makes us healthier and happier; it improves the economics for businesses that take part while collective health and happiness reduces state expenditure on services that currently prop us up when work makes us sick. Working less will be generative for the places where we live; we will have time to nurture social bonds and it could help us regenerate our ecosystems. And technology can help support these new working patterns.

In fact, the evidence that we can and should reimagine working time is so long standing and convincing we have to ask ourselves why we keep forgetting. Why has this work revolution not already happened?

Psychologists often tell us how hard it is to believe data that does not coincide with our understanding of how things should be. We often literally cannot hear or see things that do not accord with our common sense. Perhaps our thinking about work (and workers) has become so mechanistic we find it hard to grasp that humans (unlike machines) may be more efficient if they do less.

Something else is important too. Work – as I will come back to later in the book – is widely written about and theorised as an economic practice, the L for labour in the equations of economists that few of us dare quarrel with. But work is a cultural idea. The time experiments, like our search for meaning and our desire to care for one another, demonstrate that it is not simply economic equations which drive the patterns of work. When we dig a little deeper, we can see that work is rarely organised according to objective data, but rather according to more hidden beliefs and designs. In the end it doesn't matter that the five-day working week is a relatively recent and not particularly successful invention, or that shorter working weeks are better for everyone economically if you simply believe as a matter of principle and personal conviction that everyone should work as hard as possible.

In Sweden, politics interrupted Gothenburg's four-day week experiment in 2017. The evidence that shorter working hours was improving services and worker wellbeing did not sit well with the incoming right-wing government's cultural message about the importance of work and a fully flexible (that is, constantly available) workforce. The new government ignored the independent evaluation and curtailed the experiment. All was not lost, because other city councils, encouraged by the data, have since emulated the model, but it's clear that work practice does not respond to data alone. New imaginings, collective dreams and a constant re-statement of data is required to bring about a work revolution. We have all three to hand. Perhaps the next stage is to spend more time practising other ways of living – it's one of the reasons the Imagineers turned next to the importance of play.

Principle Five: Play – A Precarious Magic

One evening in Detroit, I hosted an Imagining in Mexicantown. It's where I meet Javier. 'Play?' he asked quizzically, picking up a green card depicting a game and looking round at his friends at the table. 'Most of us don't have that option right now. We're working hard labour,' he explained while placing the card decisively in a spot that signified 'play' to be of the utmost importance to a good working life.

Across all the Imaginings, the cards which denoted play were chosen decisively and placed on the table with intent. These were cards which showed ball games or board games, travel, knitting and pottery. The hobbies card had a space for people to write in their own. Running, reading – 'Have you read *The Count of Monte Cristo?*' Palash had asked me when I met him with his fellow delivery riders in Barking. 'It's my favourite – you have to feed your mind' – painting, football, birdwatching, playing in a band – everyone discussed the things they enjoy, the things which provide a spacious sense of ease and pleasure; the things we do 'just because'.

But choosing the card does not mean you are actually playing or have the space to do so. When Javier and his peers talked about 'hard labour' as we ate home-made tamales, they were distinguishing the long hours and total work they endure in their unsafe and illegal construction jobs from what they call 'regular work': a regulated, approximately eight-hour working day, the sort of working life they dream of, secured by the basics and which allows time for play.

Javier is twenty-four years old, eloquent, warm and smart. 'I came top of my class,' he told me, 'but I had a tough time: I was overweight, I had this accent, I was bullied.' Sporting a box-fresh white T-shirt and college cap worn backwards, Javier is studying mechanical engineering. I spot the blue Ford logo on his T-shirt – I had been at the car plant earlier that day. 'Like, I wish – I wish I worked for Ford,' he said. 'It's my dream – you know, they want to go full electric.' At the plant, I'd been told about the urgent need for more workers. Recruitment needs are particularly pressing on the high-tech line that will build the new electric pick-up truck, on which hopes of growth are predicated. Javier, clever, sorted and mature beyond his years, seems like someone who could one day be running Ford, never mind hoping to work there. But right now, it's a dream: neither his degree, his eloquence nor his demeanour will be enough.

Javier is a 'dreamer', the name for one of three and a half million undocumented young people who entered the US illegally as children. He was a toddler when he came from Mexico with his parents. His life chart detailed his family's repeated attempts to get legal status and how his parents had divorced under the stress. 'I have learnt that life will hit you in so many ways,' he told me. At twenty, it looked like he would get settled status under the DACA (Deferred Action for Childhood Arrivals) process, but two years later the process was frozen. His visa status makes college hard. Despite excellent grades, he is not eligible for grants or scholarships and has to find $15,000 a year to pay his fees, which is why, like his peers, he is juggling so much work: a construction job in the week, gardening at the weekend, his studies in between.

'It's good you are here,' Javier's friend Lucho broke in. 'You can hear about how it is.' (Lucho had already told me about his long and terrifying night, left alone in a flooded water main.) 'We have a lot of aspirations, passions, love for things, but hard labour is dependent on your body, how far you can push it. At the end of the day you can't focus on anything else. You're just scrolling, scrolling.' Lucho mimed with his thumbs the experience of a catatonic slump on the sofa, phone in hand. For these young men, the physicality of the work, the long hours, the often dangerous and unregulated conditions, and living on high alert as illegal citizens, is exhausting.

Play is the opposite of doomscrolling – 'It is not time off, it's not a recovery needed to work again, it's another dimension,' the friends tell me. 'Play is freedom, it gives you energy, pleasure.' Primo, large and shy, breaks in: 'Like, I play Mexican backgammon with my elders – you know, it's like a passion, I don't even think why I'm doing, it, I'm just in it.' The men warm to their theme, talking about the times they have been able to play: on the football pitch, at a festival, sharing an ice cream in the park. Play is about courtship and a little flirting. It's also a space for serendipitous connections: 'You meet people, you start to chat without pressure,' Javier explains. 'It's about relationships and when you get the chance, this is so important – for example, I figured out this way how I could go to college, despite my status.'

When I listened to these young men talk, I realised that play is not – as we often think – simply the opposite of work. If play has an opposite, it would be the 'juggle, juggle', a feeling of being on edge, over-worked or enervated by bad work. When the British psychoanalyst Donald Winnicott studied children at play, an activity he believed was vital for healthy human development, he was concerned to observe that 'the "deprived child" is notoriously restless and unable to play'. Over-worked, distracted by devices, caught in the never-ending cycle of care and work, we can feel the same: deprived and unable to play.

Playing in the digital revolution

Technology, its inventors often boast, will give us time for leisure. The dishwasher, the microwave, even Alexa who will turn on the lights, are each sold to us with a promise that they will save time that we can then use for something more pleasurable. But is technology actually the shadow side of play, stealing time while also subtly altering our ability to be 'just in it'?

Just as the play cards always went down on the table with precision and easy laughter, so the technology cards brought indecision and consternation. Participants kept their fingers on cards which showed computers, phones and other devices, moving them up, down and round the table in a shifting uncertainty, unable to let go or decide their role and importance. 'Did you see that?' Vontisha, one of my co-facilitators, asked me after a Baltimore Imagining, referring to the indecision the technology cards had provoked. 'It happens every single time.'

'No app, no work,' someone might comment ruefully, acknowledging that the card had to be chosen. 'We would ditch them [the apps and devices] if we could.' If play defines the good life, even when we are not playing, technology is the ambivalent opposite: always present, a stealer of time, relationships and the reflective space that play creates. 'You know what technology means: you don't talk to your partner or your kids, you don't even watch a movie, there's just scrolling, scrolling, scrolling where talking and the other things used to be,' lamented a group of technical engineers who joined me from a green energy company in Grimsby.

With each technology revolution there have been new fears about the possible demise of play. In the 1950s, as automation took hold, there was a perception, almost a panic, that the immense physical and mental pressures of modern work would lead to a state called 'total work'. 'Is there a sphere of human activity, one might even say of human existence, that does not need to be justified by inclusion in a five-year plan?' the German philosopher Josef Pieper asked in 1965, in an academic but widely read treatise that argued for a renewed understanding of leisure and the space for play as the basis for culture in any good society.

The play or leisure that Pieper celebrated – and feared was being lost – is not something we inevitably find just because we have time off at the weekend or a holiday. He describes instead an attitude of mind, 'the capacity to steep oneself in the whole of creation'. He distinguished play when we are at peace and immersed in what we are doing from idleness, which he described as an inner dis-ease which makes play impossible. Javier and his friends do not use the lofty language of inner peace, neither do they describe themselves as being steeped in creation, but their definitions of play as 'doing things just because', of 'losing oneself in genial activity', just like their descriptions of 'hard labour', echo Pieper's work. They also fear that technology, the endless scrolling that Lucho describes, is creating lassitude and an inability to play.

Modern computing is ironically an invention that developed and continues to advance through a form of play: simulated and actual war games. Its playful potential caught the attention of the early commercial coders in Silicon Valley. The 1970s counter-culture guru Stewart Brand was transfixed by what he saw late one night at Xerox Parc. He watched as coders and engineers re-arranged their desks and gleefully hacked their computers together in order to play illicit and rudimentary games of their own creation long into the night.

Brand wrote about what he had witnessed in *Rolling Stone* magazine, much to the dismay of the coders whose bosses had no idea about these 'fanatical' play sessions and who immediately tried to put a stop to them. Brand didn't care. He had glimpsed something bigger: that the future of the digital revolution would be personal computing because everyone would want to play, and fortunes would be made by those who could find a way to put smaller, more affordable devices in everyone's hands. Brand was widely revered in Silicon Valley circles, and he powerfully shaped the direction of technology investment, popularising his vision through the *Whole Earth Catalog* and well-attended hacker conferences. Steve Jobs was just one of the acolytes in the audience.

Decades on, almost every pocket has a phone and every phone is a portal to games and social diversion while the gaming industry is worth twice the dollar value of the film industry. Jack, a game designer who was part of the Barnsley digital hub, extolled the storytelling techniques, the visual ingenuity, the new and deeply layered sound worlds which are emerging through gaming. But he also admitted he might not last long: game designers have widely reported troubles of anxiety and memory loss, and most cannot withstand work in the industry beyond five years.

Many others who came to the Imaginings are less convinced that digital games count as play, lamenting that they have lost their sons in particular to gaming addiction and more than one person blamed their own relationship breakdown on the same affliction. Gaming is a world that feels from the outside a little dangerous. Suspicion is heightened by a generational divide. It is mostly the young who are playing, and sometimes as I listen to people's fears I think about those 'no ball games' signs placed on the walls of housing up and down the country by grumpy elders. I wonder if the games of each new generation do not seem like play to those who are older.

The delivery riders who I met in Barking tell me that this is wrong-headed. They are crystal clear on the divide between play, gaming and what they hate most: gamification. Gamification is a form of enforced work-play which includes different forms of competitive challenge: the real-time ratings, point-scoring and other detested mini competitions designed to get more out of the worker. Every Uber rider must chase their star ratings if they are to keep the app 'open' and retain the possibility of working. Even a fall to 4.5 stars can be hazardous. When the demand for drivers is high they may also be offered 'challenges' which encourage them to drive and achieve a score for rides which may result in a bonus. 'This technology, it is playing with us,' Palash told me when we met in Barking. 'Uber owns the technology and the rules, so it is Uber that is *playing*.' But true play, as Palash points out, is something different and one of its defining characteristics is the freedom to own, to make and to re-make the rules (something which is found in the best digital games).

I still don't know if digital technology can offer us true play, but I have learnt that play is a space apart in which traditional hierarchies can't apply; an activity that is oxygenating, life-giving, a deep part of our flourishing.

A place apart

'In this uncontainable life where everything is everything, you need a place apart and a place where you can play and re-invent. For me it's the Fitties,' the artist Sarah Palmer tells me at an Imagining in Grimsby, referring to the small isthmus of beach and marsh where she has a summer chalet. She chooses the play card and another, a drawing of a brain, with the words 'time to think', defining a space apart as both a physical place to get away and a place of imaginative escape.

'You've got to create separation, find space for a different energy,' Charlotte Bowen, founder and owner of The Culture House, concurred, before adding, 'Freedom from technology is part of this.' She talks of the frustrations of a world where we are expected to don a 'work persona', usually spending hours behind a screen, as distinct from a 'playful persona'. 'It's a weird thing we have to do, we're holistic beings and we connect with each other through play, yet we have to squeeze ourselves into being someone else at least five days a week.' The Culture House is a Grimsby organisation that takes art and culture to the streets. It's an almost impossible conjuring act: finding funding, bringing people together, making sure everyone is included and surprised. This is work driven by an ethic of play, a commitment to place and a belief that Grimbarians are curious and open to new and playful experiences. To sustain the work, Charlotte, like Sarah, is conscious that she has to find and make her own playful places. She has returned to her home town after working in London.

Grimsby is nestled next to Cleethorpes, a seaside town long associated with play. The railways and the wealth of the 1870s – the gilded age of the belle époque, which followed the third technology revolution – encouraged many to travel from industrial towns to take a seaside holiday. Cleethorpes provided a beautiful pier, donkey rides, dance halls and long sandy beaches. Wealthy and often more bohemian Grimbarians preferred to erect lavish bell tents a little further along the coast, decamping for the summer with servants and all other household necessities in tow. Fathers returned to the town on their bicycles each day to work. A little further still, on a long spit of once common land known as Anthony's Bank, local working-class people began to holiday, making their own encampments and chalets with anything to hand. This was the land that became the 'Fitties', a word which means salt marsh in north-east Lincolnshire.

Today it is an Arcadian place of painted chalets, each one different from its neighbour, sitting in small, tended plots. Gates and fences are adorned with eclectic artworks made from flotsam which is washed up on the wide shores. The house with the blue door is Sarah's summer home. 'I started to come here when my son was little,' Sarah tells me. 'You feel far away, and free.' Sarah's home is also her much needed 'place apart' where she can make art and play with new projects and ideas. She's not alone. Poets, artists, former miners and trawlermen alike take up residence from early summer until the autumn, swooping in like swallows each year to nest in a temporary life of ease.

Grimsby's Scandinavian-style idyll is not well known. The town is more famous as the home of Britain's industrial fishing. The industry's demise started in the 1970s. Today the port is owned by an international conglomerate and the docks are used by other international companies who maintain offshore wind farms and land the catches of vast trawlers from Iceland and Norway: their cargo is processed in Grimsby and then re-loaded, frozen, to continue on its global journey. What was once the world's largest ice factory, a red-brick palace built in 1900, stands immense in the middle of the site, a monument to former, grander times.

The loss of the fishing industry is a trauma still deeply felt. Seventy per cent of north-east Lincolnshire voted for Brexit, believing Boris Johnson's promises that the fishing industry would be restored. Recovery was never within his power; fishing quotas are a complex international negotiation, while Grimsby had in any case long lost its own trawlers and those like Lisa's father who once took care of their crews and could impart the skills to another generation. Grimsby did not gain a renewed economy but a grant to do up its shopping centre, under the government's Levelling Up scheme. For many, a further sense of betrayal set in.

But the past has potential, and for Sarah the story is not yet finished. The industrial fishing grew from an earlier forgotten way of life, generated by the landscape and things held in common: the waters and the salt grazing. Grimsby has the wide estuaries of the Humber, rare chalk streams and what are locally called 'blow wells', artesian fresh water springs uniquely found in these marginal coastal lands. The landscape is spaciously beautiful and attracts rare wild life and thousands of migrating birds. A space apart, a space of play has generated for Sarah a new imagining, a sort of stealing back. Her new work is a response to loss and a love story for a landscape that makes a different, in her words 'less muscular', future seem possible.

Both Sarah and Charlotte bind play to creative work that seeks to draw the public into new stories about Grimsby's future. In a series of events titled Our Future Starts Here, The Culture House brings national artists together with home-grown dance, theatre and multi-media installations bringing alive ideas of Gaia and deeper earth forces, all curated to provoke new and collective imaginings of sustainable futures. These events provide a temporary place apart for residents who are also invited to be playful.

The artistic emphasis is on play, but the imaginative energy connects with a wider network of community action. Several of the artists who joined the Imagining also work for community projects collaborating with Billy Dasein, the founder of East Marsh United (EMU) and the Grimsby-born tech entrepreneur Jason Stockwood. EMU are organising a community buy-out of derelict houses on the East Marsh. The houses are restored by a local team and rented at a social rent. Stockwood has bought Grimsby Town Football Club, one of the oldest clubs in the country but which, at the time of the purchase was languishing in ninety-second place (out of a national league of ninety-three), with public stands that were threatening to collapse. The club was, in Stockwood's eyes, one of the last remaining social institutions that he remembered from his youth, and it was about to go bankrupt. Buying the club was a poor investment financially but rich for play. The Mariners – as the team are known – are back in the second division, match days are sold out and, at the weekends, the club once again provides the town with another sort of place apart.

Playing to survive; playing to evolve

'Play is the actual means of our survival,' the London-based artist and activist Lucy Neal told me. Lucy is the author of a rich manifesto, *Playing for Time*. She has thought deeply about a subject that I had not in truth considered much before the Imaginings. In the spirit of my journeys and still working 'in the opposite direction', I wanted to share with her the emphasis that was put on play at the Imaginings and to ask her why she thought this aspect of life was emerging everywhere as a founding principle of a good working life.

If the technology revolution is eating play, Lucy believes that the ecology revolution will be nourished by it. We need to imagine other, better and abundant worlds and these are most likely to be conjured in play, she tells me, talking about work that has similarities to the projects of the Grimsby artists. We cannot build or move into these worlds unless we rehearse them. Play gives us a chance to try out a different part of ourselves, perhaps dress up, use props, live as if we are somewhere or someone else; we improvise, improve and build. Play in this sense is a bit like the pilgrimage – everyday concerns are put aside and for an interlude we can, if we like, turn things upside down, preparing for a future way of living.

In Detroit, Grace Lee Boggs (who railed against the idea of Do What You Love – DWYL) also recognised play and creativity as central to any work revolution. In the 1970s, Boggs and her husband James, an auto worker and labour organiser who moved to Detroit from Alabama, argued that the idea of a work revolution itself needed to be reimagined. Work protest and work organising, as formally practised by the union movement was, in their view, ill-suited to creating alternatives which should be rooted in new values as opposed to the acquisition of material possessions. They saw early the paradigm changes now affecting work and they started to distinguish between what they called 'protest organising' aimed at protecting existing work and work values, and 'visionary organising' aimed at allowing 'a more human, human being' to develop. At the heart of visionary organising would be play and the creative activities that would encourage the invention of new work lives.

It's no surprise that the collective energy and magic of play is found in many social movements, which like games often seem generous and a little anarchic. 'Beneath the streets there is the beach,' the Parisian beatniks of 1968 famously chanted as they hurled cobblestones. It was both a reality – to their amusement, they found sand beneath the stones – and alluded to their sense of play: future life would be a beach. Today's global movements, protesting injustice in all its forms, share many of the same characteristics, bringing much needed energy and imagination to politics. The artworks and collectively made structures that are typical of Extinction Rebellion protests, for example, are part of the carnival atmosphere – a manifestation of the better life they draw to public attention, while their creativity can diffuse tension. It is hard to arrest a twenty-foot pink octopus.

Who plays; who imagines?

Grace Boggs was, like Lucy Neal, also concerned with who has time for and is allowed to play. Today extreme work – 'hard labour' – prevents play. Many who came to the Imaginings who work in 'greedy' corporate jobs are also missing out on play. They select play cards as they talk about golf bags, Peloton bikes and other expensive kit that lies unused at home. The energy and mien required for a playful life is addled by long hours in air-conditioned office suites, while the lack of play contributes to stress and to a feeling of being jaded at work and by life itself.

But I realise it is women who consistently play less. 'Mom spends beach vacation assuming all household duties in closer proximity to the ocean' ran a spoof headline in *The Onion*. It came to mind as I listened to the discussion of play. Women talked mostly about the play they were organising for others: for children, wider family, birthday celebrations. Men contributed wholeheartedly to these activities – I met more dad weekend football coaches than I could count – but their own play was usually something organised away from home, somewhere more sacrosanct: even if only at the gym, or in the pub watching a game with mates.

What might have happened if women had fought for the right to play, rather than to work? It's a question that intrigues the writer Rebecca Abrams. 'All work and no play make Jack a dull boy,' she writes, 'but what about Jill?' She set out to study women and their everyday play for a decade. All the women in her study struggle to play alongside the demands of work and care. Abrams observes how women find it particularly hard to remember how to immerse themselves in playful activity after the childbearing years. I am not surprised – like many mothers, I can remember having the first half hour of freedom returned to me and finding myself at a loss, no longer quite sure how to use it. Even now, with a spare pocket of time, I am more likely to put on another load of laundry than sit down with a novel. I am not alone.

Abrams finds not only that women share a paucity of play, but that play is like a muscle and atrophies with disuse. Out of practice and longing to simply slump on the sofa after organising the play for everyone else, mothers in particular lose the muscle. Abrams is convinced this really matters, because she discovered that the women who are flourishing most are those who have managed to cultivate a playful attitude to life.

Those who have studied the science of play would concur: play, while it needs to be improvisational and unburdened by a sense of usefulness, to bring joy, is a serious matter. Stuart Brown, a psychiatrist and the founder of the US National Institute for Play, writes about the importance of play 'for its own sake' but he is also keen to emphasise the role of play in human development. Animals that play have been shown to be able to better navigate their worlds, and for humans play enhances children's development, making young people both academically and socially smarter, as well as more resilient. In Abrams's study, the women who are able to play are also more adaptable and optimistic: traits we all need in times of uncertainty and transition.

'It matters who imagines. It matters what stories make

worlds, what worlds make stories,' writes the feminist scholar of technology Donna Haraway. This is what Javier and Lucho, the young construction workers I met in Detroit, are saying when they tell me how much it means that I am listening to their stories. It is why the uneven distribution of time to play requires urgent attention. Play helps us develop, it makes us healthy and it's a form of power: those who are playing are imaginatively shaping our future.

The Imaginings are experienced as a form of play. Participants enjoy themselves and want to stay longer. There is also an awareness that a skill is being honed. 'We have never asked ourselves these things before,' I'm often told, a reflection that carries a realisation that we can and should imagine; that an afternoon or evening which has felt like fun is important. Something similar occurs to many who generously help me host the Imaginings. Community organisations, innovation hubs, public servants and businesses offer me space and sometimes facilitation support. They often reflect afterwards, with surprise, that without realising it they are no longer imagining in their life or work, that they have become less creative. The grind of delivery, raising money and meeting targets can crowd out imagination, even if we know our work depends upon it.

Research shows that these uneasy feelings about a loss of creativity are borne out in reality. There has been a steady and persistent decline in creativity which is widely attributed to the decline in play. The data shows that creative thinking and IQ rose concomitantly for decades, but at some point between 1990 and 1998 they parted ways. It seems that all is well until we enter school, at which point our imaginative worlds are devalued and undermined. 'We are not here to play about,' teachers regularly admonish their small charges, and research finds that by the start of secondary school at age eleven, most British children find it hard to tell a story. These same children may well be taken on a supervised trip to a museum or art gallery, but they are not encouraged to invent, run free, play and imagine.

Play and its sibling, imagination, help us navigate the world and give us the tools to shape it. Just as importantly, play is fun. To be human is to seek enjoyment, pleasure, different ways of being with each other. It is why *Sapiens integra* cannot imagine thriving in a life that does not have space to play. Play remains precarious – always squeezed by other claims on our time and attention. And play is transient – if we encumber our play with too much expectation (or with transactional goals) the magic disappears.

In the ancient world, despite these acknowledged fugitive qualities, play was a matter for important consideration, and regarded as the fulcrum of a flourishing life. 'Life must be lived as play,' Plato commanded, while for Aristotle the good life would be impossible if we are *'unleisurely'*. In the twenty-first century play must once again be placed at the heart of a good life. We will create better futures. We will almost certainly radically reduce our mental health crises, and we will also be better workers, not just because so much modern work requires a playful imagination, but because we would be rested, happy and nourished.

Principle Six: Organising in Place

In the second part of the Imaginings, I replaced the cards with a blank paper tablecloth and I asked each small group to design an organisation they believed could bring their imagined good work life into being.

This exercise, as I noted earlier, initially provoked consternation and some nervous laughter. Most people who came to an Imagining were doubtful that they had the skills to design an organisation, but the talking and then the designing started. On every table a new organisation emerged – one that would create good work and good lives, through rooting a new form of work organisation in place.

The House

'Come on in.' Laurie beckons me with a broad smile. 'Put your things down,' she says, ushering me into what feels like a large living room.

We are in The House. Three floors of deep red brick, this requisitioned industrial building rises proudly behind the high street. The top floor is the Night Club – a centre for learning, used by young people during the day, but particularly busy at night when many take the courses they need to change their work or move on to higher education. The middle floor is the Transition Club, with an advice centre: 'We can get legal help, financial support and business advice, we can also get professional counselling for any aspect of our lives – and there are rooms to hold meetings and to co-work,' Laurie explains. The ground floor hosts a children's centre, large and small spaces for parties and spaces that are run by and for young people. 'And that door there,' Laurie continues, pointing to what I thought was a bookcase, but can now see is a door, 'that's our human library. We go in there to "borrow" each other, sometimes to try out new jobs or just to get some life advice. It's brilliant – you can find everything in that library.'

The House has been designed by Laurie and her colleagues, with the intention of transforming work in the town they call home. If root shock is about the decimation of place when the good work goes, The House is about nurturing rootstock. It's an organisation that will grow people, work and place, in an understanding that all three are inseparably bound together.

'To make sure people from every neighbourhood can get good work, to create more good work and to transform our town, we need to know each other and organise in new ways,' Laurie continues. 'Here everyone is welcome – it's a sort of home from home and our members include those in work, out of work, those with connections and experience and those just starting out. Everyone knows something and has a piece of this jigsaw.'

As we continue the tour, I'm shown the children's centre, which is a local cooperative, started with funds The House can lend for new locally owned ventures. I also see a music production studio; the offices of a community food network that is supporting local growers; and – something Laurie is particularly proud of – the headquarters of a new eco-tourism agency. 'You know it felt risky before to change

your job, never mind start something new, but now we have
the practical support, venture funds and a community, come
what may.'

Laurie describes how The House is run – 'one member,
one vote'. 'It's cumbersome sometimes and we had to learn
a lot about our differences but it really works.' The House
itself was gifted by the local council in an asset transfer and,
most importantly, a significant capital fund was part of the
structure, enabling The House to be financially independent
and to loan to start-up businesses. Members pay dues and The
House also makes money through the provision of community internet services: 'We learnt in the pandemic how many
people weren't connected – it's crazy, businesses gave schools
laptops without realising that at home so many could not
afford to connect.' Next year will see The House invest in
community power generation. The House has been running
for ten years so far and has its sights set on the long term.

'This is a place to dream and then, together, make things
happen!' Laurie ends with a verbal flourish. She takes a
breath. 'Have I forgotten anything?' she asks her team-mates.
Everyone looks down at the paper tablecloth. We have almost
forgotten that we are not standing in the building that Laurie
has conjured in our minds, but round a table, where in front
of us the elements Laurie describes are pictured in words,
drawings and torn-out magazine images stuck onto the paper
tablecloth.

The House is a vision of a new form of work organising.
It appeared in multiple iterations: in Baltimore, a version of
was called The Glue; in Barking, The Raiders; in Barnsley,
The Time Machine. These organisations and many more
take the principles of good work: the need for the basics, for
care, for work with meaning, for time and for play, and bring
them together in a new organisation that celebrates the sixth

principle, the individuality, importance and creative potential of place. At the Imaginings, place is a protagonist in the work story, a repository of ideas and relationships that can actively re-shape work.

In the places I journey to, it is not simply that good work has disappeared. The bigger challenge is that when and if new investment materialises, it rarely creates sustained good local work. Sometimes external investors have little interest in local work. In Grimsby, a port now registered to conglomerates in the Far East means a set of owners with a strategic asset (a useful base from which international teams can maintain wind turbines, for example), with little interest in local people and their work. Sometimes the intention on behalf of investors is to create good work but local skills are lacking, as is the social infrastructure which might connect local people with new opportunities.

In Barrow, for example, successive investments in new submarine contracts create employment (jobs that can be counted and entered into national datasets in the Treasury). But Barrow is not unusual in that the higher-paid jobs are frequently taken by those who live far away. In 2019 a new Holiday Inn opened to house these BAE workers who stay in the town from Monday to Thursday. Their salaries fuel the billion-dollar revenue of the multi-national IHG hotel group and, at the weekends they spend in the already prosperous places these workers call home, but comparatively little trickles into the local economy in Barrow. Macro-level data can tell a story of investment in work that feels very different on the ground.

The labour economist and Harvard professor Dani Rodrik has argued that the idea that external investment in new economic sectors or big business automatically leads to good local jobs is simply wishful thinking. It is one of a number of assumptions in industrial policy that needs rethinking. In similar vein, and in an off-the-cuff but prescient comment, the German economist Isabella Weber has stated that to hope national level macroeconomic policies simply translate into micro, local level economic flourishing is like planting crops without worrying about local irrigation.

Anchoring investment in ways that creates good local work requires new forms of social infrastructure to ensure both the learning required and the relationships between communities, business (and between local businesses) and the state are nurtured. Strong local social infrastructure also creates and sustains vibrant places, where those with skills want to live and stay. The iterations of The House instinctively address these issues in their design and position themselves as part of the solution to the current disconnect between investment, industrial policy and good local work.

And there is another reason the designs emphasise place. Today, the institutional landscape in every place I visit is unstable, feeding the wider sense that life itself is uncertain. Philanthropy comes and goes; local government reconfigures and shrinks in the face of austerity and ideology; unions find it hard to maintain a presence when the 'big' work goes, while national initiatives, from regional development bodies to promises of levelling up or green new deals, are tied to political tides that wash in and then out, shifting the sands but leaving the landscape little changed. There is a hunger for strong institutions that are not dependent on weather made elsewhere.

'No one is coming over the hill to rescue us,' I was told yet again, an acknowledgement that there are no big or easy answers, but this time, creative change needs to start not with looking expectantly over the hill, but with what is to hand in place: people, their ideas and their capacity to organise.

Work organising

It is hard to imagine the gains of the twentieth century – fair pay, regulated hours, the birth of the welfare state – without the rise and collective power of the trade union movement.

The founders of the trade union movement drew inspiration from earlier struggles – critically the Chartists' agitation for full male suffrage and Robert Owen's early nineteenth-century dreams of a worker utopia. They also understood that the Industrial Revolution and factory work in particular had changed the rules of the game. They could see that the guilds, the work organisations which had so successfully protected the skills and wages of master craftsmen, would no longer protect mass labour rights in new industrial settings, much less ensure that workers could have a share of the prodigious wealth industrialisation was generating.

With the rise of mass industrial technology, power was consolidated in the hands of industry owners and in new work practices and contracts which made the skills of any individual worker indistinguishable (and therefore vulnerable). At the same time, vast new places of work (the factories, the mines and industrial shipyards) provided opportunities for workers to come together in influential numbers, in order to agitate for new contracts and conditions. At stake were tactics, organisational design, membership and the definition of good work: each needed to be re-thought, and trade unions were responsible for a decisive evolution in the form of work organising in order to re-shape work.

The tablecloth organisations produced in every location show a similar adroit understanding that we are once again in a new era as technology and ecological imperatives shift investment, the location of work, the terms on which new work is offered and ways in which power is concentrated. Those who come to the Imaginings have observed and often viscerally experienced these realignments, fomenting a desire to once again create a new form of work organisation that can meet the moment.

The first step is to invert the locus of power. The twentieth-century trade union is a vertically integrated organisation; members are organised by work type or profession, with national headquarters managing research, budgets and agendas. The twenty-first-century House starts instead in place, reclaiming the importance of local decision-making and local agendas, and organising horizontally to draw in as many local people as possible.

It has become common in Britain and America to talk about 'left behind' places, a label that jars in neighbourhoods from Barrow to Baltimore. The stereotypes sting because residents have an intense local pride in people and place – places they have actively chosen to live in or to return to, not places where they have been 'left'. Generic labels like 'left behind' are also hated because they add to a sense that each place in its individuality and humanity is invisible to those with power. 'Do they even know we are here?' I'm asked in Barrow. 'Do they just imagine we are some small racist mining town?' I'm asked in Barnsley. There are dark things, and people talk about those things – from gun crime in the US to knife crime in the UK, the gaps on the high street where businesses used to be. And there is a strong and proud sense that many solutions can be home-grown, with a place like The House to draw on and expand local ties and ideas.

The House will secure the basics and will expand to take in wider life concerns, the need to rethink *learning* in particular and to secure a role in creating, anchoring and *designing* the work itself.

Really learning

When Laurie shows me the Night Club on the top floor of The House, she is responding to a widely felt need to find new routes into all forms of learning.

In the view of those who came to the Imaginings, what's missing are not only excellent and adequate resources – teachers, apprenticeships, high-quality and diverse courses, financing for study and second chances – but something much trickier: the social glue that silently communicates to everyone the validity of the endeavour, that learning is a real promise of a good working life whether you choose to leave or stay. Every imagined 'House' positioned itself to embrace this critical challenge: organising new forms of learning; creating links to those in good work (the exchange) and providing the cultural glue; 'a reminder that we here and we have potential', that it is worth taking the time to study.

'A DIFFERENT LEARNING SYSTEM', a group of participants in Grimsby wrote in capital letters across the top of their work organisation. This group have minimum-wage jobs packing components for a very successful start-up that sells home energy meters. They have read about the good green jobs that have been promised to the region and they want to think about how they can form a local organisation in order to 'really learn' (they again use the words so often repeated) and position themselves for that work. Like many Imagineers from all places, they talked simultaneously about the challenges: places of learning that don't always feel welcoming, are hard to reach on public transport, a fear that the courses aren't actually the ones they need.

'Really learning' means putting aside presumptions of what people might like to study – from aeronautic engineering to the creative and emotional skills required in this revolution – and how far they can go. As I travelled, I frequently heard politicians lament a perceived lack of 'aspiration' among younger people in particular. 'How can we have a better educated population?' one prominent local leader asked me. 'Our young people lack ambition.'

'Why would we want those "noddy certificates"?' young people would often retort. The Imaginings showed that most young people are confident and ambitious; what they can't currently see are paths between the learning on offer and the work they dream of. At the Imaginings, employees and local employers alike did not see the problem as one of ambition. Instead, they understood the lack of connection between local learning strategies and local people. The need is for diversity in provision and strong social connections to support learners at every age and stage.

'Really learning' means allowing people to aim high. It might look something like the G.I. Bill, which supported American army veterans to transition back into civilian life at the end of the Second World War. The bill, which was grossly disfigured by the lack of support for Black veterans and prompted by fear of unrest rather than an unwavering commitment to education, was nonetheless a radical piece of US education policy. Generous financial support was offered ($500 a year when Harvard fees were $400 a year) because policymakers expected a low take-up. It was assumed that most veterans would choose cheaper vocational courses. But trusted to choose their future for themselves, they aimed high, signing up to study science, law, engineering and liberal arts. As the American economy rode the wave of a new technology revolution these veterans were acquiring just the skills they and their country needed.

'Really learning' also depends on the element almost never discussed by politicians: social glue. In Detroit, Javier and his friends wrote 'Herramientas/Intercambio' ('Tools/ Exchange') in bold letters at the top of the organisation they designed. Education and specifically degree certificates were the tools required but, as they had learnt, certificates are not useful without a strong social network, the exchange part of the equation. 'You can have a degree, but if you don't know people, at the end of the day you are not going to succeed,' Javier told me, a view widely shared by his friends, who chime in: 'It's not what you know, it's who you know', 'You're going to succeed through connections'. Their organisation, like countless others, had a human library to facilitate social exchange and create paths between their learning and local opportunities.

When I heard Laurie describe The House and its Night Club, and as I made my pilgrimages, I did not know that workers had in fact designed an earlier version. In the closing decades of the nineteenth century, 'houses of the people' flourished across Europe, and one of their core purposes was to support local education. Revolutions, as Hannah Arendt reminds us, move forwards and backwards, and the discovery and reinvention of forgotten or once discarded ideas is part of the pattern.

'Everyone who enters marvels,' wrote a nineteenth-century visitor to the Maison du Peuple in Brussels, describing a 'veritable palace of light . . . a reminder that they [the workers] are grand and powerful'. Not every house, maison or casa was as grand as the Maison du Peuple, an art nouveau masterpiece designed by Victor Horta who was the starchitect – the Frank Gehry or Zaha Hadid – of his day. But every one was designed to be generous, in order to bring local people together, to reflect back the importance of work and workers and to transform opportunities in that place.

In the belle époque, workers were widely asking how they

could take up new roles in society; how they could expand their lives and the futures of the places they were from. In response, the nineteenth-century houses were designed as places where people studied together, consciously preparing for a new future. It was widely understood that in order for local places to flourish, local people needed the tools, the learning but also the broader cultural validation that learning together would bring: a strong sense that the commitment of time and effort was worth it because together everyone would (and did) rise.

Togetherness was also designed into the houses for another reason. Members were encouraged to socialise across generations and traditional hierarchies of class and occupation because there was a belief that this wider mixing would germinate new ideas and connections, which in turn would lead to the design of new work. Interestingly, at the Imaginings there was also an explicit demand to find ways to connect across divides and generations. In Grimsby, for example, participants talked about those in their community with different politics: 'They have a reason. We need to get to know each other and talk.' In other places in Britain many talked about refugees in local hotels and wanted to include them in the conversation, concerned about their isolation and also sure that everyone has ideas that will help redesign work.

Designing the work

The House, like its predecessors, is designed to grow local workers and to grow new forms of work. There is a long history in Britain and the United States of workers organising to create better work, with the explicit intention of shaping the direction of technological development. Two of the most famous, although largely forgotten, examples are rooted in places where the Imaginings took place: Barrow and Detroit.

In Barrow, the company that is now BAE Systems was once the privately owned Vickers, and in the 1970s Vickers virtually owned the town. Even Barrow's fourth-division football club and at least one of its pubs was listed as a company asset, and Vickers's perceived role in turning other companies away, to make sure there was no competition or alternative choices for skilled workers, was widely resented.

When the government announced a programme of nationalisation of key industries, the plan had strong local support. Workers believed they would recover autonomy and have a voice in the future direction of their town and their work. As one worker recalls, 'They thought, this was it. What a surprise they were going to get. They thought nationalisation would bring everything they'd fought for. But within a very short space of time they found out that they'd swapped one boss for another.'

When workers realised nothing had changed in the balance of power or value of work within the company, there was disappointment at first, and then organised reflection, which led to a remarkable plan for worker-led industrial transition: the Workers' Report. Nationalisation did prove to be galvanising. But not quite in the way imagined.

Rejecting the company logic that 'leads Vickers to sell arms to anyone who will buy – both sides if possible!', worker committees researched how their technology could be used differently. In collaboration with the expertise of local NHS workers, they developed plans to produce affordable dialysis machines. With science already showing the environmental challenges of the oil-fuelled combustion engine, workers also developed plans to produce the world's first hybrid electric vehicles.

The Workers' Report did not come to fruition in Barrow. Management decided that a better strategy to deal with rising competition from Japan and elsewhere in Asia was to downsize the workforce. (Ironically in the Japanese case, their competitive edge was due in part to the realisation that, as the CEO of Toyota noted, every worker is coming with a 'free brain', and the consequent adoption of worker participation in work design.) Redundancies followed in 1980s, the pain of which is remembered today and was recorded at the Imaginings.

The Workers' Report shows the potential skill and foresight workers can bring both to the design of work and to shaping the direction of technological innovation. The ideas were taken up in London in the 1980s, when the Industrial Investment Board pioneered a series of very successful city-wide investments that brought together a worker analysis of industrial transition, a commitment to socially useful production and new forms of worker democracy.

In Detroit, the UAW (United Automobile Workers' Union) offered a similar masterclass of worker-led industrial re-organisation in the face of crisis. In 1940, following the invasion of France and the first London bombings that were to become the Blitz, President Roosevelt realised that the United States needed to mobilise in support of Europe. He called for the manufacture of fifty thousand military aircraft. The ambition was staggering – in 1940, fifty thousand planes had not yet been made in total anywhere in the world. A dramatic shift in work and production capacity would be required to achieve the vision.

How long would it take to switch to plane manufacturing, President Roosevelt asked auto industry CEOs. The auto industry stalled. Henry Ford was personally offered a multi-million-dollar contract to build aircraft engines for

Rolls-Royce. He turned it down point blank. Industry leaders weren't interested in accepting subsidies for war production, which they viewed as a short-term distraction from their real business of building a steadily expanding auto industry with its necessary workforce.

Walter Reuther, a leader in the UAW, saw an opportunity. Workers had been campaigning and mobilising to improve their working conditions. Reuther realised that the need for planes put the bargaining power in their hands. His political instincts told him that strikes would be unpopular but that the need to transition manufacturing could be seized to change both what was being produced and worker conditions.

The Reuther Plan, as the union-led proposals were known, was to build five hundred planes a day. The genius of the proposal was that it addressed auto industry fears that their core manufacturing would be disrupted. Reuther assured the CEOs that planes were, in his words, just 'an automobile with wings'. These automobiles with wings would be built not by switching production out of cars in any one factory, but by networking together spare capacity across all car plants, thereby adding production space for planes while maintaining car production. Only the unions could network and coordinate the thousands of workers needed across plants at sufficient speed to implement the plan. Reuther proposed that, in return, workers would be offered a long-sought-after annual wage and a voice in government-funded investment decisions, and that all plants would be unionised.

The public marvelled at the plan, while the national press hailed the idea as 'the most constructive proposal ever to come from organised labour'. Lobbying behind the scenes meant that the plans were not implemented exactly as they had been proposed, but it did not matter – the unions had broken a deadlock. Military production was scaled up and worker rights were agreed. President Eisenhower would later write to Reuther, praising this 'magnificent performance' as the basis by which a war transition in work and the economy was brought about.

The Workers' Report generated by Barrow's workers, like the Detroit-generated Reuther Plan, was a form of visionary organising. Just as Grace Lee Boggs and James Boggs had advocated, workers came together not only to ask for better conditions but with proposals to transform the work and the values which underpin it. Individuals I met are doing the same today: Jos de Blok in his work on care, Saket Soni in his work with the storm chasers and April Lewis in the way she is organising the Baltimore Open Works makerspace are among those following this path.

In the union movement there are also those who are asking similar questions and experimenting in the ways in which they work. Decades of anti-union legislation in both the United States and Britain have curtailed the remit of unions, making it much harder to do creative, propositional work, but a new generation of leaders are working in new coalitions with new tactics. Instead of waiting for seeds from elsewhere, these leaders and workers look at what is growing in their soil and ask questions about what could be nurtured and propagated. The first step is always to think about how to 'widen the frame' of connections, opportunities and experience.

Widening the frame

Erica Smiley — or Smiley, as she known to pretty much everyone — has spent most of her life organising in one way or another. As some remember childhood games, Smiley, who grew up in Greensboro, North Carolina, remembers a sit-in to support Black Kmart workers experiencing racial

discrimination. North Carolina is a state with very low un-
ionisation and the Kmart workers realised that going through
formal channels was unlikely to get results. They called instead on their neighbours and community to support them.
Many responded, including Smiley's youth group. The sheer
numbers that showed up forced the Kmart distribution centre
to negotiate and the workers won their rights. For Smiley it
was a memorable early lesson about what can happen when
communities – neighbours, customers, workers, church con-
gregations, wider family and friends – organise horizontally
in place.

Later, at school, Smiley felt she was 'other'. She experienced racism – her mother had to fight to get her into the
school programmes she rightly belonged in – and then in turn
Smiley had to fight her mother, who was not at first delighted
to find that her deep-voiced, sports-mad daughter was not
going to conform to all gender norms and certainly did not
want to follow in the family line as a beauty queen.

Smiley did not want to be limited by other people's ideas
of her life path, and she did not want anyone else to be limited either. I think this partly explains why she is so alive to
the shifting environment that surrounds work organisations.
The context of work has changed, she argues – we are doing
different work, under different conditions, and technology is
a big part of this – but just as important is the change in the
way we see ourselves. We think differently now about who
we want to be. This is a huge opportunity.

In this new context, to organise as workers is just not
enough. 'Few people will name "worker" first when identi-
fying who they are,' Smiley explains. 'They may say, "I am a
woman", "I am Black" or "I am Muslim". And in the same
way, they don't just want to organise around narrow work
concerns: pay and conditions, for example. Workers want

to secure these basics *and* to organise around care, housing, recreation and justice.'

Smiley's everyday connection to workers is another reason she is forging a new organisational path. Jobs with Justice, where Smiley works, has a network of two hundred thousand community organisers and a democratic structure which means that all campaigns are generated through local members. Smiley works through a set of close local networks whose fine-grained, hyper-local insights drive the organising agendas. One of the organisers in her network is Kimberly Mitchell, who works at the Macy's department store in Washington DC. Kimberly describes Macy's as her second home: she's worked there a long time and the company and her fellow workers are important to her. Kimberly is also a single parent, a home owner, a part-time small business owner and has been a carer for her mother and grandmother. 'The word "worker" is not a good word to me. It can sometimes feel patronising,' she says, 'as if workers are the category that have to sit around being told what to do.' But it's more than that: 'If all you see when you meet me is that I'm a worker you're missing the entire point. I am a whole person.'

Smiley talks about the Great Awakening, and this is what she thinks we need to wake up to: we are workers who want decent pay, predictable hours, meaning and dignity, but we also want to develop as our full selves, caring for our families, supporting our communities, having time for leisure and play. To create a work revolution in this century, Smiley believes we need new organisations that are 'life-wide' – she uses exactly the term that many at the Imaginings also used.

Widening the frame is how those who came to the Imaginings describe their designs and their desires. It is not just that The House includes everyone; it also has a wide and locally set agenda that encompasses issues of care and repair, meaning, learning and play. Many organisations are drawn within a large heart.

Adapt. Re-use. Rethink: these are the codes of Smiley's twenty-first-century organising. Through research and practice she urges us to extend the idea of what we can collectively bargain for and at the same time to rethink who we can ally with, reaching out to and including others who are not like us. Her work offers a manifesto which looks forwards in the shrewd recognition that a movement in this century is made up of many – including those in the care sector, women and many Black workers – who were legally excluded from the protections of the last century and who therefore are not seeking to restore organising to its former glory but rather to create something that can evolve to meet the challenges of now.

This new horizontal organising draws on the strength of place – you are much more likely to tie your energy to people you know and a place you care about. Critically, the organising proposed at the Imaginings not only 'widened the frame' to neighbours, it also included – on carefully de-bated terms – the inclusion of local business leaders. Such an organisation needs a very different structure, financing and governance – these aspects too were debated as the tablecloth organisations took shape.

All voices heard

Democratic structures were at the heart of every tablecloth design, to ensure a wide membership included all voices. Vertical organisational charts were crossed out and replaced with new organisational diagrams which visually represented horizontal structures; organisation 'for the people, by the people'.

This structure is not inward looking: The House is imagined as a node in a wider network designed to include similar organisations nationally and beyond. The ambition is for dense and overlapping infrastructure. Everywhere I was asked by the Imagineers what I had seen elsewhere. There is a thirst for knowledge on work innovations and a desire to connect to others travelling in the same direction. Attachment to place is not to be conflated with introverted localism. But there is an understanding that the local house must be in order first – able to stand on its own feet, and this in turn means independent structures and capital.

Membership subscriptions would cement a sense of ownership. But the decline in the value of most people's wages means worker subscriptions are unlikely to be sufficient, particularly for organisations aiming to be inclusive of everyone. Local business should pay dues. It was argued that new organisations which can support a culture of local learning and collaborative economic partnership are in the interests of local business. Local government would have a role, transferring assets that would capitalise the organisation. This last point is vital. The new work organisation cannot be caught in a spiral of constant fundraising and would also need sufficient funds to invest in start-ups.

Everywhere the search was for a new model of organisation that would be democratic and worker-owned, while financially viable, able to intervene in and create a new economy. I had heard of someone pioneering just this sort of organisation – what I would come to learn is a 'modern mutual' – and when the Imaginings took me to the United States, I went to meet her.

Sara Horowitz is a lawyer by training, and she was excited and then astonished when she was offered her first professional position in the early 1990s. Astonished because the contract did not include health benefits, paid holidays or any form of sick pay. How could this be, she asked herself. She was going to be working for a law firm. It turned out that she would not be classed as an employee but an independent contractor and so, like the domestic workers and agricultural labourers left out of early union law, the new definition that would soon become widespread – freelancer – would exclude her from basic work rights.

Sara, however, comes from a line of union organisers. The first Sara Horowitz was an immigrant garment worker who arrived in the United States from a small town on the Russian–Polish border at the start of the twentieth century. She was on the run from antisemitism and had a small son in tow. This little boy, named Israel, would become Sara's grandfather, and one of the founders and eventual vice-president of the International Ladies' Garment Workers' Union. It was obvious to Sara that freelancers needed to organise and that she should follow in her family footsteps.

The Freelancers Union that she founded in 1995 today has over half a million paying members who are assured of a basic safety net including health benefits and insurance to cover their work. But this is only part of the story. From the beginning Sara's vision was to secure the basics and to think beyond. 'I want art, nature, leisure and education,' Sara's great-grandmother had told her son when he started out organising, 'and the union needs to deliver all this.' Sara's ear was therefore already attuned when she heard something similar from the freelancers she was working with: 'a desire to lead a 360-degree life'. Freelancers wanted to change the status of their work *and* they wanted control of their time, to care for themselves and others. They wanted to lead twenty-first-century lives that felt fundamentally human. Sara realised this mission would require a different organisational structure and a new economic model.

Sara set out on her own journey. She was looking for examples of sustainable cooperation based on trust and reciprocity. She was surprised to find that cooperative forms of organising once existed everywhere, including in the United States. 'We were mutualists first,' Sara writes in her book *Mutualism*, 'before we were capitalists or socialists.' From hunter-gatherers to the former slaves who set up the Free African Societies, many people have organised themselves cooperatively for their survival.

At the Imaginings no one used the term mutual and I had not yet met Sara or read her book, but The House, The Time Machine, The Raiders, The Glue and the many other organisations drawn with wit and precision on the tablecloths shared a set of organising characteristics that made them mutualist. They would include everyone from the place; they would be democratic; 'all voices heard'; 'one member, one vote'; and they would be financially independent – able to intervene in the local economy. The Raiders, for example, intend to develop and own the technology platform on which their work is based, while Barnsley's Time Machine committed to investing in a Barnsley Dividend.

Strength in numbers, a long-term commitment to place and financial independence prepares The House – and all modern mutuals – for perhaps their most important role: renegotiating relationships of power, in particular with business.

Making common cause with business

How to engage with business leaders and financial power? Taking to the barricades is perceived to be energising but ultimately futile. 'If anyone wants to stick it to the man, it would be me, but I just don't think there is "a man" any more,' commented one Imagineer, pithily summarising a widely held view. 'We are like slaves shouting at the Roman centurions,' another described with hands aloft, gesturing to what they saw as the tragicomic pointlessness of most work protest strategies.

Participants are not fatalistic in the face of economic interests, but they are attuned to the way power has shifted – how, for example, decisions that affect them are often made in other places; how local bosses can also find their hands are tied; and how laws go unenforced, whatever the abstract promises.

Addressing structures of national and global power starts with new local strategies of engagement. Strategies can start small. One would be to negotiate on new ground. 'When we have been able to discuss things with our managers in different surroundings [outside work], we have had very different sorts of conversations,' Martin told me early on at the Barnsley window factory. The House would invite conversations in a safe, worker-owned space.

Another strategy would be to build on the pragmatic understanding that we are all humans and, particularly in regional cities and towns, that everyone is 'in this together'. Smiley would agree. She points out that just as we are all workers and are more than workers, so employers live multiple identities. 'Employers are the same: they also carry similar complexity in what moves them, often being more antagonistic in their identity as an employer than, say, as a person of faith or a member of the LGBTQIA+ community. Within this complexity lies opportunity.'

Twentieth-century work organisations mirrored the way that power was organised inside the industrial businesses they were fighting against. Hierarchical and antagonistic cultures created opposition strategies that could often, very successfully, wrest some form of worker control. Today power is more diffuse. The boundaries between 'us' and 'them' are sometimes clear cut, but not always. And those who came to the Imaginings (many of whom were union members) argued that change today is more likely to come through careful strategies of collaboration. An alchemy of technological possibility, the ripening of worker imaginations and a new reckoning on the part of business leaders are, in the view of most Imagineers, the realistic ingredients of good new work. No one in The House expects power to give way but they do think that new tactical alliances are possible.

Catalyte is a Baltimore-based business that is combining all three elements of this alchemy. In 2000 the company posted an advert targeted at selected low-income Baltimore neighbourhoods. It promised a salary of $12 an hour to train as a coder, followed by a guaranteed job on a higher wage.

'I saw that advert,' Adriana told me, 'and I was sure it was a scam.' At the time she was working long hours as a casino hostess. Open and friendly, she was good at her job but was paid less than the minimum federal wage ($7.25 an hour) and every month was getting deeper into debt. Little by little, Adriana felt her life starting to slip out of control. Unable to make ends meet, she defaulted on her rent and found herself sofa-surfing with friends. Her former partner considered the arrangement unsuitable for their small daughter, and to Adriana's heartbreak he wrested custody of the little girl from her.

It was the salary that made Adriana think the advert could not be for real. The idea that someone would pay her above minimum wage just to train seemed impossible. She was also pretty sure she was not a tech person. But the advert continued to circle through Adriana's mind in the days and weeks that followed. What if it was real? The money would mean a completely different life and perhaps the chance of what Adriana most wanted: to regain custody of her daughter. In despair and sure she could not sink any lower, Adriana decided to go for it. When I meet her at Catalyte's offices she has long been an expert coder. 'I love it,' she tells me. Coding, for her, 'is like playing with a big puzzle'. Adriana also has her daughter back.

Catalyte is a company at the forefront of digital innovation, using AI and machine learning to develop some of the most advanced software in the world. Clients include corporate giants such as Nike and Microsoft. The company was founded by Mike Rosenbaum, a Harvard lawyer and entrepreneur who worked in Moscow in what he calls the 'wild decade' of the 1990s. These were years of coup attempts, dramatic currency fluctuations and a context in which some amassed enormous wealth as lucrative assets were grabbed from the collapsing Soviet order. It was an experience which prompted Rosenbaum to think deeply about economic transitions as he witnessed up close how work, business, towns, cities, even national economies, can change rapidly and seismically, leaving many behind. He also understood the connections between economic and social success: inequality and instability do not for long provide a good environment for business.

When Rosenbaum moved to Baltimore, he was struck by parallel dynamics in his new home city. To him, there was a Wild West winner-takes-all-vibe. He was fascinated and appalled by the racial, spatial and economic divisions that surrounded him. He wanted to understand better this place he now called home, and to think about his role in its transformation.

Baltimore is a divided place. When I stood with April Lewis at the top of the steps of Open Works, I could see its geography unfold. A white core is wealthy and flourishing, with the Johns Hopkins medi-tech complex at its heart. In the Black wings east and west of this centre it's a different story. These are the neighbourhoods made famous by *The Wire*, the gritty TV show written by a former city police reporter and starring many of the city's residents alongside Idris Elba, who played the charismatic drug baron Stringer Bell. Poverty has gripped these neighbourhoods since the closure of GM Steel. The original GM Bethlem site is now an Amazon fulfilment centre and today most people who grow up in the wings face a bitter choice between two bad options: low-paid insecure service jobs, or a place in the retinue of the real drug baron, most likely followed by jail.

Mike Rosenbaum – like fellow residents April and Philip, the former felon turned janitor – could see that in Baltimore place is destiny. It would be almost impossible to make your way from the West Baltimore neighbourhoods of *The Wire* to, say, a professional job at Johns Hopkins. For Rosenbaum this was a justice issue, but it was also a business challenge. He could see that the city had enormous untapped talent, the kind of talent that he would need to grow a thriving business. Rosenbaum reasoned that, if a technology revolution (the decline of steel and the rise of medi-tech) had distorted the city then he would use this century's technology (specifically artificial intelligence) to build a business that could fix the problem.

Catalyte's success is based on the development of a bespoke machine learning tool that can identify the ability to code. The company places adverts in tough neighbourhoods and online in ways designed to reach potential software engineers from underinvested communities and other typically over-looked groups. Targeting by zip code, they invite people to take their test. No school completion certificates or proof of formal education are required: the AI can identify a potential coder with 94 per cent accuracy. Succeeding in the test is a pass to paid training and support in moving into a highly paid job. To date Catalyte has reached almost a quarter of a million people in Baltimore and across the United States as their work expands.

Hiring and training from deprived neighbourhoods has been a smart tactic. A company like Catalyte faces enormous competition for talent and Rosenbaum and CEO Jacob Hsu – who relocated from Silicon Valley – have been able to find the workers required for exponential growth. Critically, they have understood that to sustain a team in a place like Baltimore might start with innovative hiring, but also that the crew, once hired, will need to be nourished.

Catalyte graduates can earn six-figure salaries. Adriana found the transition into training and then work (she both codes for Catalyte and trains others) to be smooth. A combination of her extrovert personality and love of the work made her feel like she was swimming with the current. Her friend Brianna, striking with a balletic poise, but shy, found the transition much harder. When Brianna graduated from the training, she was placed by Catalyte at a leading DC law firm. Like Adriana, she loves her work, but readily admits that she could not have held down the job without the ongoing team mentoring and care. 'It's a hard culture and a tough place for a young Black woman from East Baltimore,' she told me, explaining how everything about the corporate culture, from how to dress to what would be an appropriate lunch at her desk, felt alien to her at first. 'But everyone [at Catalyte] is there for me – I'm learning the culture, and how to give myself some grace.'

I'm energised by meeting Rosenbaum and Hsu, and I tell anyone who will listen about my experience at Catalyte. I'm disappointed to find that, while people are fascinated by the story, they at once file it in the 'exceptional' box. There is a pervasive sense that these business leaders are interesting but too far from the norm to offer wider lessons.

Rosenbaum and Hsu are certainly compelling individuals: deep thinking and with back stories that drive their values. Hsu is the son of Taiwanese immigrants. His father, who arrived in the United States in 1973, wanted to be an academic economist but found his way blocked by racism. He took a job at Ford instead, where he was more welcome: all Asian immigrants were perceived to be good as 'the IT guy'. Swallowing disappointment and another form of racism, Hsu's father got down to work. His brilliance was spotted and he was transferred to Silicon Valley, where Jacob was born. In California his father became a highly respected pioneer of satellite technology. The bigger lesson was not lost on Jacob, who believes in thinking differently about where talent is found and nurtured. It's why Jake, as he is known to his friends, jumped at the chance to join Mike Rosenbaum as Catalyte's CEO.

I think Rosenbaum and Hsu are, however, filed as 'exceptional' for a different reason. We have come to expect successful tech leaders to resemble immature brats with little regard for their employees, much less the places they live. Tesla founder and CEO of X Elon Musk, apparently happy to fire employees on a whim and more interested in colonising Mars than fixing homelessness in his home town, is one example. Another is Jeff Bezos: 'I want to thank every Amazon employee and every Amazon customer because you guys paid for all this,' the founder of Amazon announced without any apparent sense of irony, launching his own space flight. With a sense of bitter disappointment these are the personalities and mindsets we have come to see as the norm, the template for today's digital leaders.

Technology revolutions nonetheless create competing possibilities and this space in turn creates competing ideas about what it means to lead. Every technology revolution has its robber barons. They colonise space and resources, exploit workers and local populations, before in many cases attempting to launder their reputations through philanthropy – we can think of the Carnegies and the Rockefellers in earlier revolutions. But these same moments of rupture also produce more interesting individuals, the forebears of Rosenbaum and Hsu.

Canal investors, mill owners, chemists, cereal and chocolate magnates alike have challenged the received wisdom of their day, changing assumptions around work. These leaders are sometimes recognised by their peers as visionary: business owners tried to meet the somewhat reclusive William Kellogg and many flocked to see his six-hour day in action. More often they are seen as little short of mad. When contemporaries referred to Robert Owen, the Welsh textile magnate and utopian thinker who made his fortune in the steam revolution, as a 'journeyman prophet', they were not being entirely reverential. Hindsight is kinder. It is those leaders whose ideas are, at the time, seen as in some way exceptional or outlandish, who have in the longer run reset economies and re-shaped the social contract. I call these business leaders New Industrialists.

New Industrialists

New Industrialists understand the moment they are living in. They have a breadth of curiosity and depth of intellect that goes beyond their work and profession; a quality sometimes called 'hinterland' in politicians. It enables these leaders to interrogate their context and to grasp that social and economic volatility is a signal of deeper change that requires a pivot in thinking about business values, the role of workers and the place they are from. Mike Rosenbaum reads widely and is influenced, for example, by Carlota Perez and her analysis of technology revolutions, and the research of the 'happiness guru', economist Richard Layard. Layard argues that economic activity should be measured by how much wellbeing is produced and advocates strongly for new thinking on apprenticeships.

New Industrialists believe in action. Grasping that technology in particular is shifting the rules of economics and the aspirations of society, they do not pronounce or give business interviews; instead they invest their own time and money in large-scale local experiments. Rosenbaum could have joined the board of any number of Baltimore charitable enterprises as a platform for his views while he burnished his reputation and fortune as a lawyer. Instead he chose the riskier New Industrialist path – the creation of a business that would change the dynamics in a new sector: computer coding, AI and software development.

The third characteristic of New Industrialists is closely connected: their dominant motivation is business, not altruism. Perhaps the best-known New Industrialist is Henry Ford. At the forefront of the mass production revolution, he realised that economic success would require a new deal for the worker. Ford was convinced that higher wages would be the critical driver of a new business model: decently paid workers would be customers for his cars. The company's management board were convinced that higher wages would be certain business suicide. The two locked horns and in the end, unable to get his way through negotiation, Ford took his board to court.

Ford's ruthless determination is admired by some and

abhorred by others. Ford was an antisemite and violent, not above shooting at his own workers when they tried to or-ganise or otherwise get in his way. His motives in providing everything from higher wages to high-quality education was transactional: it would drive his new business. In Britain, the chemist John Boot pioneered the paid weekend, taking up an idea that workers had long agitated for because he too realised a social innovation would solve a business problem. His business experienced significant fluctuations in demand which were costly because they required the constant letting go of workers in down times and then a need to hire and train again. Boot realised that retaining paid workers in a new pattern would reduce his costs of churn and drive business profits.

Other New Industrialists are driven by business, and they have more complex objectives. Sara Breedlove (perhaps better known as Madam C. J. Walker) was reputedly the first female self-made millionaire in America: she saw the oppor-tunity of the chemical revolution to develop a new beauty industry. Born in the cotton fields of the American South, her goal was to grow a national business, and her business model was based on an innovative idea. Just as Rosenbaum could see exponential growth needed a different network of talent, Breedlove could see her fortune could only be made by reaching customers – women – in a new way: house-to-house sales. She would give thousands of African American women well-paid and dignified new jobs as commissioned sales agents, thereby building her own empire while trans-forming employment opportunities for Black women. As she told Booker T. Washington in a speech we would like to imagine a Silicon Valley CEO giving today, 'I am in the business world not just for myself alone, but to do all the good I can for the uplift of my race.'

New Industrialists like Breedlove often came from poverty and they were determined to make their fortunes and lift others with them. Modest roots also set other New Industrialists apart from their peers. Robert Owen, the youngest of six children, came from a family who could not afford schooling. It seemed natural to him to question the contract with his workers, who after all were people very much like him. He recognised his investment in education would transform both his business and the lives of people he knew.

There is a tension in the relationship: New Industrialists tend to want just enough change to preserve prevailing economic structures of ownership and profit. Joseph Rowntree was not alone in building new villages for workers in his English factory, while turning a blind eye to the shocking conditions of those who worked on his plantations in the colonies. Company productivity did not demand similar experimentation in far-away places.

New Industrialists do not aim to disrupt the established structures of power. They are the first among their contemporaries to accurately judge their times, to see that business as usual is not an option, and make changes so that they and their industries can thrive. But whatever their intentions, the genie escapes the bottle. The experiments of New Industrialists open vital spaces for wider thinking and action that cannot always be controlled. In these spaces and with these figures, workers can make common cause. Discernment is necessary, but the alliances provide an opportunity that is a critical ingredient in every work revolution.

When I set out on my journeys I wanted to find the contemporary Fords, Rowntrees and Breedloves. History suggested that these figures would be found in businesses at the heart of the new technology revolution in Silicon Valley. I was disappointed. Until I realised I wasn't looking in the right way. Technology is a common denominator – every New Industrialist is at the forefront of their new technology, understanding its potential and the social and economic changes of which it is part. And there is another denominator that matters just as much: rootedness in place. From Rowntree to Rosenbaum, innovation is driven by a connection to place, by ideas that grow through relationships and imaginations made in a place and a desire to change the fortunes of the place and its people.

All work happens somewhere. But no leader can really know what happens in places their businesses depend upon but which they rarely see. A global technology company headquartered in Silicon Valley might, for example, depend on servers parked in Arizona. This is not where business surplus is made, this is not the place where the corporate leader will visit, and so a visceral connection to what is happening in that place, to work, communities and to natural resources, is lost. 'Those big boxes were planted down one day and just as suddenly they will be picked up,' the digital founder Craig Burgess tells me, referring to the distribution centres in his home town of Barnsley. He decries their lack of roots and horizontal connections to the local economy. All design, marketing, human resource work and other services they require is commissioned in an unknown headquarters somewhere else; no further work or progression is created for the town. Craig contrasts the 'boxes' with the work of the digital hub which is generating good work through connections with local business.

We are at an inflection point. Many business leaders are asking the bigger questions that motivate Rosenbaum and Hsu: how can we address the inequities in the places we work? How can we motivate our workers by thinking differently about meaning? How is talent grown (as opposed to found and plucked)? And how can we reduce the wider environmental impact of our work in such a way that our grandchildren will survive and paths of generative productivity can develop?

Of course, not all the answers to these big questions áre found in place: they depend on wide networks and relationships, which I turn to in the next chapter. But – as the Imaginings demonstrate – the rootstock for both a just transition and new and just work is found in place.

Staying behind is 'an art, an invention, a practice', writes the Italian anthropologist Vito Teti, who has developed the concept of *restanza* to describe a constructive attachment to place. Staying behind, in this world view, is not being left behind, it's a choice and a form of adventure. Staying means being aware of shared histories, tending what remains and building a future alongside others who choose to stay, to return or to arrive. It's intense but also joyful, because staying inevitably means bonding with others who have made the same active choice.

Belonging to a place that is not conventionally considered to be powerful – one of Baltimore's wings, for example, or Barrow, a place most Britons struggle to locate on a map – can also shape a different mindset: insight, new ways of thinking and a commitment to neighbours and alternative ideas that have been long in the making. Many of these ideas showed up at the Imaginings, where more than one participant reflected on 'staying behind' as an active choice of resistance, a refusal to be the ideal twenty-first-century worker, expected to move wherever the work takes them.

Simultaneously, working in locations more conventionally seen as powerful – London board rooms or a Silicon Valley tech campus – I met participants who came from the same places I had journeyed to: Grimsby, for example, or Detroit. Some of these people feel lucky to have got away, while others dream that one day they can return. A work revolution would, by growing good work in all places, make these choices less stark.

Rooting twenty-first-century work

We imagined twentieth-century work as the foundation stone upon which we could, individually, build a good life. The House implicitly acknowledges that this stone has slipped away. In its place, twenty-first-century work is imagined differently, a binding root that loops us to others, to new parts of our lives, to thriving local economies and out to bigger networks. Roots are strong and malleable; they rarely move or break. When the inevitable storms come, they anchor us in a place.

The House signals an investment – of time, capital and emotion – in new forms of social institution that can bring people together in a place to grow these roots. At the Imaginings, the new work organisations shared a set of common principles: they are place-based; they secure the basics; they attend to wider wellbeing; they have a role in creating work and new economies; they are democratic and capitalised. They are also always envisioned as part of a rich forest of institutions, connected to each other, to existing unions, to youth clubs and other civic places. They thrive because they are not in a desert; their own roots are entwined in a bigger ecosystem. They are the seed, the starting point for growing good working lives in this century.

With this more organic understanding of work, the attention becomes the soil in which good work grows: its structure, its oxygen, its nutrients – and the need for gardeners to bring the new alive. I turn, then, in the final chapters of this book to these gardeners: the role that workers, intellectuals, business leaders and the state can play in bringing about this work revolution.

Part III

A Common Fate

Designing the Just Transition

Can we reimagine our working lives? That's the question that sits at the heart of this book. The journeys showed me that we can indeed radically reimagine our working lives and that we are collectively seeking ways to live very differently. The journeys also confirmed that we are in the doldrums, the period that Carlota Perez identifies in every technology revolution when we feel stuck: injustice is acute, divisions between geographies are deep, political populism grows and the lived realities for many are painful.

How, then, can we transition from the ways that we currently live and work to those that are imagined and embodied in the six principles generated at the Imaginings? And how could we do this in a just way, being mindful that we do not unwittingly stitch the injustices of the twentieth century into the social and economic infrastructure of the twenty-first?

In the fissures that have opened with new technology, with our desires for justice and our hopes to live with a different form of generative natural abundance, we have the chance to shape a turning point and to create a rich and common fate.

Pivoting from an era that no longer serves us to something better requires new dreams we can coalesce around and, crucially, it requires the concerted action of four groups: workers; intellectuals, whose thinking can extend our horizons of what is possible while building bridges between other agents; business leaders; and the state.

In a just transition each of these groups has a particular and important role to play and in closing this book, I set out an agenda for action.

Workers

Transitions start every time with worker voice, imagination and organisation. From the abolition of slavery to the genesis of the New Deal, from the creation of European welfare states to the introduction of equalities legislation, seeds of change are first planted by workers who – in the face of considerable odds – come together to dream of a better life and then to organise. In the same way, at the Imaginings workers moved from ideas (the principles) to the design of organisations (the houses) that would enable action. It is not necessary to recap the previous chapters here, but I want to emphasise two specific aspects.

First, that workers understand what this current paradigm shift demands. In the nineteenth century, workers who organised within guilds argued that they were uniquely and highly skilled, and therefore should be well rewarded. In the twentieth century, strength came in numbers, to unionised workers, and the proposition shifted to one which might be crudely summarised as 'we are strong and we will break you'. In the twenty-first century, workers who are acutely aware that old divisions in status, pay and certainty are crumbling, have a different organising principle. The houses embody a belief that workers and places grow together. The new organisations redesign the rules of cooperation to give workers a voice – not simply a voice of protest but one of creativity. The houses are the basis for a worker-led transition.

Second, many, many workers have already made significant changes, either through a desire to seek a better life or because they have lived in places where industrial transition has been imposed. They know what is required for the journey: psychological and social support, funded and high-quality learning, financial support for a period of re-training or learning, family care support, solidarity and hope. The houses were in many ways envisaged as transition clubs, to provide these things in place. But workers also know that wider networks and relationships to business, to finance and to the state are required.

In the 1970s the journalist Studs Terkel made a journey across America which in some ways was not dissimilar to my own. Terkel asked American workers from all walks of life to talk to him about their days. He wrote, 'I was constantly astonished by the extraordinary dreams of ordinary people.' In my own case, I was not astonished by the sophistication of dreams or by the level of creativity – all my previous work shows me that ideas are everywhere, if we take the time to listen – but I was surprised by the extent to which new dreams are shared in common. Unfortunately, and to our wider detriment, these ideas are not often heard.

'It's becoming harder to find new ideas,' the labour economist John Van Reenen told his peers at a global gathering on technology and labour policy that I attended during the pilgrimages. I was taken aback. Van Reenen is widely regarded as an intellectual powerhouse, and he was discussing the challenges of innovation frontiers. Was he looking in the wrong place, or at the very least starting at the wrong end, I wondered. At this conference academics presented fascinating papers tracking global trends in the size of firms, the movement of wages and the impact of technology. Workers were not invited to present their ideas, but the Imaginings show how their insights married with those of academics and intellectuals could create different breakthroughs in the ways we are thinking about and organising the transformation of work. These are the new ideas.

Organic intellectuals

Change is fomented by ideas. Intellectuals have two significant roles to play in a process of transition. They can widen what is deemed practically possible or plausible – political theorists call this the Overton window, named for Joseph Overton, an American conservative thinker who, in the 1990s, demonstrated that what we believe to be practical is not fixed and moves with big ideas. And intellectuals can act as important bridge-builders between workers, the state and curious business leaders. Thinkers who can connect rigorous research to lived reality have a particularly significant role to play. I call these thinkers organic intellectuals. Organic intellectuals are found within academia, in the workplace and in community-based organisations.

We are living in a time of rich intellectual ferment. New ideas and breakthroughs, from physics to social psychology, biology to anthropology, are re-shaping our understanding of ourselves as humans and of the ways we are connected to one another and to nature. These are ideas that stretch what we desire from work and life, and they are the basis of the new human template *Sapiens integra*. *Sapiens integra* is itself a new idea that more completely describes who we are today. New ideas are also moulding how we understand the idea of change and transition. Biologists and social psychologists are showing us that our thoughts are not innate, but are instead flexible, continually shaped by our social connections and in particular by the design of our collective institutions. We change our minds.

And we are changing our minds about one of the disciplines most pertinent to work: economics. There is a revolution in economics, emanating from a group of scholars whose ideas – although not formally connected, or indeed always in full agreement – are re-drawing the rules of the discipline. Strikingly, most of these scholars are women. This group includes Diane Coyle, Mariana Mazzucato, Kate Raworth and Isabella Weber among many others. It also includes Carlota Perez and Elinor Ostrom.

The implications of Ostrom's work on the commons for how we think about human nature, the design of institutions and collective economic possibility is profound and has particularly influenced Kate Raworth. Her work is guiding the thinking and practice worldwide of those who want to grow a new economics that can care for and replenish natural systems. Raworth has developed the concept of Doughnut Economics: a set of twenty-first-century economic principles that could enable us to flourish within the ecological boundaries of the planet. The principles address injustice while offering new norms to curb activity that extracts natural resources through unsustainable means. Inequality, Raworth argues, is a system design failure: a well-designed economy is one in which everyone shares in the value created (as opposed to the current model, where value accrues to a few who may or may not share it).

When Kate Raworth lectures at Oxford, the university's largest teaching hall does not offer sufficient capacity for the students who sign up. Everywhere I go, people ask me, 'Do you know Kate?' Community and state leaders alike are eager to be connected to Raworth and to work with these new principles.

The core principle of this new economics is to rethink the goal. Economies are currently benchmarked according to their success at increasing national output as measured by GDP (gross domestic product) but, as Raworth points out, growth that uses resources at a rate that puts human survival at risk or which counts work activity which is damaging to humans is not a viable goal. In recent decades GDP has grown in the US and the UK, even when standards of living and wellbeing have fallen. GDP data has painted a picture of material growth at the national level – that is, not experienced within communities where prices are rising and incomes falling. In response, Diane Coyle has also made the case for a profound rethink. In *GDP: A Brief but Affectionate History*, she has argued that GDP is a blunt twentieth-century tool that cannot address what she sees as the core twenty-first-century concerns: a new economics of place and the social shaping of technology.

Mariana Mazzucato is another critical intellectual whose advice is sought globally – by governments, finance ministers and central bankers. Mazzucato challenges our ideas about where and how value is created. Economies and value, she argues, are generated by workers and through early state investment, not solely (or even primarily) by gifted entrepreneurs or markets. But we have confused value with price and so we have failed to recognise the collective effort that has enabled all modern inventions, and consequently we have failed to share the rewards. The implications of Mazzucato's work are profound, suggesting that a new relationship is required between workers (the primary generators of value), the state (who can seed value-led innovation) and markets, or business (who must recalibrate), as partners in promoting the wider life-enhancing social outcomes we want.

This deep innovation in mainstream economics has not received the wider public attention it deserves, perhaps because it is largely led by women in a discipline that is dominated by men. Famously, when Ostrom was awarded the Nobel Prize, male doctoral students scratched their heads: they had not heard of her. It is also noteworthy that many of these women have operated on the edges of academia. The industrialised timescales of our universities demand constant and rapid publication, making it hard to do the long-run deep work practised by Perez and Ostrom, while vertical silos – again part of the university's industrial design – make the interdisciplinary collaboration required to tackle today's complex problems much harder. Younger academics who came to the Imaginings frequently complained about their gig worker status: they earn low salaries and have long and often unpredictable teaching hours, while their value is judged by a publication schedule that makes it hard to find time to think.

Despite these very real challenges, a heterodox economics has broken through, often making powerful links to advances in psychology, technology and ecology while also embracing questions of ethics and the challenge of inequality in particular. This new economic thinking really matters because economics is the language of policymaking, shaping the rules of investment, ideas about business success and above all assumptions about work.

Big ideas stretch horizons and make revolutionary change possible largely through making the new seem no longer revolutionary, but simply common sense. Organic intellectuals, with their combination of place rooted practice allied to rigorous thinking are expert at moving the 'new' onto the centre ground.

Onion Collective shows us how this organic practice can bridge economic thinking with local transition. The collective was founded by women from Watchet in Somerset. Living in a small, loved but gritty town nestled between the sea and the wilds of Exmoor, the women watched as their community experienced a collective grief and sense of loss when the paper mill, the main source of employment, closed. When the promised 'rescue' – an external investment in a harbour regeneration project – failed to materialise, they took matters into their own hands. Onion Collective set about creating new forms of purposeful work. They have built a beautiful community-owned arts centre in the harbour – the East Quay – and worked to develop a bio-mill based on innovative fungal technology on the site of the old paper mill. They also partner with a gaming studio, Free Ice Cream, to deliver a community tech platform, infrastructure that can be used by communities locally and nationally to build connections and resilience. The intention is to offer local sustainable work, attaching people to each other, to the place they are from, to nature and to a local industrial history of making useful things.

Onion Collective are a source of inspiration because they are creating good work in an inclusive local economy, rooted in the imaginings of the community itself, and simultaneously drawing on new ideas in economics. Onion Collective call this attachment economics. As Jess Prendergrast, one of the founders, explains, 'Attachment is central to viewing economics through a community lens – these are attachments to place, attachments to people and attachments through time.'

Others are experimenting in similar vein. They include those pioneering restoration economics (thinking about the economics of regenerative and shared land use); the Foundational Economy Collective (working with the principles of *restanza* mentioned in the previous chapter); and the Women's Budget Group (who, among other things, have pioneered work on the economics of care).

Transition is a form of migration. It involves leaving things behind, including ideas we once cherished. And it involves finding new ideas we can coalesce around. Organic intellectuals provide us with new ways of thinking about the world and it's notable that enlightened business leaders, in particular New Industrialists, are deeply engaged with and curious about this new thinking.

Enlightened business leaders

The third group who must take bold action is the business community. I have already described the critical role of vanguard business leaders – the New Industrialists – who understand the nature of the paradigm change in which we are living, and therefore the need for a new social contract to enable workers and their businesses to grow.

A just transition requires the active collaboration of a wider circle of business leaders beyond these pioneers. The innovation agenda includes: new contracts based on the six principles of the good working life; pioneering new ways of growing talent and capability; experimenting with new forms of worker democracy and ownership; and advocating for new forms of growth that are generative for the business, for workers and for the places in which workers live.

Seeking New Industrialists, and with questions about the role of business in this transition, I interviewed local business leaders and some of those heading the global corporations that are setting work agendas. I started with Satya Nadella who, as the chief executive of Microsoft, runs a company whose products – early personal computers, software, cloud computing, AI – provide the tools for much of modern-day work. In Silicon Valley, Nadella has a reputation as one of the more thoughtful tech leaders and he has written his own book in a 'quest to imagine a better future for everyone' and rediscover 'Microsoft's soul'.

I asked Nadella what he thought his and Microsoft's role might be in the design of a new social contract. He responded first by talking about 'surplus' and his mission to generate more surplus in all the places in which Microsoft operates. Then, more interestingly, Nadella talked about his guru, Colin Mayer. Mayer is a modest and deeply thoughtful Oxford business professor who is asking big questions about the design of corporations. He argues that the corporation is an extraordinary institution that has a unique capacity to deliver the things it invents and imagines. He also believes that, in recent times, corporations have taken the wrong fork in the road. Corporations must be in the business of solving problems, not creating them, and this is where things have gone wrong.

The corporation, according to Mayer, has been captured by a narrow economic school of thought – neoliberalism – which started in Chicago in the 1930s and took flight in the 1980s, dictating the syllabus of every business school. Friedrich Hayek, a contemporary of William Beveridge at the London School of Economics, and later Milton Friedman, the Nobel-winning economist at Chicago, are seen as the founding fathers of neoliberal economics, a theory which among other things champions the market and profit motives in all areas of life. Neoliberalism drove the deindustrialisation policies implemented by Margaret Thatcher in Britain and Ronald Reagan in the United States. Such is its reach that its tenets also became orthodoxy on the left, with a British Labour government, for example, introducing market principles into public services.

In 2016 the International Monetary Fund, long seen as *the* standard bearer for neoliberal theories, started to distance themselves from what they also saw as a failed idea. But not before two generations of business leaders had been inculcated in a very particular way of thinking which states that the purpose of the corporation is profit: business must be shaped for *Homo economicus* and cultures of ruthless maximisation of all assets. Mayer points out that this almost religious adherence to profit maximisation, now akin to a law of nature, is most unnatural, not least because a relentless pursuit of profit against all other measures holds within it the potential for destruction.

Mayer argues for a recovery of the true purpose of the corporation, in which profit plays a role, but only one role among many, and he, like Mazzucato, advocates for an acknowledgement that the firm accumulates wealth through investments made by virtually every member of society, and the labour of workers. Today, he writes, the corporation is 'inhuman' and our wider distrust of it makes us anxious.

Mayer's agenda to return humanity and values to business is shared by many successful business leaders. There is a distinction, widely held but rarely officially articulated, between good business and bad or parasitic business. In the United States, almost every business leader I met referenced the work of the Harvard economist Raj Chetty, expressing concern at Chetty's findings which show that social mobility in the US has stalled and that neither school nor work is providing a route forward. They were asking themselves what their role is, as business leaders.

In Britain, in 2011 the Labour politician Ed Miliband differentiated between what he called 'predatory capitalism' – bad business that extracts value, such as through low wages – and 'productive capitalism' – good business that is profitable, good for workers and producing goods and services that are of benefit to society. Miliband's remarks were not popular at the time with his political peers, who were afraid that the ideas might seem anti-business and therefore vote-losing. More than a decade later, the Imaginings show that this distinction is widely understood and is important in rebuilding trust in business and illuminating a path that many would like to follow.

Good business leaders understand that what is good for business is good for workers: the two are mutually reinforcing. The first role of business, then, in designing the transition, must be to accept the invitation offered by the new work organisations to join a different dialogue; to explore how work and business could improve together. Other structural responses would include ensuring that every company board has a member with the skills to understand worker perspectives and build partnerships and conversation. Standard questionnaires and value exercises do not reveal any truth or creative potential, but small steps which are commonplace in other European countries but not currently in Britain or the United States, such as worker representation on boards, should and could be widely adopted.

The next step is to think differently about how people might be collectively supported to grow, and the role of business in this endeavour. The famous management guru Peter Drucker used to ask the CEOs attending his conference whether they thought they had 'dead wood' on their teams and in their companies. Most would raise their hands. Then came his riposte: 'Were they dead wood when you hired them, or did they become so under your command?' For two decades at Davos I have listened as business leaders discuss the 'war' for what they perceive to be scarce talent. Something has always struck me as awry. Many speak as if the challenge is exogenous to their businesses; a problem generated elsewhere, meaning that the production line passing in front of them does not have the correctly prepared 'hands' or 'brains' for them to choose. The Imaginings show that those business leaders who roll up their sleeves, nurturing talent and engaging with the new motivations, with the desire to learn and ideas of their workforce, are very successful. This is the path to a new contract.

Many are experimenting with new forms of worker democracy within a wider search for business innovation. B Corp, for example, is a US and UK certification system for for-profit businesses which commit to a set of stringent social and environmental standards – which include their contracts with workers, suppliers and stakeholders – and to transparently declaring their progress. B Corps have their critics but the transparency and oversight exceed that of other business indices such as corporate social responsibility (CSR) and environmental, social and governance (ESG) frameworks, which Mazzucato, among others, has criticised as being 'just talk'.

Experiments in new and diverse forms of business ownership are also growing and important, not least because one of the clearest indicators of worker voice and share of value is, not surprisingly, worker share of ownership.

Guy Singh-Watson is a pioneer of employee ownership and another New Industrialist. Inheriting a farm in the rolling valleys of Devon, he has regularly shared the highs, lows and politics of farming in a newsletter that is delivered weekly in a vegetable box to thousands of families, including mine. His search for an alternative and profitable way of doing good business started in 1990, when he had a run-in with a supermarket giant. 'I asked a supermarket buyer if we could delay an appointment by a day and he put the phone down on me,' Singh-Watson writes. 'I rang back and he said: "Look, sonny, when we whistle, you jump and ask how high."'

That was it. Singh-Watson decided to invest in the seasonal vegetable box delivery system that his company is now known for. Today his farm, Riverford, is part of an extensive cooperative network of growers and producers that deliver directly to people's homes. He has grown a high-value business and invested not only in his workforce but in wider generative projects (annually £1.8 million of profit is invested in regenerative agriculture projects and experiments which include the development of fully compostable packaging). In 2018 Singh-Watson took a further radical step, selling 74 per cent of the business to his workforce at a reduced market value. Ignoring the venture capitalists who now circled, just as the supermarkets had done twenty years before (food delivery, like care, disaster repair and makerspaces is a sector increasingly attracting the debt financing of global capital), Singh-Watson decided that the future of the business belonged with the workers who had grown its success.

Employee ownership trusts, the structure used at Riverford, recognise (as argued by the heterodox economists) that the business has been made by the workers and that business acquisition or similar routes to growth not only fail to reward workers, they frequently put jobs at risk, given the emphasis in traditional company structures on reducing labour costs and numbers.

Guy Singh-Watson has been a pioneer in the farming sector, doing business with profit, workers and ecology in mind. In his values and vision, he is laudable but not alone. In the UK there are 1,600 employee-owned businesses, and in 2022 the government received 430 applications from business owners who wanted to go down the same route. Perhaps this is not surprising, given that research shows employee-owned businesses generate higher productivity, increased employee engagement and wellbeing and higher rates of innovation.

Mutual and cooperative structures are another alternative with the proven ability to create good work. The Basque region in Spain, once a place riven by the economic and political fragmentation which epitomises the idea of 'left behind', is today a vibrant place characterised by a dynamic and equitable economy. At the heart of the region is Mondragon, the world's largest industrial cooperative ecosystem. More than eighty thousand people are employed in a network of industries ranging from agriculture to advanced engineering, with annual revenues of over US$11 billion. While the name may not be internationally recognised, one in three European cars contain parts made by the cooperative, 90 per cent of European aircraft run on Mondragon technology solutions and one third of Europe's solar panels are manufactured by the group.

One of the defining features of Mondragon includes the 1:6 ratio that governs the difference in salaries between wages at the top and bottom of the group. Another is the capital fund which can be used to invest in the local region. Cooperatives in the group give a 10 per cent return (pre-tax from profits) to a mutual investment fund. Funds have been used to create a globally renowned university, as well as providing start-up funding for new businesses and for innovation.

In the mutual sector, this alternative form of capital is called indivisible reserves. In Italy, where 9 per cent of the economy is held by cooperatives, indivisible reserves are a form of finance protected in the state constitution. Each Italian cooperative returns 3 per cent of their revenue to cooperative capital funds. Every new cooperative is eligible to get start-up funding from this pool. The result is a capital market which can create new businesses that offer good work and model new forms of ownership. In turn, each successful business 'pays forward', enabling a vibrant place-based economy, just as the Imagineers presented in their house designs. On a smaller scale, this cooperative culture already exists in other places. In Baltimore, for example, Red Emma's, a worker cooperative, generates a fund that it uses for a radical programme of community education.

'We are no different to anyone else,' Ander Etxeberria Otadui told me when I visited Mondragon, keen to dispel notions that mutual organisation is in any way remarkable or reliant on people who are in some way unusually good or 'angelic'. 'It's not something special in the water and we go home and quarrel with our partners just like anyone else. But what we do have are good business structures and what we know, is this is a way to grow good, profitable businesses and good work – we want profit, but it's what we do with that money.'

Good business, like good economics, is about rethinking the goal. At Mondragon the goal is to create human wellness through the creation of good long-term work, and that requires strong, profitable business. Mondragon is a business system that – like Kate Raworth's proposed twenty-first-century economy – is just by design. Value accrues to all the workers within the cooperative. Members have social protection – pensions, health insurance and support to upskill. If, as does happen, a business closes, workers are offered positions in other parts of the cooperative or the chance to re-train. (The goal will be to save the workers not the business.) In the eighty-year history of Mondragon, no worker has required support from the welfare state due to the loss of work.

One of the biggest challenges business leaders currently face is what economists would call information asymmetry. 'Remember when we used to meet in the Winter Gardens – even the Rolling Stones came to play,' a group of Grimsby business leaders who joined me for dinner reminisced. They were all highly networked at the national level but nonetheless mourned the lack of local social infrastructure – the clubs, the restaurant where you knew you would see your peers and hear about the latest innovations while deepening the relationships necessary for business. Many business leaders feel cut off from ideas and capital which would allow them to plough the different furrow they instinctively lean towards. Everywhere I was struck by how often those I met were unaware of experimental success, even in their own region, and how hungry leaders were for the social connection that being part of a bigger story and network would provide.

'Greed is dead' announced the economist Paul Collier, one of Colin Mayer's Oxford colleagues, in 2020. His pronouncement may have been a little previous and a little optimistic but it does seem as if the tide is turning on extreme wealth, with important implications for workers and indeed for business leaders. The production of billionaires requires a range of business mechanisms including extreme resource use, tax evasion, low pay and often cruel exploitation. Having made their wealth, the consumption patterns of billionaires are also a cause of concern: their lifestyles, which typically include such things as the ownership of multiple residences and the frequent use of private jets, diminish our collective chances of halting runaway climate change. Extreme wealth also generates public anger and strong anti-business sentiments that find voice in tumult and populist politics, making a transition much harder. In 2024 world leaders at the G20 summit agreed to design taxes on wealth, policies which have been pushed by workers and by coalitions of the wealthy, the so-called 'patriotic millionaires', in Britain and the United States.

The pioneering New Industrialists of earlier eras were part of what we might think of as a moral economy: they created wealth, they became wealthy themselves and they invested in their business and the people and places where their businesses were located. This moral economy is what we need to create today. Just as earlier technology revolutions saw the simultaneous growth of both robber barons who the state had to tame alongside more enlightened industrialists, so today we see both forms of business growing. The role of the state and public policy, which I turn to next, must be to actively support enlightened business through appropriate fiscal and investment policies, and through clearly articulating with business leaders, the merits of a new social contract for all sides. Wealth is an Anglo-Saxon word that means life: the richness of life, all lives. This is the mission of twenty-first-century business.

A dynamic state

There can be no turning point, no pivot towards new working lives and new forms of flourishing without a dynamic state, able to shape the frameworks within which we live and within which business and investment take place. In this transition the state must hold a broad vision to carry us forward; it must invest in the new institutions required (including work organisations); it needs to provide us the workers with new forms of income at points of personal transition and with the 'real learning' that will equip us for the future; it must ensure the basics; and it must both uphold and restructure the rules required by the new realities. I am going to consider each element of this remit in turn, but first it seems necessary to ask, can the state fulfil its role? In both the United States and Britain, we commonly ask whether the state is too small or too large. In a time of transition, we need to ask a different question: is the state sufficiently dynamic?

Questions regarding the state are challenging, not least because trust in government is at an all-time low and still declining. Feelings that public and political systems around us are rigged to benefit those with more wealth and power are widespread. There is a perception that politicians in particular put their personal advancement above a commitment to the public good. In both Britain and the United States the political access granted to lobbyists and CEOs of fossil fuel companies and tech behemoths is another cause of popular concern.

Local state actors are often, although not always, more trusted. In particular I have noted on my journeys that trust does still reside in those who have deep local roots and come from the places they represent or work within. I have already described the way that local government has innovated, for example in creating Barnsley's digital hub or Kilmarnock's vibrant work. In the Basque region, a strong and close relationship with regional government is part of Mondragon's success. State leaders, like business leaders, are not all cut from the same cloth – nor do they have the same resources to hand – but the bigger picture remains one of widespread disillusion.

State structures do not help. Like the university, government is an industrial organisation, ill-suited to modern challenges. The time horizons of modern democratic government make it hard to respond to long-term challenges such as the ecological crisis, while vertical and hierarchical governance structures of command and control, inherited from the nineteenth century, make for adversarial cultures and militate against creating the forms of mission, dialogue and broad alliance that are needed for problem-solving and for shaping a common future. In Britain the challenges are exacerbated by an overly centralised bureaucratic model with extraordinary power concentrated in London and in the hands of a small group of like-minded officials in the

Treasury, who are distant in geography and imagination from those they are meant to serve.

The limitations on both sides are clear: collective distrust faces outdated, dysfunctional state structures, with good people on both sides hampered in their work. The state bureaucracy must be modernised to lead and govern in a technological age. This critical work is a subject on which the state is already offered clear analysis and advice. The state also appears to require stronger connection to and engagement with new ideas. Too many of today's political leaders seem to be uncertain as to how they might use cultural and social power to shape technology in particular. Many state actors continue to work within frameworks which once again focus too strongly on the 'tools' of this technology revolution, thereby misunderstanding wider cultural and social currents which could shape economies in ways that work better for communities.

How to plan for and navigate a just transition may be the biggest political question of our time. And the task is urgent because making a transition without state support is unthinkable. The scale of the macro challenges we face – in technology, ecology and justice – mean that only the state can bring the coalitions and resources to bear at the appropriate scale. We already know the brutal ending of the story of unmanaged techno-industrial transition of the 1980s and we can't repeat it.

When people transition alone, the economic, social and psycho-spiritual costs are enormous. The history of technologically driven deindustrialisation shows the grim harvest for people and for place that is transmitted between generations: poor health, ennui and the ripple effects of unbalanced economies. When Martin and his colleagues in the window factory in Barnsley described the way their 'stuffing was knocked out', or workers at BAE Systems talked about the 'nothing' that was left when thousands of jobs were lost in

Barrow, they were describing the transition that started in the 1980s. A monumental struggle between the miners and a Conservative government determined to force through an energy transition as a prequel to a wider deindustrialisation of the economy accepted high unemployment, the loss of good work and deep social divides as necessary casualties. The entry of China to the World Trade Organization in 2001, bringing competition from six hundred million new workers, all prepared to accept – or coerced into accepting – very low wages saw the state apparently powerless, accepting the flight of swathes of the last remaining skilled industrial jobs.

A crisis created by unmanaged transition not only creates trauma and despair for communities involved; it is hard to repair. In Britain, the New Labour governments of the late 1990s and early 2000s had a utopian belief that digital technology would somehow bring jobs to decimated regions, but in reality the market alone would not and could not make this happen. As political advisors later confessed, the party did not understand the scale of the crisis. Those in 'left behind' places turned against Labour and their lack of understanding, which enabled the Conservative Party to regain office vowing to 'level up' everywhere left behind, including those places that have formed the core of my journey. But, once again, a place-based policy turned out to be little more than a hollow slogan. As the Conservative government's own paper on levelling up acknowledged in 2022, more than twenty-five years on, the 'wrenching, structural changes' imposed in the 1980s have not healed. In 2024 the Conservative Party lost the general election. Moving into the second quarter of this century, a different approach is still awaited.

In the past, the state has brought imagination, convening power and resource to points of transition: moments where the need to divest from established systems of production and work seemed fiendishly complicated, perhaps impossible.

One of those moments was in the eighteenth century, when every person in Britain was complicit in the slave economy, just as today every person is complicit in the carbon economy. We are of course not all working in the business of oil extraction, just as in the eighteenth century not every citizen was a slave owner. But the webs of our economies are tangled and complex; we rely on products, pensions, transport, technology, home energy and food systems that are oil based. In the same way, slavery underpinned all aspects of the economy in the eighteenth century. The economy of every town and every household, banking, investments, manufacturing and basic goods from cloth to sugar were all part of a triangular colonial trade, the apex of which was a market for people which fuelled all other aspects of commerce. Adding to the complexity, the slave traders themselves were trusted men of distinction, the 'leading humanitarians of their age': fathers, respected municipal leaders, founders of schools and orphanages.

Slaves, with almost unimaginable bravery, ignited the work revolution that led to the eventual abolition of slavery. Their heroic acts of resistance in the plantations of the Caribbean and elsewhere led to the formation of the anti-slavery movement in Britain, which by the 1790s was attracting widespread public attention and considerable sympathy. But – just as is the case for the climate movement today – it was much easier to acknowledge the problem than know what to do about it. Eric Williams's *Capitalism and Slavery*, which I referred to in earlier chapters, tracks the ambivalence and incoherence of peers and political representatives who in theory wanted to end the slave economy but were terrified that the consequences would be national bankruptcy, mass unemployment or worse.

In the eighteenth century, people had to come together to transition from one economy to another, to make the seemingly impossible possible. Enslaved workers led revolts and imaginings in the form of protests and pamphlets, and stimulated public support. Intellectuals such as Diderot and Montesquieu argued that slavery could not be justified on either moral or economic grounds, shifting the parameters of wider thinking and 'common sense'. The state, under pressure, stepped up to shape the growing consensus against slavery as an economic opportunity, actively steering public and private investment towards new (innovative and risky) technology. It was a strategy that fostered the Industrial Revolution. The state also funded compensation at scale for the slave owners who freed their slaves. Today we are rightly outraged that the slaves were not compensated, but in the realpolitik of the time, compensating the business owners was an unjust solution that enabled a just cause.

What should the state do today, when economic, social and ecological transitions are required on a similar scale? In Germany, the then chancellor Angela Merkel asked this question in 2018, when she directed the country's civil, industrial and political leaders to establish the Coal Commission and to forge a plan for energy transition. Together an agreement was negotiated to halve coal use by 2030 and phase coal out completely by 2038. This plan would entail tens of thousands of workers losing their well-paid mining jobs. It might have seemed an impossible task to negotiate at the outset, but high trust in a strong system of bargaining, in which unions and workers felt they had a genuine voice and the open timeframe given to the negotiation process all played a critical role in reaching an ambitious plan for transition.

Merkel brought billions of euros to the negotiating table to fund high-quality re-training and early retirement packages.

Firms across the supply chain were also compensated. But it was not just money that was on offer. Something else was critical too: a shared future imaginary. In sharp contrast to the Thatcherite forced and violent closures of the coal mines and industry in the 1980s, the German conversation was not one of how to retreat or close a sector but rather one of how to collaboratively reimagine Germany's modern green high-wage industrial economy. The state, recognising they did not have all the answers, invested in a long-term participatory process to develop new forms of work and economy. The result was financing for innovation, for local social infrastructure (from childcare to new bike lanes) and the regional growth of two new high-value (high-wage) sectors of the economy: astrophysics and biochemical engineering.

The German process is far from perfect. The International Panel on Climate Change reported that the timescales are still too slow. More recently, a bigger challenge has emerged. War in Ukraine brought energy insecurity to Europe, and as Germany lost its access to Russian gas, the pressure to resume coal mining grew and a new mine was opened at Lutzerath. Even hard-won victories can slip backwards, but without the state there is no convening and no sustained forward momentum. Pacific nations on the front line of climate change – whose territories are about to be submerged – have picked up the baton, developing the world's first national blueprints for transition and demonstrating again the indispensable role of the state in convening what must be a deep and wide participatory process.

Today the state must invite us into a shared vision; one which weaves an honest appraisal of the challenges together with real possibility and a dynamic course of action. A shared story of the future gives hope, it brings alive the guiding values and it sets a direction of travel in times when not everything can yet be known. Investment in the vision in the form of concerted action and the deployment of resource is also critical: this cannot be another empty story of opportunity.

Investment must start by liberating local potential in a recognition that, while national industrial strategies have an important role to play as part of a dynamic strategy, they struggle to create work, or to make connections between local people and new economic sectors. The dynamic state will shape an investment strategy that recognises place as a protagonist in the future, in the way that everyone who came to the Imaginings – workers and enlightened business leaders – understood was necessary.

Drawing together the shared visions leads me to a proposal: the state should invest in all citizens and workers in two ways: through the provision of transition incomes and through a new valuing of collective learning. Both these interventions might be thought of as what the economists Sam Bowles and Wendy Carlin call 'emblematic policies' – they are clearly not sufficient interventions in and of themselves to create a transition but their distinctive nature marks the paradigm shift; they demonstrate new values and a shift in economic policy in action. They catalyse good work and the broader transition.

Transition incomes, paid by the state, will allow us to take time out to learn, to re-train or to move into work that has high social value but does not yet have an equivalent economic value. Imagine, for example, airline stewards who can become carers: they have the skills but they are unlikely to swap their current higher pay for the not yet reorganised or revalued care economy. However, the paradigm shifts of our world require a strong care workforce and a greatly diminished civil aviation aircrew: transition incomes would make possible (within a broader strategy) such required shifts from high carbon to low carbon work. In other sectors and places where extractive work such as oil production is currently concentrated, transition incomes would be a critical part of a strategy similar to that pioneered by Merkel in Germany.

Transition incomes have a personal role and were suggested at the Imaginings as a necessary condition to pursue a 'second chance'. They would make it possible to experiment and re-learn in the way that the technology revolution and the climate emergency require. In Scandinavia a strong welfare state encourages very high levels of entrepreneurialism. Workers are not afraid to take risks, knowing that if they fail, they will be well supported until they find other work or start a new venture. In Britain and the United States learning is expensive (which I come to below) and the added costs of finding childcare mean that opportunities to transition are not available to the low paid and women in particular.

A transition income would support individuals but, most importantly, it is a collective, national commitment to change, and to a just and green economy. Anyone wanting to make the switch would be eligible for the support. The income could be paid at a level well above the living wage because, unlike universal basic income, not every citizen would require it, nor would requirements be simultaneous or time unlimited.

Transition also requires a new and imaginative model of learning. Learning which is picked up, continued and easily accessed at different points of life must become the norm. High-quality learning equipping us for the work which this technology revolution will offer is necessary (emulating in some respects the post-war US offer to veterans). This new model of integral education will offer no distinctions between intellectual, manual and practical studies, recognising that this century's requirements include creativity and emotional and relational skills as well as a wide set of technical core competencies. The new model will privilege learning above formal schooling and certificates (leaving behind the credentialism that the philosopher Michael Sandel writes about so scathingly and which is also treated with withering disdain at the Imaginings). Radically reimagined access points will also need to be designed, enabling smart young people to connect to work in ways which are everywhere currently missing.

In every technology revolution a dynamic state can see the need to invest in a small number of core areas that will enable the transition, fuelling the economy, work and new cultures.

In the twentieth-century oil-based revolution the emphasis was on possessions and in particular on home ownership. Governments in Britain and the United States heavily subsidised housebuilding and loans for house purchase (through the expansion of mortgages and the invention of new tax incentives). This policy ensured a stable workforce – everyone could find somewhere to live in the places of new industry. And it had another, arguably more important function: home ownership drove cultural patterns of consumption and the shape of the new technology revolution. Every home owner needed furnishings, white goods and a car in the drive. I think of the house as a totemic good, driving forward the last technology revolution – given its role in economic productivity and security, in generating work (through the demand for possessions) and through its cultural role which drove a new vision of the good life.

In this technology revolution, learning is the totemic good as the focus moves from possessions to knowledge and experience. A just transition requires deep and wide investment in learning on the part of the state. Learning will underpin the new experience economy, driving new forms of productivity and meeting new cultural desires for wellbeing and our *Sapiens integra* dreams of development. But this investment will only happen with a cultural repositioning of learning, as no longer a cost but a collective good.

As the twentieth century progressed we increasingly came to think of education as a private endeavour; a personal competition to achieve test scores and a consumption good that would, if we were lucky and/or could buy our way into the best schools and courses, position us for well-paid work. But education cannot be positioned or evaluated in this way. The social, economic and political costs of leaving young people and those in older industries out of the new story through different forms of educational exclusion and learning failure is a brake on transition and keeps us all in the doldrums.

A desire to be 'really learning' was continually articulated at the Imaginings, as was the desire for 'second chances'. Both are dependent on this re-positioning and redesign of learning as a collective good. Both are dependent on multiple and accessible paths in and out of learning throughout our lives, just as the non-linear life designed by the grave-digger Jonny in the first Imagining depicted. From schools, to universities, to apprenticeships, from the Night Clubs in The Houses to as yet unimagined forms of learning, the state must facilitate and support a revolution for the just transition.

Framed by a guiding story, the state must finally, but critically, focus on designing and enforcing the rules.

There is no good working life without the basics and all workers are looking to the state to enforce minimum (or, better still, living) wages, health and safety laws, fair contracts and freedom from surveillance. Enforcing the rules also means closing regulatory loopholes: the gaps in which companies pay significant dividends or command share buyback schemes while finding ways to avoid recognising their workers as employees or reducing earnings and rights in other ways. 'Worker' must be recognised as one category, regardless of contract status, and every worker must be sure of the basics. This is a fundamental step in repairing trust between citizen and state, and in ensuring good working lives.

The design and enforcement of just fiscal rules, ensuring that business as well as citizens contribute to the collective good, is also a basic role of the state. Many have written about this important strategic role. Critical measures for a just transition will include an end to subsidies for fossil fuel extraction and a redesign of the tax regime to favour taxes on the use of scarce natural resources, and on wealth as opposed to labour. Many of those whose work has already been discussed, including Kate Raworth and Thomas Piketty, have set out how these taxes could be designed, and Piketty has modelled their potential impact. This new tax regime would support the investments required in learning, transition incomes and the capitalising of place-based work organisations. The path towards these new regimes, which many law-makers in the United States and the European Union, along with world leaders of the G20, are seeking, requires in turn each state's adherence to international rules and to strong international relationships.

Carlota Perez repeatedly emphasises the unique and critical role that the state must play in 'tilting the playing field'. In other words, it is the state that can introduce the legislation and infrastructure that will direct the development of technology, and it is the state that can direct investment into the new: smart, green, generative forms of growth. The state can also ensure a plural and diverse economy, one that benefits households, communities and those pioneering new forms of good business in all places. Today we have a monoculture: every economy must be structured according to the rules of the market. But workers at the Imaginings, alongside New Industrialists, have diverse ways of thinking about the ownership of technology, about new forms of care economy and mutually owned finance and investment. A dynamic state will nurture all these models.

The state, like workers, organic intellectuals and enlightened business leaders must embrace imagination and experimentation, allowing commonly shared visions of the new to be born and practised.

None of these actors can resolve our challenges in isolation, but each has a critical part to play. Each has rich histories, experiments and role models to draw on, in order to take connected actions that will bring the principles of a good working life into being: meeting the ecological moment, shaping the technology revolution and ensuring the transition is just. Each are capable of revolutionary thought – the practice of thinking together and combining both old and new to meaningfully move forward. This frees us from ideas which no longer serve us and forges a new story of our common fate, bringing us together and enabling the radical re-conception of work.

Twenty-First-Century Work: A Radical Re-Conception

I came to the end of my journeys, and I wanted to share the stories I had heard. Pilgrims have this tendency. These stories, the ones I call unofficial, are rich in possibility and they are practical – these are ideas that could be implemented; they speak to hopes that are widely shared and they directly address the crises we are facing. They are so different in content and tenor to the official stories: strategies of work creation which do not benefit local people tied to state-funded programmes which attempt to persuade us to take a job, any job, regardless of the conditions or the work's purpose. Official stories continue as if the wider context in which we live has not dramatically changed. I wanted to tell a story about a different future, one which draws together personal hopes, community and bigger system shifts.

I wrote a book proposal, and my editor took it to the meeting where decisions are made about which books to publish. A book about work and above all about hope – everyone liked the idea. But my working title, 'The Workers' Revolution', would have to go. The editors, publicists and others who attended the meeting did not think of themselves as 'workers' and they wanted to commission a book in which everyone could see themselves in the future I was painting. I agreed, of course. I certainly wasn't wedded to the title and this book is about and for everyone. But I was also intrigued at this rejection of the 'worker' label.

The Imaginings show that we all want good and meaningful work to be part of our lives, *and* we want to de-centre this work to make sure we have the space and time to attend to all those other things that allow us to flourish and feel happy. Almost no one wants to be defined by their work alone. As Kimberly Mitchell, working at Macy's department store, told the union organiser Erica Smiley, you diminish me if you just see me as a worker.

But I wondered if the rejection of the 'worker' label at the publishing meeting implicitly carried something else: no one at the meeting saw themselves as a worker; because the 'worker' label has increasingly been used only to describe those whose work is of low status and who earn low pay. 'I want a profession,' a long-term unemployed and middle-aged man told me in no uncertain terms when, decades ago, I first started exploring services that support people to find work. This individual was making clear that he would not just accept any job; he was not just a worker, he wanted work with meaning, and above all to be accorded the respect and dignity that a profession would bring.

Labels matter (and titles will certainly determine the books we read) but the distinctions between forms of work, blue- or white-collar, jobs or professions, have become increasingly blurred. At the same time, attempts to see us as disparate parts – hands (workers) or heads (professionals) – increasingly jars. In my journeys I planned initially to meet with certain categories of worker: low paid, skilled, digital, for example, but it was hard to draw absolute distinctions, partly because many people have done lots of different work, but more because the conditions which govern work are shifting. A professional in a law firm can, as the young Sara Horowitz experienced, find themselves in effect to be a self-employed gig worker.

The forces of change challenge us all. No one will escape an ecological crisis that removes all forms of certainty from what we will eat, to what work will remain or whether we can travel to meet one another. Similarly, AI will continue to transfigure work in the CEO's corner office just as much as it will change working from home, in a makerspace or for the delivery rider on the street. In particular, technology, until its course is changed, will continue to eat into the basics for every worker, everywhere. We are living in a time of transition – a moment in history when diverse forces, including those of technology, ecology and injustice that I have explored in this book, impact everyone. Bonding together to bend the arc of future work towards those qualities and conditions that would enable us to flourish is in our common interest. The more of us who join together, the richer our lives can be. Work is a collaborative project and the conditions which broadly shape work and life shape us all. We are workers and we share a common fate.

An inclusive community of fate, writes the political scientist Margaret Levi, is not an ideal; it doesn't require ubiquitous love for each other, but it does require action on behalf of that fate. It requires, in Levi's words, 'being ready'.

In closing, although this is in reality the beginning, and drawing on the six shared principles of a good working life that emerged at the Imaginings – a commitment to securing the basics; to work with meaning; a re-configuration of time, a re-valuing of care and repair; a commitment to play and to place – I want to draw out six further points of connection, the cross-threads of our shared story, that if acted upon would enable us to radically re-conceptualise our working lives and, together, move into a stronger, richer common future.

First, **let's not pretend**. Change is happening and we need to see these changes as they really are, alive to the possibilities and to the sometimes harsh realities that need to be confronted. Paradigm change – times of momentous transition – are times when we can rethink and renew our ideas, our values, our institutions and the patterns by which we live our days and take care of each other. We owe it to one another not to pretend. There are dark things, as many who came to the Imaginings pointed out, and we need to see those things in order to reckon with them. And there are even bigger possibilities that we can only see and act on if we listen beyond the loudest official voices and then act together.

We must **put aside ideas that no longer serve us**. These ideas, many of which underpinned twentieth-century work patterns, that promoted over-work and over-use of the natural resources, that accepted the good work of some would be predicated on the exploitation of others. These ideas have exhausted all of us and are exhausting our ecological systems.

Specifically, we need to lay to rest *Homo economicus* and nourish *Sapiens integra* instead. We are social, we want to connect and take care of each other, we do sometimes want to compete and we want to grow. We benefit – even in competition – from the rules of reciprocity and mutual collaboration. Developments across a wide range of disciplines tell us that *Sapiens integra* better defines the humans we are. *Sapiens integra* came to the Imaginings and conjured ideas and systems that would serve us now.

We can **rethink the purpose of work**. We are not cogs in a machine; our purpose is not simply to contribute to an abstract number that defines economic growth, without regard to whether this numerical ranking is creating wellbeing and nurturing our people and lands. We are head, hands and heart, and the purpose of our work is to grow these capabilities while contributing to economic systems that can support good lives and rich places. Our purpose is to do the work which nurtures and repairs our systems for ourselves and the generations to follow.

Rethinking the purpose of work will alter the status of work. In particular, the work of care and repair is likely to be recognised and valued for its true importance.

As the twentieth century progressed, we came to see work as a narrow economic bargain. We trained and competed for jobs which we hoped would bring us individual success and material security. The quality of this work and its purpose, the collective webs on which it depended, were rarely mentioned. L is for labour in the twentieth-century economists' equations – a unit of input into the sum of growth much like any other component: machines, minerals or software.

In this century we are reframing work, which we can now see is a cultural and collective project as much as an individual economic task. Work is social: it is where we make ourselves. We are seeking work with meaning in which we can contribute to a greater purpose. We want work which is just and does not harm the wider social and ecological systems we recognise we are part of. Just as we want to be head, hands and heart, so we want to be emotionally and socially connected to bigger collective endeavours. We can also see clearly that what happens to us – whether we succeed at school or in our work – depends on shared systems and infrastructure: on geography, politics, the intellectual currents that shape what is or is not acceptable. Part of our collective work – our action on behalf of our common fate – is to re-shape these systems.

We can reject the simple bargain of time for money, in

part because money no longer affords us our dreams but also because we want to make new and different non-economised forms of abundance in differently patterned lives.

We can and must **redesign the patterning of our days**, allowing us time to work, to rest, to play, to care. These are the principles of the good working life, on a par, and which taken together will ensure economic productivity and good lives, vibrant places, renewed ecologies and people. Without this redesign we are investing every year in a costly exercise of damage – to ourselves and to our environment. We are currently trying to meet these costs, of escalating anxiety, physical frailty, failure at school and at work, while failing to attend to the root cause: the design of good working lives. This imbalance was my starting point, the impulse for my journeys.

We need to **redesign our institutions**. The shape of our institutions frames what action is possible. The houses designed at the Imaginings, with their wide membership, broad networks, active and locally shaped agendas and with the control of capital reserves which would enable intervention within the local economy, were created to contend with shifts in financial and spatial power which have come with successive waves of technology. The design, which emphasised a move away from traditional hierarchies to structures which enable inclusive and everyday decision-making, additionally renew the practice of democracy in place-based institutions.

Our institutions also shape us. They convey what matters – competition or collaboration, for example; they govern who we meet – whether we rub shoulders across generations and with people 'not like us'. Good working lives are, as I have noted, dependent in each new era on new adaptive designs that can grapple with and shape the new technological, social and economic realities.

Our institutions must be multiple, plural and abundant. It's important to emphasise, in an era where social institutions have often been positioned as a luxury, that these new institutions are a prerequisite of both economic and social flourishing. They must sit within abundant landscapes that include and take care of what already exists. Parks, libraries, schools, playgrounds, unions, clubs of all sorts need support and sometimes repair. It is the abundance of institutions and the networks between them that will allow good working lives to not only take root, but to spread. Institutions are also like trees, unlikely to last long standing alone without companions and their nutrients.

And finally, we need to **renew our means and modes of collaboration**. Collaboration starts with what connects us. 'It's been a bit eye-opening to see and hear everyone's views – it's good,' an Imagineer commented in Grimsby. It was a common observation, drawing attention to our lack of space and opportunity to hear each other's creative ideas. At the Imaginings ideas of collaboration started from common ground – work and the place in which we live – and then opened to considerations of difference and how others (who it was always acknowledged might think differently) could be drawn in to a more expansive common fate. The starting point was what connects as opposed to what separates.

Organising often draws strength from the opposite starting point: the ability to define a common enemy: 'the bosses', 'the foreigners'. Historically, the experience of coming together to defeat an enemy has also provided the turning point; the point at which societies come together with a new reckoning and change course. The last two world wars were cataclysmic, creating just such a coming together, re-shaping technology, economies and our social contract with one another. If we have a common challenge today, it is climate change, the existential nature of which, if faced honestly, provides us with the urgent impulse for concerted action.

To act, we need this impetus, and we need to renew the way we collaborate. An arresting and important aspect of the Imaginings was a shared desire to find new ways of listening, talking and working that would forge horizontal alliances between workers, intellectuals, business and the state. 'We haven't thought this way before,' was a frequent remark, closely followed by 'What can we do next?'

Working outside the structures of formal power, with no fixed agenda and with tools to spark collective imagination, enabled the emergence of new stories and possibilities. These were stories that were shared across walks of life and political divides.

Managers and corporate leaders have generated their own Imaginings and have also been intrigued to hear stories and insights that do not emerge from employee surveys or corporate value exercises. Senior professionals recognise that these unheard and unofficial stories are behind behaviours and motivations they see in the workplace. I have never allowed observers at the Imaginings; we cannot talk freely if someone else is listening. But in Barrow, I had to waive my rule, given the sensitive nature of the work at the Yard. I asked the representative from HR if she would mind sitting to the side, in what was really a large cupboard. Participants rapidly forgot her presence, but when she emerged, she declared herself to be somewhat shocked. 'We [in management] can never hear ideas like this,' she told me, 'but these ideas would be transformative for us.' In this century worker creativity is one of the most important assets of any company and every worker wants to be recognised for the ideas they can bring.

We need creativity to find answers to our challenges and to re-shape our lives. The Imaginings tapped into experience, ideas, beliefs; they drew on the everyday and on deeper wiring – memories of when things were shared or in some way differently organised. To shape our common fate, all of us need the space and the tools to imagine and to re-make our realities.

'All reality is made up,' concluded the anthropologist Michael Taussig after making his pilgrimage. Held up in the storm-light of my first Imagining in Kilmarnock or the sunlight of my last Imagining in Detroit, I learnt that what we take to be the reality of work today does appear to be nothing more than a thinly veiled fiction, which could so easily be spun into something richer. It is this work, this collective revolution, that must now begin.

Notes

Who Wants to Reimagine Work?

4   *'greedy jobs':* Claudia Goldin, the Nobel-winning economist, has borrowed the term 'greedy jobs' from sociologists Lewis Coser and Rose Laub Coser, who coined the concept to describe work which seeks 'exclusive and undivided loyalty'. Rose Coser described motherhood as this form of work and Goldin, whose research centres challenge of gender justice at work, has noted how greedy jobs penalise those with child care responsibilities in particular.

4   *its own psychological pressures:* Heather Boushey, in *Finding Time*, documents the long hours and social costs experienced by the 'overworked rich', and in *The Challenge of Affluence* the economic historian Avner Offer describes what he called 'the hedonic treadmill': the rich have money but, furtively still trying to keep up with their peers, they don't feel better.

4   *still predominantly women:* Slaughter, *Unfinished Business*. The original article, published in the *Atlantic* in 2012 and titled 'Why Women Still Can't Have It All', remains one of the magazine's most-read articles of all time, such is the continual and widespread experience of the challenges Slaughter describes.

6   *Beveridge:* I have drawn on Jose Harris's definitive and fascinating biography of Beveridge.

8   *Today the welfare state:* 'DWP Benefits Statistics: August 2022', Department for Work & Pensions. The Joseph Rowntree Foundation reports that two thirds (68 per cent) of working-age adults living in poverty live in a household where someone is in

work. See *UK Poverty 2025: The Essential Guide to Understanding Poverty in the UK* (London: Joseph Rowntree Foundation, 2025), p. 77. This is a 55 per cent increase in in-work poverty since the turn of this century (p. 82).

9   *Levelling Up:* 'Levelling Up' was a political policy first articulated in the 2019 Conservative Party manifesto that aimed to reduce the economic imbalances between geographic areas and social groups across the United Kingdom. The following Labour government dropped the name but has remained focused on the intent within the Ministry of Housing, Communities and Local Government.

10 *Suicide rates in Ayrshire:* National Records of Scotland reveal that East Ayrshire was one of only four Scottish council areas where the local death rate outstripped that for Scotland as a whole over the five years from 2018 to 2022. Craig Borland, 'East Ayrshire "probable suicide" rate above Scottish average', *Cumnock Chronicle*, 5 September 2023.

12 *'re-arranging', 'brotherhood':* As quoted in Turner, *Dramas, Fields, and Metaphors.* Turner, an anthropologist, was particularly interested in the idea of a pilgrimage journey as a form of *communitas*: a social process through which those participating could bond around new ideas. Michael Taussig also refers to his anthropological method as a pilgrimage in *The Magic of the State.*

19 *on a par:* Ruth Chang, the philosopher and chair of jurisprudence at Oxford University, developed this important concept of 'on a par' to challenge and guide better public decision making in situations of what she calls 'hard choices'. See Chang, 'Hard Choices'.

Why Now? Imagining in Times of Rupture and Opportunity

24 *predicting a dystopian future:* Susskind, *A World Without Work.* Other notable voices of doom include Erik Brynjolfsson and Andrew McAfee, who have pioneered the idea of the great decoupling. Their arguments focus on how tasks are being broken down within jobs, raising output but ensuring workers who now do only one part of a former job, do not and will not benefit: see Amy Bernstein and Anand Raman, 'The Great Decoupling: An Interview with Erik Brynjolfsson and Andrew MacAfee', *Harvard Business Review*,

June 2015. Carlota Perez has taken apart their arguments in a series of very readable blog posts on her website.

24 *machines … will encroach:* Susskind points out there is an entire field known as 'affective computing' that is dedicated to building systems that can do this (*A World Without Work*, p. 85). Such systems are touted as, for example, a potential response to the care crisis which I discuss in Principle Three: Care and Repair.

24 *Autor … points out:* See Autor, 'Why Are There Still So Many Jobs?'

24 *Autor also argues:* In *New Frontiers*, Autor and his colleagues argue that workers employed in new work are more educated and higher paid – even conditional on education – than workers employed in preexisting job titles in the same detailed occupational categories. This pattern suggests that new work may be more skilled, specialised and potentially better remunerated than pre-existing work. Others who agree with this thesis include Eric Hazan and his colleagues at McKinsey Global Institute: see their report, 'A New Future of Work: The Race to Deploy AI and Raise Skills in Europe and Beyond', 21 May 2024.

25 *At IKEA, for example:* 'IKEA's Contact Center Agents Become Interior Designers', CX Today, 15 June 2023.

25 *'tools first':* The World Economic Forum's work on technology typifies a 'tools first' approach, with its focus on AI, for example, which is also framed as an unstoppable force giving rise to policy questions that ask how we might adapt to AI rather than how we might adapt AI.

25 *inventors of the microchip:* Two independent inventors who were not working together invented the integrated circuit known as the microchip. Jack Kilby, an engineer with a background in ceramic-based silk screen circuit boards and transistor-based hearing aids, started working for Texas Instruments in 1958. A year earlier, research engineer Robert Noyce had co-founded the Fairchild Semiconductor Corporation. From 1958 to 1959, both electrical engineers were working on an answer to the same dilemma: how to make more of less: greater computational power was needed for all forms of engineering. O'Mara, *The Code*.

28 *Carlota identified:* Perez, *Technological Revolutions and Financial Capital*, 'Technological Revolutions and Techno-Economic

Paradigms' and 'Capitalism, Technology and a Green Global Age'. It's important to emphasise that the effects of the social revolutions are felt in ripples; the old and the new (the desire for the new car and the electric bike) overlap.

28 *the digital revolution born in the 1970s:* In Perez's formulation, AI is not a new revolution but a development within the fifth revolution. See Perez, 'What is AI's Place in History?', Project Syndicate, 11 March 2024.

29 *a 'turning point':* Perez charts the rise of new sectors of society with each revolution: the first (steam) saw the rise of merchants, makers, engineers, entrepreneurs and naval officials; the second (railways) created new urban lifestyles and work which included booksellers, milliners, tutors; the third (steel) created a new skilled worker aristocracy in engineering and white-collar professional work; the fourth (mass production) created a blue-collar workforce who were decently paid in order to create a market for consumption goods. Perez predicts the fifth (digital) revolution will see a rise in well-paid smart green high-tech jobs, which will include an emphasis on repair. See Perez and Tamsin Murray Leach, 'A Smart Green "European Way of Life": The Path for Growth, Jobs and Wellbeing', Beyond the Technology Revolution working paper, March 2018. Also Perez, *The Social Shaping of Technological Revolutions.*

30 *organic intellectuals:* Gramsci developed the concept of the 'organic intellectual' in his prison notebooks, distinguishing intellectuals who through their working-class base allied their thinking to broader interests of the places and classes they were from, in contrast with 'traditional' professional intellectuals whose position had a certain inter-class aura, which conceals their attachment to established hierarchies and their class interests. Gramsci thought intellectuals could perform an essential mediating function in class struggles. In my own work I also suggest that intellectuals can play a critical role in mediating, widening the window of what seems possible, and in linking ideas to practice. Critical thinkers who can do the latter are those I call 'organic intellectuals'. I return to these ideas in the closing chapter.

30 *not a story of techno-determinism:* It's important to note that Perez is

not alone in pushing back against ideas of techno-determinism. Many economists insist that technology is shaped by wider forces (as opposed to being the dominant shaping force). Diane Coyle, for example, argues that 'all technology is social' and nothing is inevitable in terms of what gets adopted or how. She gives the example of electricity: it's not a new technology, but many countries can't deliver stable supplies to their citizens because the task is socially and institutionally – not technologically – demanding. *Markets, State and People*, pp. 88–91.

31   *Scientists agree:* See, for example, this survey of academic scientist's studies of the current state of planetary boundaries: Katherine Richardson et al., 'Earth Beyond Six of Nine Planetary Boundaries, *Science Advances*, 9:37 (2023). Scientists differ in their estimates of the number of species facing extinction (predictions vary between 28 per cent and 48 per cent); they agree that the loss of abundance and the precipitous decline in certain pollinators, for example, presents a grave threat.

31   *patterns of human migration:* Vince, *Nomad Century.* Zurich Insurance Group suggest that conflicts driven by climate change could generate upwards of a billion economic migrants in the next thirty years: see Sean McAllister, 'There Could Be 1.2 Billion Climate Refugees by 2050. Here's What You Need to Know', *Zurich Magazine*, 23 October 2024. The International Organization for Migration suggest there may be 200 million climate migrants by 2050: 'Environmental Migration', IOM Environmental Migration Portal.

32   *There is an immediate and urgent need:* In 2015, 196 nations came together in Paris to sign the Paris Agreement, a legally binding treaty to reduce carbon emissions. So far attempts at mitigation have been limited. In 2024 the world saw the first year-long breach of the 1.5-degree warming limit, with every month breaking record temperatures.

32   *'algorithmic pollution':* The Digiconomist Bitcoin Energy Consumption Index estimates that, in 2022, a single Bitcoin transaction generates the same carbon footprint as 1.73 million Visa transactions – equivalent to the same power consumption the average US household uses in 48.1 days.

32   *lithium mining:* Lithium deposits are largely found under indigenous
      land, from Australia to Bolivia. The mining process is extremely
      water intensive in places where water is a scarce commodity and
      involves the release of powerful toxins into the atmosphere and the
      lungs of workers. Lithium and cobalt mining (both are required
      for battery technology) involves child labour and very low wages
      or conditions of modern slavery as reported, for example, by
      Amnesty International in 2016 ('Exposed: Child Labour Behind
      Smart Phone and Electric Car Batteries', 19 January 2016) and
      by Global Witness in 2023 ('A Rush for Lithium in Africa Risks
      Fuelling Corruption and Failing Citizens', 14 November 2023).
      These new forms of modern mining – like the previous extraction
      of oil – are to date enriching global corporations but having little
      effect on the everyday economy for those who live in the poorer
      parts of the world where these, precious elements are concentrated.

34   *communities continually reinvent:* In *A Paradise Built in Hell*, Solnit
      writes about the 'extraordinary communities' that arise in times
      of disaster, taking examples from the San Francisco earthquake
      of 1906 and the more recent devastation wrought by Hurricane
      Katrina in 2005.

34   *Think like a forest:* Ghosh, *The Nutmeg's Curse*. Ghosh argues that
      in the current environmental crisis there are no safe havens;
      our future is predicated on coming together and sharing in new
      ways. He takes inspiration from the ideas of the economist Elinor
      Ostrom, whose work I discuss in Principle Three: Care and
      Repair.

35   *Work is causing:* See, for example, 'Fact Sheet 11: Work Insecurity',
      ILO Socio-Economic Security Programme. In 2021 WHO and
      ILO produced their first ever joint report looking at the health
      challenges that are resulting from long working hours and stress.
      Frank Pega et al., 'Global, Regional, and National Burdens of
      Ischemic Heart Disease and Stroke Attributable to Exposure to
      Long Working Hours for 194 Countries, 2000–2016', *Environment
      International*, 154 (September 2021).

36   *Millions of households:* In *UK Poverty 2024*, the annual review of
      UK poverty statistics, the Joseph Rowntree Foundation show that
      two thirds of households in poverty have at least one full-time

working adult. One million children in Britain are growing up in destitution, with NHS data additionally showing British children are growth stunted in comparison with their European peers: 'The Food Foundation Report Highlights Impact of Britain's Food Policy Disaster', Nuffield Foundation, 19 July 2022. 3.4 million households in Britain do not earn enough to feed their families. 3.5 million live in fuel poverty. More recently the geographer and Oxford University professor Danny Dorling has also drawn attention to the growth stunting of British children who are growing up in conditions of extreme inequality in 'The Lives of Seven Children Tell the Story of UK Inequality', *Jacobin*, 30 June 2024, and *Seven Children*.

36 *In the US:* According to the Bureau of Labor Statistics, more than thirty-seven million US citizens live in poverty, of whom 6.3 million are in work. Women, and the Latino and Black populations are over-represented in the numbers of the working poor. 'A Profile of the Working Poor, 2020', BLS Reports, September 2022. Twenty-seven million US workers have no health insurance, and approximately half of those experiencing homelessness have a job. See 'National Uninsured Rate at 8.2 Percent in the First Quarter of 2024', ASPE Office of Health Policy Data Point, August 2024, and 'Data & Trends', United States Interagency Council on Homelessness.

36 *Those in low-paid work:* Karel Williams and his colleagues have made detailed and excellent studies which show how in Britain stagnant wages have combined with underfunded public services and a housing crisis to put a decent life beyond the reach of millions, arguing 'the low-paid need more than a pay rise'. They propose a foundational liveability framework which connects income, essential services and social infrastructure, and argue that it is these three pillars rather than economic growth (GDP) which should be measured, in order to direct a just economy. Calafati et al., *When Nothing Works*.

36 *takes a physical toll:* See Marmot et al., *Health Equity in England,* which shows the effects of 'iso-strain', the psychosocial hazards of low-paid work in which stressors include low pay, little control over the work and high job instability, with resulting high levels of general ill health, depression, cardiovascular disease, coronary heart disease

and musculoskeletal disorders. In 2015, nine million work days were lost in Britain to stress, more than the days lost in the Thatcher-era strikes.

36 *live on average ten years less:* Marmot, *The Health Gap.* I discuss these issues in more depth in Principle Four: Time.

36 *17 per cent of working age adults:* 'Prescribed Medicines Review: Summary', Public Health England, 3 December 2020. This figure rises to one in six adults in areas of the UK where there is a scarcity of good work. The Resolution Foundation has tracked the complex links between work and mental health in young people, in Charlie McCurdy & Louise Murphy, *We've Only Just Begun: Action to Improve Young People's Mental Health, Education and Employment* (February 2024). See also the Health Foundation's research on the links between low paid work and poor physical and mental health, 'Relationship Between Low-Quality Jobs and Health', 20 June 2024.

37 *Research from Europe and the United States:* A 2021 survey by Generation found that 'employers prefer staff under forty-five who are a better cultural fit'. These same firms agreed that older workers perform just as well, they just don't want to hire them: see Camilla Cavendish, 'Tempting Back Older Workers Means Ditching Business as Usual', *Financial Times*, 3 February 2023. In the UK, the Chartered Management Institute has found that only four in ten managers are open to employing someone between the age of fifty and sixty-four.

37 *politicians urge older people:* In the UK the Department of Work & Pensions spends significant sums on programmes designed to 'push' older workers back into the labour market. In 2022 – the last figures available – the budget was £22 million. These programmes tackle older people's motivations and skills but they consistently ignore the demand side: employers who will not consider older workers.

37 *More than a quarter of a million:* 260,000 older workers, according to the UK Centre for Ageing Better. In the United States there are more older people in work – the Pew Center report 19 per cent of over-65s are working, which they attribute to negligible pensions and other benefits – but 80 per cent of older workers say

they experience age discrimination at work. Rebecca Perron, 'Age Discrimination Persists Among African American, Hispanic and Asian American Workers 50-Puls, AARP, 18 October 2024 (updated 15 January 2025). The American Psychological Association report that age is one of the last acceptable prejudices, so engrained that many don't notice it. Kirsten Weir, 'Ageism is One of the Last Socially Acceptable Prejudices. Psychologists are Working to Change That', *Monitor on Psychology*, 54:2 (March 2023).

37   *one in three workers:* Andy Haldane, 'The Political Love-In with Business is Long Overdue', *Financial Times*, 9 February 2024.

37   *Young workers:* 39 per cent of those under thirty no longer expect work to bring them rewards. Nearly half of Gen Z (those born between 1997 and 2012) and four in ten Millennials (the oldest of whom were born in 1980) say that they feel stressed most or all of the time. See 2023 Deloitte Gen Z and Millennial Survey.

37   *work that conflicts with their values:* Deloitte undertook the biggest survey of younger workers (23,000 workers across 44 countries), which showed that more than 80 per cent will not take work that does not align with their values. See 2023 Deloitte Gen Z and Millennial Survey.

37   *knotted most closely together:* These are not factors that can be easily isolated as Kimberlé Crenshaw's path-breaking work on intersectionality demonstrated. Crenshaw's earliest research looked at intersectionality in a Ford industrial plant.

37   *an enduring impact:* Bauluz et al., *Spatial Wage Inequality in North America and Western Europe.* The authors point out that this impact of geography is stronger in the UK than in the US, Canada, France or Germany, determined in no small part by wider institutional factors and the centralisation of political power and institutions that is also unique to the UK. Paul Collier documents how the Treasury has an exceptional grip over all UK policy despite being far more socially exclusive than other parts of the civil service – in his words, 'wildly unrepresentative of Britain's population', with northerners in particular systematically under-represented in ways which make it impossible to create good policy (*Left Behind*, p. 46).

38   *have been graphically documented:* In *Deaths of Despair and the Future of Capitalism*, Case and Deaton show how despair is related not simply

to the increase in poverty but the longer-term undoing of a way of life that was rooted in work which has disappeared. Sandel's *The Tyranny of Merit*, tells a similar story, as do personal memoirs such as J. D. Vance's criticised but bestselling *Hillbilly Elegy* and Fiona Hill's *There is Nothing for You Here*. Hill, a former senior White House advisor, comes from Bishop Auckland, a former mining town in County Durham, and the title of her book was her father's warning: she needed to leave in order to live a good life.

38   *cultural mockery:* Many of the places to which I have journeyed have been the subject of films where crude portrayals of local life and people create anger. The sociologist Imogen Tyler has written about the complex ways in which work dehumanises and stigmatises: 'stigma is about the movement between external and internal processes of devaluation' (*Stigma*, p. 239). Ada Harvey Wingfield has written an important case study of how these subtle and granular processes of racism work in the US health and care systems, creating extreme psychic pressures on workers.

38   *one third of London's primary school pupils:* In 2019, ten years into a national programme of austerity, a British national teacher's survey recorded that 97 per cent of teachers had seen a 'dramatic increase in poverty and were regularly helping to feed and clothe children', while they were dealing with fatigue and hunger in the classroom (Tyler, *Stigma*, p. 167).

39   *dismissed as 'interpretation': Capitalism and Slavery* is based on Eric Williams's Oxford University doctoral thesis, completed in 1938. The book traces the connections between slavery and industrialisation, and those between colonial extraction and the development of new industries such as rum distillation. It was published in the US in 1944, but it was another twenty years before *Capitalism and Slavery* found a British publisher. Today it is a modern classic. Williams led his country, Trinidad and Tobago, to independence, becoming the first prime minister of the liberated islands in 1962.

39   *transfers wealth while shifting exploitation:* This work includes the new mining for rare earths, the increasingly low-paid work of factory production and new categories of work such as content moderation. This work is located in the Philippines, Kenya and Uganda, places where large numbers of talented but unemployed

young people can be persuaded to view hours of the most depraved and distressing content in order to tag it and remove it from the internet for very low wages and at enormous cost to their mental health and self-esteem. Factory production has similarly been off-shored to places where wages are lower and conditions are out of sight. Stories reach us of the nets hung around the outside of the towering dormitory buildings at Foxconn, where Apple iPhones are assembled. Along with counselling and a written commitment from employees not to jump, the nets are designed to catch the workers who can no longer bear the pressure of repeated intolerable tasks and who attempt to throw themselves to the ground and end their lives.

39 *Piketty's research shows:* Piketty also draws a line of continuity between slave-holding, colonialism and modern wealth.

39 *By the 2020s:* Lawrence Mishel and Jori Kandra, 'CEO Pay Has Skyrocketed 1,322% Since 1978', Economic Policy Institute, 10 August 2021. In the UK, the High Pay Centre reported in 2024 that the median FTSE 100 CEO is now paid 120 times the median worker. 'FTSE 100 CEO Pay Reaches New High', HPC, 11 August 2024.

39 *the trend is identical:* In the US and UK the real value of wages has declined for workers in first decades of the twenty-first century, falling by an average 2 per cent a year for low- and median-income workers since 2008. See, for example, Martin Armstrong, 'Which OECD Countries are Facing the Sharpest Falls in Real Wages?', World Economic Forum, 20 December 2022, and Stephen Machin, 'Wage Controversies: Real Wage Stagnation, Inequality and Labour Market Institutions', *LSE Public Policy Review*, 3:2 (2024).

39 *data shows these disparities are harmful:* One reason that those who are very wealthy are among those calling for a re-evaluation of taxation and in particular taxation on wealth as opposed to income. 'Nearly Three Quarters of Millionaires Polled in G20 Countries Support Higher Taxes on Wealth, Over Half Think Extreme Wealth is a "Threat to Democracy"', Oxfam International press release, 17 January 2024.See also Avner Offer, who has written about the individual and social challenges of affluence.

40 *when disparities become too great:* In 2024 Wilkinson and Pickett updated their research showing how inequality is detrimental to health, economies and the climate: 'The Spirit Level at 15', Equality Trust, 22 July 2024.

40 *meaningful opportunities are vanishing:* In situations of rampant socioeconomic inequality that are the norm in Britain and the United States today you cannot simply say people are responsible for their own fates, or pretend that experts in any field are neutral. Sandel writes: 'the diminished economic and cultural status of working people is not the result of inexorable forces, it is the way elites have governed' (*The Tyranny of Merit*, p. 22).

40 *Piketty's research:* I am drawing here on Piketty's later book, *A Brief History of Equality*, in which he writes for a more general reader.

41 *they want to repair:* In *The Dawn of Everything*, Graeber and Wengrow suggest that the term 'inequality' frames social problems and divisions in such a way that they can in theory be addressed by technocratic reform. Inequality, they write, assumes that 'no real vision of social transformation is even on the table', it's one reason that the term is so appealing to elites. In contrast, movements for justice, I would suggest, have in their sights a creation of a new system, even if they cannot yet describe all of its components.

42 *When William Beveridge travelled:* I tell this story in *Radical Help*.

43 *'in a practice of thinking together':* Arendt, *On Revolution*, p. 224. In her book *Renewal*, Anne-Marie Slaughter similarly describes a process of looking forwards and backwards with radical honesty to create a new future.

Principle One: Securing the Basics

48 *One third of Barking's current residents:* Data taken from the UK national census 2021. 'How Life Has Changed in Barking and Dagenham: Census 2021', Office for National Statistics, 19 January 2023.

48 *earning a living wage:* Everyone who came to the Imaginings was compensated for their time. In many instances employers allowed workers space in their paid working hours; in others, people came to community centres keen to participate and I offered supper. In

the case of these gig workers, I compensated their time at the rate of the London living wage.

50 *The World Bank estimates:* 'Self-Employed, Total (% of Total Employment) (Modeled ILO Estimate)', World Bank Group. It is estimated that 38 per cent of US workers now work freelance, and 46 per cent of UK workers, although UK datasets focus on the self-employed, which is not identical to being freelance. Edward Segal, 'What to Know About the Freelance Workforce as it Grows and Changes', *Forbes*, 14 May 2024; 'The Self-Employed Landscape 2022', IPSE.

51 *more likely to be in debt:* The average savings in Britain are £11,000 per adult and data from the Joseph Rowntree Foundation shows the average British worker is more likely to have debt than savings: 'Fact Sheet: Dangerous New Phase for Families in Debt – UK's Economic Insecurity by Numbers', 3 August 2023. In the United States the picture is more skewed, with 25 per cent of the population having savings over $100,000 but one in three workers having no savings. In addition, with no national health service, US low paid workers have a much-reduced safety net.

51 *are relatively modest and uncontested:* I believe what I hear, because the nature of the methods I use mean that people challenge each other and arrive at a 'truth'.

52 *a critical factor:* In Britain the anthropologist Henrietta Moore and the social policy expert Anna Coote have argued for universal basic services to be considered as an integral part of family income and wellbeing.

52 *access to affordable digital infrastructure:* Rachel Coldicutt of Careful Trouble has done leading research in the UK on digital infrastructure and widespread lack of access. See Anna Dent, 'The Real Cost of Home Broadband', Promising Trouble, 6 September 2023.

52 *Sen's research shows:* Sen set out his approach to poverty in his 1979 Tanner Lecture, 'Equality of What?' and summarises the approach in his 1983 article 'Poor, Relatively Speaking'.

52 *pay the rent:* Although conversely in some places where housing is more affordable, such as Grimsby, workers complained that there is a culture of low pay because employers know housing costs are low. I was told, but cannot verify, that there is no living-wage

employer in Grimsby and there was resentment that the low pay/
low housing cost equation is used to limit potential earnings that
might offer new horizons.

53   *One third of British workers:* Lindsay Judge and Hannah Slaughter,
      *Enforce for Good: Effectively Enforcing Labour Market Rights in the
      2020s and Beyond*, Resolution Foundation, April 2023. As ever,
      unjust wages do not fall evenly. More than a third of British young
      people earn below the minimum wage and two thirds of young
      mothers with children. Almost half of those with a physical dis-
      ability are trapped in poorly paid work. And wage differentials
      are marked by race: Black and brown workers earn less than their
      white peers. In Britain those who were born outside the country –
      like the gig workers who joined me in Barking – earn less again.

53   *adherence to safety standards: Enforce for Good*, the Resolution
      Foundation report of 2023, finds that productivity is higher in
      companies that do enforce legal standards, making it clear that
      cutting corners is not only terrible for workers, it is bad for business
      and for national economies.

55   *basics start to slip out of reach:* Teachers, for example, have seen their
      wages decline in real terms by 14 per cent between 2010 and 2021
      (Calafati et al., *When Nothing Works*); the *BMJ* points to data which
      shows that doctors' salaries have declined by 25 per cent over the
      same period; freelance journalists report that on average they now
      earn £17,500 a year. Each of these professions once guaranteed a
      middle-class family lifestyle.

55   *a wider undoing of the work contract:* In her book *Uberland* ethnog-
      rapher Alex Rosenblat argues that while few people, relatively
      speaking, have driven or ridden for Uber, the work practices the
      company has introduced are slowly infiltrating the wider economy
      and the rest of our lives.

55   *feel a widespread despair:* In her book *Can't Even*, Anne Helen
      Petersen, a freelance writer and cultural critic, tracks the mani-
      festation of millennial burnout rooted in a widespread experience
      of being unable to find or maintain some sort of equilibrium: 'for
      our kids, in our relationships, in our financial lives'.

56   *British Gas:* In 2021 British Gas engineers were subject to the no-
      torious and currently legal practice of 'fire and rehire' whereby a

company can offer its existing employees new contracts with new terms, which may include lower wages and longer or less predictable hours. Employees who do not accept the new conditions are fired.

56 *Billions are being invested:* In 2019, the Harvard Business School professor Shoshana Zuboff wrote an alarming and groundbreaking book documenting the rise of 'surveillance capitalism' – in her view a parasitic and rogue form of capitalism that is nullifying norms and rights for workers and all citizens in ways which threaten the possibility of a democratic contract and society. The book is forensic in its examination of how surveillance has grown and developed, and less forthcoming on solutions, but one which Zuboff recommends and I look at later in this book is the need for new forms of collaboration and institution-making that can specifically confront new forms of techno-corporate power.

56 *in the United States:* Virginia Eubanks and Alexandra Mateescu, '"We Don't Deserve This": New App Places US Caregivers Under Digital Surveillance', *Guardian*, 28 July 2021.

56 *Surveillance algorithms are used:* Ben Makuch, 'How McDonald's Spies on Organizing Workers', *Vice*, 5 March 2021. Indigo Olivier, 'McDonald's Spies on Union Activists – That's How Scared They Are of Workers' Rights', *Guardian*, 2 March 2021. Research from Coworker.org looked at the implications of 550 technology products that appeared in workplaces in 2019 and 2020, funded by capital from pension funds to private equity: Wilneida Negrón, *Little Tech is Coming for Workers: A Framework for Reclaiming and Building Worker Power* (2021).

57 *These technologies impact:* Negrón, *Little Tech is Coming for Workers*, p. 39. In a lecture delivered at the University of Michigan in February 2022, equality campaigner Bama Athreya highlighted what she termed 'algorithmic cruelty': the way in which many customers also make the work of platform workers harder with tough ratings and practices such as promising tips to delivery riders or Instacart workers which are cancelled at the last moment.

57 *The discovery of these devices:* 'Wells Fargo Fires Workers for "Simulating" Being at Their Keyboards', *Financial Times*, 13 June 2024.

58 *research showing:* Ernst Ekkehard, 'The AI Trilemma: Saving the Planet Without Ruining Our Jobs', *Frontiers in Artificial Intelligence*, 19:5 (October 2022).

58 *Documents leaked from Amazon:* See, for example, Avery Ellis, 'Exclusive: Amazon's Attrition Costs $8 Billion Annually According to Leaked Documents. And It Gets Worse', Engadget, 17 October 2022. For a sense of scale, the company's net profit for its 2021 fiscal year was $33.36 billion. According to another internal memo leaked to the *Guardian*, attrition rates are such that Amazon is predicted to run out of a possible pool of workers in each place warehouses are located. Michael Sainato, 'Amazon Could Run Out of Workers in Two Years, Internal Memo Suggests', *Guardian*, 22 June 2022.

59 *Securing the basics:* Jeetu and Palash also argued this is better for customers who they believe are also 'ripped off' by sharp practices, for example when deliveries are doubled up to reduce pay, the second customer is most likely to receive slow and cold food. The worker will be blamed but the customer will also be unhappy.

Principle Two: Meaning

65 *'isostrain':* See, for example, *Fair Society, Healthy Lives: The Marmot Review* (London: Institute of Health Equity, 2010), p. 72.

66 *we start to feel adrift:* See also Frankl, *The Unheard Cry for Meaning*. In the 1970s the psychoanalyst Victor Frankl diagnosed unemployment as a specific neurosis which leads to human beings feeling useless. Today, useless – or as the London consultants call it, pointless – work leads to similar feelings of uselessness and that life itself is without meaning.

66 *'It is not only the labour':* Karl Marx, *Capital* (1867/1887), Volume 1, p. 481.

66 *'It's almost irrational':* Armstrong, *The New Poverty*, p. 174.

69 *7 per cent of the vegetables we grow:* 'United Kingdom Food Security Report 2021. Theme 2: UK Food Supply Sources', Department for Environment, Food & Rural Affairs, 22 October 2024.

69 *energy-intensive cold chain links:* In *Frostbite*, Nicola Twilley coins the term 'artificial cryosphere' to describe the pervasive, invisible and

global cold chains that move our food around the world. What we think of as 'fresh' is increasingly man-made and energy intensive. After potatoes, frozen peas are the most highly consumed vegetable in the UK.

71 *important for the future of national economies:* See Kattel et al., *How to Make an Entrepreneurial State.*

71 *it can be a challenge: Guardian* journalist Aditya Chakraborty profiled a number of UK makerspaces in 2018. He noted both their importance in an industrial eco-system and the way rising land prices and therefore rents make their existence continually precarious in Britain. 'Meet Britain's Willy Wonkas: The Ideas Factory That Could Save UK Industry', *Guardian*, 28 March 2018.

73 *encouraged to don a personality:* The feminist scholar Arlie Russell Hochschild famously documented similar processes where workers in a wide range of industries are forced to manage emotions and feelings as part of their work in order to reassure others.

74 *one of America's few women firefighters:* In the United States only 4 per cent of firefighters are women. Discrimination – a view that women are not strong enough to do the work – means that few women are hired and those who are face constant harassment from male colleagues. In 2023 the Baltimore fire department were taken to court on sexual harassment charges, a case which the prosecutors won ('US Settles Sexual harassment Claims Against Baltimore County Fire Department', *Insurance Journal*, 11 September 2023). In Britain, rampant sexual harassment in the fire service has also come to light, with a union survey showing a third of women firefighters have to regularly face degrading sexual harassment in various forms, often feeling unsafe and unsure as to whether those same colleagues would support them in an emergency situation. For women firefighting is not work which meets the basics. Rajeev Syal, 'Almost Third of Female Firefighters Have Faced Harassment at FBU Events, Report Finds', *Guardian*, 7 February 2024.

75 *'Initially it was widely assumed':* Rawsthorn also notes that much of this work (with bio-materials) is inspired by natural processes, or by ancient and indigenous design making traditions. Nikolai Kotlarczyk, 'Alice Rawsthorn on the Future of Craft', The Mindcraft Project, 11 March 2024.

76   *'It's as if'*: Graeber, 'On the Phenomenon of Bullshit Jobs'.

78   *AI is just warming up:* Susskind and Susskind, *The Future of the Professions.*

79   *These workers:* Women did not take the industrial demarcations that largely excluded them from better paid work without protest. The first generation of feminists, the so-called materialist feminists, challenged two core aspects of industrialisation: the physical separation of the household from the public sphere and the economic separation of the domestic economy. 'The private kitchen must go the way of the spinning wheel, of which it is the contemporary,' argued the American playwright and pamphleteer Zona Gale. With a slogan of 'homes without kitchens and towns without housework', a line of remarkable women agitated for six decades for new feminist cities that would be designed around shared kitchens, laundries and child care centres. Their history is told by Dolores Hayden in *The Grand Domestic Revolution.* Angela Davis drew explicitly on these first-generation feminists in *Women, Race and Class*, writing women of colour back into the story and reminding white second-wave feminists that Black women did not do housework for free; this was their labour and the work/political challenge is to recognise and value it, not abolish it. With regard to invisible histories, the artist Faith Ringgold's art and story quilts tell the stories of workers that are left out of histories, including that of her father, who was forced to do non-unionised labour.

80   *Rose studied the often-destructive patterns:* Rose, *Hand, Brain and Heart.* The way in which the heart can be used to disrupt extractive models of techno-science is also explored in Puig de la Bellacasa, *Matters of Care.*

80   *brought their heads, hands and hearts together:* I am making a different argument here from that made by David Goodhart in *Head Hand Heart.* He argues that work in each form – those who work with their heads, their hands and their hearts – needs to be accorded dignity. While this is true, I learnt at the Imaginings that the bigger goal, that which brings meaning, is to design work which brings all these parts of ourselves together.

80   *Bren was a fisherman:* In his book *Eat Like a Fish*, Bren graphically describes the destruction of industrial fishing, the solidarity of the

work, the thrill of the hunting and the decline in the quality of the catch, much of which was marked 'D' for disgusting given its level of infestation by parasitic worms and lice. Fish marked with a category D sticker was sold at cut-price rates to McDonald's and became Filet-O-Fish sandwiches.

82   *breathe life back into our oceans:* Researchers at the University of California Santa Barbara found that growing seaweed in less than 4 per cent of US waters could neutralise California's agricultural emissions, while World Bank studies suggest that this new industry could provide up to fifty million jobs globally. The World Bank estimates that farming seaweed in less than 5 per cent of US waters (0.1 per cent of the world's oceans) annually could produce the protein equivalent of three trillion cheeseburgers while absorbing 135 million tons of carbon, and 10 million tons of nitrogen. 'Seaweed Aquaculture for Food Security, Income Generation and Environmental Health in Tropical Developing Countries', World Bank Group, July 2016.

83   *'Become like me':* The political theorist Roberto Unger argues that many modern families still expect children to follow the parental path while the modern state also plays a limiting role, asking everyone to 'serve' the economy, making it hard for young people to find their own course (*The Knowledge Economy*, p. 97). In 2023 Rishi Sunak, the then British prime minister, committed to abolishing university courses that did not lead to professions he personally considered served the national economy.

83   *work with purpose and meaning: Forbes* magazine, for example, has called Gen Z 'the most purpose-driven generation yet', while also noting that 74 per cent of Gen Z want to quit their jobs because they don't feel they have enough room to grow or sufficient meaning and purpose. Dena Trujillo, 'Engaging Gen-Z, Our Most Purpose-Driven Generation', *Forbes*, 15 September 2023.

84   *highly pressured sorting machine:* I borrow the term 'sorting machine' from the philosopher Michael Sandel, who has written about the ways in which these pressures among privileged youth in particular are extreme. In the US the suicide rate of young people aged twenty to twenty-four increased 36 per cent between 2000 and 2017, with more young people dying of mental illness than

homicide. See Sandel, *The Tyranny of Merit*, p. 180. In the UK, one in five young adults are now reported to be experiencing 'severe distress', with more than half of young adults in public polling saying problems related to their work are causing stress: 'One in Five Young Adults Experiencing Severe Distress in England', UCL News, 6 July 2023.

85   Homo economicus*:* Adam Smith made an early portrait of *Homo economicus* in the *Wealth of Nations* (1776) but noted that while man is 'selfish', 'there are evidently some principles in his nature which interest him in the fortune of others'. John Stuart Mill exaggerated his features in his widely read philosophical works taken up by subsequent economists including Alfred Marshall. In the 1960s, Milton Friedman acknowledged that *Homo economicus* was by now a cartoon character but argued that he was the exemplar of how we *should* behave, further entrenching his template within the design of economic models and work. Kate Raworth tells the wider story of *Homo economicus'* powerful and destructive role in mainstream economics in her book *Doughnut Economics*.

86   *recent scholarship:* For example, the physicist Carlo Rovelli has demonstrated that matter, including humans, is only held together by relationships; the biologist Dennis Noble has conducted groundbreaking research that shows both our genetic predisposition to cooperate is exceptionally well developed and the falsity of ideas of human beings as a form of genetically determined human machine. The social psychologist Cecilia Heyes has shown the way our ideas are the product of the collective mind, and the extent to which we will forgo our individual interests for the common good of the community.

87   Sapiens integra*:* Cottam, 'Welfare 5.0'.

Principle Three: Care and Repair – Tending to What Sustains Us

88   *Without care:* 'El trabajo de cuidados es imprescindible para el mantenimiento de la vida,' writes the Spanish philosopher Silvia Lopez Gil in *Las Logicas Del Cuidado*. Her work informs a wider exploration of care which takes in tasks, feelings and the need to connect to and repair our natural world explored by Joan Tronto,

Bernice Fisher, as cited by Maria Puig de la Bellacasa in *Matters of Care*. It is these richer dimensions of care and repair that are discussed at the Imaginings and which inform this chapter.

89 *It is estimated:* Fiona Harvey, 'UK Government "Failing" to Cut Carbon Emissions from Home Heating', *Guardian*, 3 February 2022.

89 *One in four:* Figures taken from the 2021 UK census. In the year recorded, pre-pandemic, half a million people left the labour market to care. 'Key Facts and Figures about Caring', Carers UK, 2024. In 2022 the Joseph Rowntree Foundation found that 44 per cent of working age adults caring for others are living in poverty, a direct result of the difficulty of balancing work and care.

91 *In Barnsley, an estimated one in five:* In June 2024 twenty-two thousand people in Barnsley were on hospital waiting lists (i.e. this does not include those waiting for care or adolescent mental health services; an estimated twenty thousand more are waiting for care services). Jack Tolson, 'Latest Waiting List Figures Released', *Barnsley Chronicle*, 25 June 2024. The Barnsley metropolitan area has a population of approximately 244,000.

91 *a bigger national emergency:* Nationally over 7.5 million people in Britain are waiting for health treatment, up from 4.2 million in pre-Covid 2019 and 2.5 million in 2010, when investment levels in health and primary care were higher. In 2024 270,000 young people were on waiting lists for child and adolescent mental health services in Britain with children routinely waiting more than two years to be seen. 'Press Notice: Over a Quarter of a Million Children Still Waiting for Mental Health Support, Children's Commissioner Warns', Children's Commissioner, 15 March 2024.

91 *Retention of staff:* One in ten people who join the NHS leaves, with the top two given reasons being the need to find work–life balance and illness. In some health professions turnover and departure is much higher: a third of midwives and a third of qualified nurses are thought not to be working. Jerome Smail and Megan Ford, 'Report Reveals "Eyewatering" Social Care Nursing Turnover', *Nursing in Practice*, 12 October 2023.

92 *a complex transaction:* The International Council of Nursing reports that these migration policies are the biggest challenge faced by

nursing globally, with much ill feeling that richer nations are pur-
suing policies of neocolonial extraction, failing to meet expected
standards or values of reciprocity. The World Bank, by contrast,
count the remittances sent home by migrating carers as a positive
economic contribution to be encouraged; none of the downsides
passed on to other family members now missing schooling or
taking on extra roles are counted.

95   *a community-based service:* Lisa runs Together for Childhood, a
programme aimed at creating communities where children can
thrive. The programme originated and is funded by NSPCC, but
local leaders have considerable autonomy over the local design and
culture of the service.

95   *children removed by social services:* I have written about the distress
caused by the escalation in the rates at which children are removed
from low-income families in *Radical Help*, an escalation with complex roots that include changes in political priorities, our collective
economic fortunes and rising inequality. Polly Curtis has also
written *Behind Closed Doors*, an excellent, nuanced and forensic
account of British social care systems that remove children from
their families at rates higher than any other Western country, and
the devastating consequences for families and wider society. The
Child Welfare Inequalities Project found that if a child lived in
the top 10 per cent area of deprivation nationally, they were ten
times more likely to be taken into care or put on a national protection plan (ACS0006: Evidence on Local Authorities' Children's
Services, Parliament.uk). East Marsh ranks in the top 1 per cent
nationally on deprivation indices.

96   *There is abundant evidence:* See, for example, Garlow and Slaughter,
'A World View of Care and a New Economics'.

96   *nurturing the smaller businesses:* Across OECD countries, SMEs
(small and medium enterprises) account for an estimated 99 per
cent of all firms, are a main source of employment and generate 50 to 60 per cent of value added on average. 'SMEs and
Entrepreneurship', OECD.

96   *the Barrow Way:* The network has been pioneered by Trina
Robson the founder of Love Barrow Families, Rebecca Rawlings
of Women Community Matters and Dave Higham of the Well

alongside others in the community and local government, advocating for change locally through mechanisms such as the Poverty Truth Commission.

98 *The vision is robust:* Numerous studies show the power and affordability of networked community responses; the data includes an evaluation of WCM by the Tavistock Institute, funded by the National Lottery ('About the Women and Girls Initiative', Tavistock Institute) and the cost impact of the Barrow Way's 'grow your own' initiative, through which a third of staff and volunteers have been recruited locally from those who have previously been supported by the network ('Growing Our Own', Barrow Women's Community Matters); my own work with families (*Radical Help*, 2018); the pioneering work in Wigan on the Deal, evaluated by the King's Fund ('Lessons from the Wigan Deal', The King's Fund); and Mark A. Smith's work in Northumbria piloting 'the liberated method' ('The Liberated Method – Rethinking Public Services', Changing Futures Northumbria, 2023). It is striking and unfortunate that no study has been made that pulls this data together in a coherent national picture which would show the efficacy of this human and horizontal way of providing care in place.

98 *Dave Higham:* He tells his story in *Rat Hell to Rat Park*.

98 *county lines gang:* County lines refer to criminal networks which move drugs from city locations to smaller towns and rural areas. Children or vulnerable young adults are coerced into carrying the drugs so that those running the lines and the drug businesses are not exposed. In some cases, the dealers also take over a house of a vulnerable adult as an office for their operations. This is called 'cuckooing' – it is a practice widely seen in many of the neighbourhoods where I work. In 2023 the Children's Commissioner for England estimated that at least twenty-seven thousand children are involved in county lines, exposing them to abuse and extreme violence.

99 *absence of hierarchy:* The importance of creating support systems in which it is not clear who is offering and who needs help is something I have written about in *Radical Help*. Circle, the community network that supports older people, is successful because members both help each other and draw on help, encouraging everyone to

join in a culture that does not feel stigmatising and which therefore builds broad capability across all members.

100   *detailed, data-rich studies:* Ostrom, *Governing the Commons* and *Beyond Markets and States.*

101   *Ostrom's work has implications:* Ostrom used her findings to develop a set of guidelines for the design of institutions in which all resources, including the time and skills of workers, could be differently shared and owned. The Ostrom Workshop at Indiana University and the team at Radical Xchange, among others, have continued to work with and extend the possibilities of what is often called polycentric governance.

102   *up to eight preschool children:* In registered early years settings this ratio can be as high as 1 adult to 13 children. See 'Early Years Foundation Stage Statutory Framework', Department for Education, 11 October 2024.

102   *The activities at the core:* Cottam, *Radical Help*, p. 38.

102   *'Capitalism is a guzzler of care':* Fraser, *Cannibal Capitalism*, p. 53.

102   *Academic research shows:* Research conducted into the increasing private investment and control of the British care sector shows the resulting vulnerabilities which include chronic under-staffing, increasing wage differentials between staff and management, and the constant compromising of safety and care which are covered up. Walker et al., 'Held to Ransom'. The techniques cited were implicated in the collapse of two large UK care providers: Southern Cross in 2011 and Four Seasons Health Care in 2019. Independent Health Foundation data corroborates the links between the very low pay of care workers, ownership and staff turnover: Lucinda Allen, Skeena Williamson, Emma Berry and Hugh Alderwick, 'The Cost of Caring: Poverty and Deprivation Among Residential Care Workers in the UK', The Health Foundation, 11 October 2022.

102   *One pound in every five:* Carmen Aguilar García and Heather Stewart, 'Revealed: The Bumper Profits Taken by English Private Nursery Chains', *Guardian*, 12 March 2024; Diane Burns et al., 'Where Does the Money Go? Financialised Chains and the Crisis in Residential Care', CRESC Public Interest Report, March 2016.

104   *A national helpline:* Alison Holt, Judith Burns and Chris Bell,

'Modern Slavery Helpline Calls Surge from Care Staff', BBC News, 23 October 2023.

104 *'I am just a number': Exposed* is a film made by Black and brown British nurses. They narrate their shocking experience of nursing through the Covid-19 pandemic, in which deaths were much higher among lower-paid and Black workers in many industries including health and care. Their visceral sense of being disposable cogs in an industry without heart is repeated and again: 'Your body is tolerated, your value is economic'; 'I'm just a number'; 'If anything happens to me, it won't be long until they find another'.

104 *'Racial outsourcing':* Wingfield, *Flatlining.*

106 *A Buurtzorg client requires:* Data from a 2009 Ernst & Young evaluation of Buurtzorg cited in Laloux, *Reinventing Organizations.*

107 *implemented in twenty-four countries:* In the UK, attempts to apply the principles of the model have struggled because NHS systems and organisations have failed to consistently enable and support teams to work with the level of managerial and budgetary autonomy and responsibility required. 'Transforming Integrated Care in the Community: Project Results', Public World.

111 *nature and local fabric:* This repeated emphasis on the need to care for nature is distinguished carefully from 'environmentalism' that is frequently seen by participants as 'just another stick to beat us with', or 'something that belongs to those people in London that earn over a hundred grand'.

111 *Care is not invisible:* The feminist Nancy Folbre has long argued that the crisis in care is rooted in the invisibility of the work – work of the 'invisible heart', as I referred to in the last chapter. This phrase is also the title of one of Folbre's books.

112 *Root shock:* Mindy Thompson Fullilove first used the term to describe the traumatic experience faced by Black people who have periodically been displaced from their homes and their communities. The British geographer John Tomaney has borrowed the term to describe the displacement and sense of social abandonment that came with the closure of the mines in his home region of County Durham.

114 *to mend people and things:* Exploring care and repair, I have met many working this way, among them Rabab Ghazoul in Cardiff,

part of the Gentle Radical collective whose projects include Turner Prize-nominated artwork at the Tate, and Al Mish'aal, a place that invites local people to share a meal and an experience as a way of making many who feel left out in a rapidly gentrifying city heard, seen and whole.

114   *a so-called storm chaser:* Sarah Stillman, 'The Migrant Workers Who Follow Climate Disasters', *New Yorker*, 1 November 2021.

115   *Saket's success:* Saket's work as a union organiser is deeply inspiring. It's a story he tells in his own book, *The Great Escape*, which reads both as a thriller and as a how-to guide for organisers in this new economy.

115   *possibility in this new and vast economy:* In the current disaster economy, community assets and the ownership of land on which damaged homes once stood is frequently bundled together with the requirements for repair and transferred to the global corporations who win the repair contracts. This loss of rights occurs most frequently in historically low-income neighbourhoods, where housing stock is poor and the damage tends to be greatest, while documents may be missing and many are uninsured. The corporates are free to demolish what remains, and developers are invited in to replace it with high-end housing.

115   *Such thinking:* In the United States, the Holding Co. have drawn attention to the size of the care economy in a similar way, valuing care at $648 billion, 'larger than the US pharmaceutical market and the US hotel, car manufacturing, and social networking industries combined', an argument that persuaded the Biden administration to see care as critical infrastructure that needed investment, as opposed to economic cost to the economy. 'Care is the Next Big Frontier', The Holding Co.

116   *the 'care-plus' economy:* Slaughter and Cottam, 'We Need a New Economic Category'.

116   *In my own work:* I tell the story of Circle in *Radical Help*.

Principle Four: Time – Rethinking it Top to Bottom

120   *Such timepieces:* For example, in *Tess of the D'Urbervilles*, Thomas Hardy tells us how Tess still lived in a world where one-handed

clocks divided the day. Time was passed not spent: it was time to fish if the tide was right, while harvesting a field was measured by the how many men would be needed for the task, not the hours it would take them. 'Spellowe [a field] can be harvested by four indifferent day workers,' records the historian E. P. Thompson in his famous essay 'Time, Work-Discipline, and Industrial Capitalism'.

120 *Sociological Department:* In 1915 Ford renamed it the Education Department in a more explicit recognition that he was 'producing the human product' – the worker – in the same way as he was producing the machines. Freeman, *Behemoth*, p. 130.

120 *'a new type of man':* Gramsci, *Selections from the Prison Notebooks*, no. 22.

122 *The six-hour day:* The story of the Kellogg's Six-Hour Day is told by Benjamin Kline Hunnicutt in *Kellogg's Six-Hour Day*. This fascinating history also includes data from the worker household surveys which I draw on below. Kellogg's experiment was in part influenced by the drive to 'Share the Work' in a global downturn, later overturned by Roosevelt's New Deal – described by Hunnicutt, as the triumph of welfare capitalism and 'jobs, jobs, jobs'. Kellogg described his own experiment as 'liberation capitalism'. He was much influenced by the Lancastrian soap magnate Lord Leverhulme, who would build a model worker town at Port Sunlight. Leverhulme believed that work should 'bring a sufficiency in wages … and such a sufficiency it leaves leisure for things of the soul' (cited in Hunnicutt, *Kellogg's Six Hour Day*, p. 29).

123 *Keynes had just predicted:* J. M. Keynes, 'Economic Possibilities for our Grandchildren' (1930), in *Essays in Persuasion* (New York: Harcourt Brace, 1932).

125 *The future is already here:* Attributed to William Gibson, the American speculative fiction writer.

125 *began to pilot a four-day working week:* Jasper Jolly, 'A Hundred UK Companies Sign Up for Four-Day Week with No Loss of Pay', *Guardian*, 27 November 2022.

126 *An evaluation led in Britain: The Results Are In: The UK's Four-Day Week Pilot*, Autonomy Research Ltd, 2023. The report details the different approaches taken to the four-day design (staggered weeks, one day of closure, de-centred). It also notes that the design process

itself leads to improvement in productivity as working processes were reviewed; most companies were able to reduce the number of meetings, improve their email etiquette and so on. One thing that did not work was for the CEO to dictate use of new 'non-work' time: companies for example that expected their employees to join corporate volunteering were disappointed; workers used the time for their own life designs.

126   *Ninety-two per cent:* The 8 per cent who did not continue with the working week piloted as part of the formal, evaluated experiment have mostly continued to trial other flexible policies. Only three companies in total in the experiment did not continue reduced working hours in some form.

126   *'desirable to achievable':* The authors' conviction that the four-day week is achievable is partly rooted in this study but also the evidence they have gathered from private and public sector experiments further afield (for example Microsoft in Japan, Unilever in New Zealand and the government of Valencia in Spain) and the growth in business productivity data collected by respected business sources such as Henley Business School (see 'The Four-Day Week: The Pandemic and the Evolution of Flexible Working' white paper).

127   *The US military:* Schulte, *Overwhelmed*, p. 109.

127   *Eighty-eight per cent: Going Public: Iceland's Journey to a Shorter Working Week*, Autonomy Ltd, June 2021.

128   *If we are rich:* See 'Carbon Billionaires: The Investment Emissions of the World's Richest People' Oxfam Policy & Practice briefing note, 7 November 2022. Michael Goldstein, 'Billionaires' Tears: Will Climate Protestors Cancel the $28 Billion Private Jet Business?', *Forbes*, 16 November 2022.

128   *triple dividend:* I borrow the term from the sociologist Judith Schor, who has researched the social and ecological benefits of shorter working weeks over decades (see, for example, *Plenitude*) and was part of the academic team evaluating the most recent UK and US four-day week experiment referred to above. In this experiment companies were asked to monitor their energy usage because previous smaller trials have shown that work energy consumption reduces. Unfortunately, given the range of

companies in size and function it was not possible to get comparative metrics.

130 *Some academics argue:* The economist Nicholas Crafts, for example, concluded that Keynes's predictions have been exceeded, given extended periods of retirement (see 'The 15-Hour Week').

130 *will rarely live long enough:* Marmot et al., *Health Equity in England*. As discussed in the opening chapters, the pattern in the UK and the US is similar, with life expectancy declining in lower-income groups and in particular in the US for minority ethnic groups: Elizabeth Arias, Betzaida Tejada-Vera, Kenneth Kochanek and Farida B. Ahmad, 'Provisional Life Expectancy Estimates for 2021', NVSS Vital Statistics Rapid Release report no. 23, August 2022. The link between work and declining health has led to public health leaders in both countries attempting to define good work.

130 *time forcibly taken from him:* Elizabeth Cohen has argued that exploding our temporal mindsets and re-allocating time is necessary and would be significant in addressing inequality and injustice. She documents the ways that injustice compounds as time incarcerated for example leads to missed schooling and work experience which is never made up in *The Political Value of Time*. My own previous work shows how those who are financially poor have their time taken from them by the state in other ways: forced queueing and the laborious form filling required to access welfare benefits is just one example.

130 *In Baltimore, more than half:* The United States culture of mass industrialised incarceration penalises young Black men from poor neighbourhoods. One in three Black Baltimoreans in prison come from one of ten neighbourhoods. 'Baltimore City, and Other Black Communities in Maryland, Disproportionately Harmed by Alarming Rates of Incarceration', Justice Policy Institute press release, 27 June 2022.

131 *according to data:* 'Health State Life Expectancies by National Deprivation Deciles, England: 2018 to 2020', Census 2021, Office of National Statistics.

133 *Home Link team:* The proposal was for truancy officers based in social services, but community insight and participation led to a

new role based out of schools (and therefore not feared) and on support, not judgement. Almost three hundred pupils and their families are supported annually, with 50 per cent of pupils needing no ongoing support, having fully reintegrated into school.

134 *an effective anti-truancy policy:* Data provided by East Ayrshire Council Education Services show that of the children truanting in 2023/24, more than 60 per cent no longer need support.

134 *Gorz advocated:* Gorz, *Reclaiming Work.*

135 *found support on the left and the right:* Guy Standing, a long-time advocate of UBI, has written a short history and argument in favour of the policy (*Basic Income*, 2017), while more recently, in *Welfare for Markets*, a wide-ranging and historical review of all cash transfer programmes and advocates, Anton Jager and Daniel Zamora Vargas have argued that the idea represents the rise of the 'transfer state', an alliance of interests which include the California digital elites, who hope to use state transfers to keep wages low and the work force flexible, as opposed to advocating for a reimagined society.

135 *seems impossible to implement:* In the UK, research undertaken by the RSA in 2020 costed a UBI blueprint demonstrating that an income of £5,000/year to every UK household (and replacing the universal credit welfare payment, but not housing, childcare subsidies or payments for disability) would cost £90 billion, a significant sum for an income that would in no way provide enough for an individual to live on. Alan Lockey and Fabian Wallace-Stephens, *A Blueprint for Good Work: Eight Ideas for a New Social Contract*, RSA, June 2020. More targeted schemes (closer to the cash transfer definitions used by Jager and Zamora Vargas in *Welfare for Markets*) have been successful: for example, in Wales young people leaving care have been provided with a cash income which an interim evaluation showed had positive outcomes (a full evaluation is expected in 2027). 'The Welsh Basic Income Pilot for Care Leavers: A Look at the First Interim Results', Autonomy Ltd, March 2024.

138 *draw a Tardis:* TARDIS stands for Time and Relative Dimension in Space. In the TV programme, the time-travelling doctor enters a blue police telephone box (designed in the 1960s) to travel across space-time, intervening in history on the side of the oppressed.

Doctor Who was first commissioned in 1963, with the most recent series expected to premiere in 2025.

140 *When white settlers arrived:* As told in Kimmerer, *Braiding Sweetgrass*, p. 181.

141 *This is the conclusion:* Gratton and Scott, *The One Hundred Year Life.*

142 *We often literally cannot hear or see:* Readers who are not convinced should take Harvard's selective attention test, designed by academics Daniel Simons and Christopher Chabris, which is easily found on YouTube.

143 *In Sweden:* Maddy Savage, 'What Really Happened When Swedes Tried Six-Hour Days?', BBC News, 8 February 2017.

Principle Five: Play – A Precarious Magic

145 *Javier is a 'dreamer':* The term 'dreamer' originally referred to the Development, Relief, and Education for Alien Minors (DREAM) Act, a piece of legislation that was intended to give immigrant youth legal status and a path to citizenship.

145 *DACA:* The DACA process was designed by President Obama in 2012 as a stop-gap solution: Dreamers would get work permits and other status such as health insurance, while their papers were processed. The scheme was frozen in 2021 after a federal judge in Texas ruled the programme illegal.

147 *'the "deprived child" is notoriously restless':* Winnicott, *Playing and Reality*, p. 101.

148 *'Is there a sphere of human activity':* Pieper's treatise was published in English in 1965 with an introduction by T. S. Eliot.

148 *'the capacity to steep oneself':* Pieper, *Leisure, the Basis of Culture*, p. 43.

148 *developed and continues to advance:* The internet was originally developed by the US military and the links between the military, games and ongoing technology development continues. It is widely recognised that the war in Ukraine which started in 2022 has provided unique opportunities for the military and private sector companies to develop their AI capabilities.

148 *Stewart Brand:* Brand was the founder of the *Whole Earth Catalog*, which Apple founder Steve Jobs memorably likened to Google, the place where the first digital generation could find articles on

everything counter-cultural. Brand is reputed to have put the 'personal' into personal computing and was influential in steering technology investment in the early decades, as recounted by Margaret O'Mara in *The Code*, her history of Silicon Valley.

149   *game designers have widely reported troubles:* Finding paid work in the game industry is also reputed to be hard. Employers capitalise on a ready supply of new recruits eager to 'do what they love'. There is a famed crunch around release dates, when for three months of the year, twenty-hour days can be the norm. Interestingly, a UK game company participated in the four-day working week experiment described in Principle Four: Time.

150   *may also be offered 'challenges':* Sarah Mason, in *Chasing the Pink*, writes from the inside about her experience of driving for Lyft, about the long history of gamification and about the ways in which the stakes are raised by customers who may not realise the devastating consequences of their actions such as giving a low rating.

152   *Poets, artists, former miners:* Fitties 'residents' include the eco-poet Harriet Tarlo, artists such as Anabel McCourt and, until her tragic death in a road accident in 2023, Judith Tucker, Robert Wyatt, founder of Soft Machine, and of course Sarah herself. I am very grateful to Sarah for sharing all her knowledge on the history of the Fitties – I hope that she will write a book about the social history of this beautiful and fascinating spit of land.

152   *not well known:* Although the Fitties are not a secret and are today in a form of peril. The council has sold the land to a private corporation and the future is uncertain, while the growth of Airbnb means that chalet rentals can make significant sums for owners, attracting new investment and a new sort of owner. The cumulative result is that the cost of chalets has increased tenfold in the last decade, threatening to make the Fitties a place out for financial reach for local people.

154   *EMU are organising:* EMU use Ethex, an online platform that crowdsources investment from a very wide community who want to put their capital to good use. Investments start at a very low level – I am myself an investor in EMU – demonstrating a new form of social economy in action.

154   *bought Grimsby Town Football Club:* Jason Stockwood has written

about his motivations for buying the football club: 'We Bought Grimsby Town FC to Help Renew the Place We Love', *Guardian*, 29 June 2021.

155 *projects of the Grimsby artists:* Lucy Neal, like many in the climate movement, sees the ecological crisis as a crisis of the imagination. See, for example, Ghosh, *The Nutmeg's Curse* and Vanessa Machado, *Hospicing Modernity*. Both write about stories and the imagination and their importance for a liveable future. The environmentalist Tim Jackson is interested in the transcendent experience that can happen when we become immersed in things we enjoy. He notes in particular that a feeling of being lost in nature or of an unexpected natural encounter (both highly valued in the Imaginings), can be a catalyst for new ways of being in the world. Also making a clear distinction between distraction and what he calls 'social snacking', Jackson suggests that we might try to reach immersive and imaginative states more intentionally through practices such as meditation or through guided experimentation with psychedelics. He believes that these intense experiences are required to imagine change in our world, in particular new ways of living and collaborating that connect to and foster a care for our environment. (See Elf and Jackson, 'Self-Transcendent Experience and Sustainable Prosperity'.)

156 *'Mom spends beach vacation':* The Onion, August 2013. The article tends to appear with some regularity in summer social media memes.

157 *play 'for its own sake':* Brown, *Play*, p. 30. The psychologist and neuroscientist Alison Gopnik makes a similar argument in her book *The Gardener and the Carpenter* (2016), arguing that play has a developmental role across species and that parenting in the US would gain from being less results driven and more open to unstructured play, which would additionally bring joy to parents and children.

157 *In Abrams's study:* Abrams, *The Playful Self.*

157 *'It matters who imagines':* In *Staying with the Trouble*, p. 12, drawing on the work of anthropologist Marilyn Strathern, Haraway writes, 'It matters who imagines. It matters what matters we use to think other matters with; it matters what stories we tell to tell other

stories with: it matters what knots knot knots, what thoughts think thoughts, what descriptions describe descriptions, what ties tie ties. It matters what stories make worlds, what worlds make stories.'

158   *creative thinking and IQ:* Hopkins, *From What Is to What If*, p. 9. In his book and on an accompanying podcast, Rob Hopkins, one of the founders of the Transition Movement, looks at both the science of imagining and at social pioneers who have transformed their places through imaginative experiments.

159   *find it hard to tell a story:* Ibid., p. 85.

159   *In the ancient world:* The Dutch historian and cultural theorist Johan Huizinga drew on this ancient philosophy in his development of the human template *Homo Ludens* (1938), arguing that play is the foundation of culture and therefore human society.

Principle Six: Organising in Place

163   *Dani Rodrik has argued:* See, for example, Rodrik, 'An Industrial Policy for Good Jobs', and Rodrik and Stantcheva, 'Fixing Capitalism's Good Jobs Problem'.

164   *Isabella Weber has stated:* @IsabellaMWeber, X, 8 November 2024.

165   *drew inspiration from earlier struggles:* Trade unions were legalised in 1872. Chartism was a national working-class protest movement of the nineteenth century, pressing for the vote in a succession of protests which were violently suppressed by government. The Chartists also explicitly fought wage cuts and waves of unemployment which came with new forms of industrialisation. Robert Owen was a Welsh textile manufacturer turned social campaigner who advocated for the cooperative movement and fought for the ideals of decent housing, regulated working days, universal education and an end to child labour.

166   *The twentieth-century trade union:* Using the schema developed by Frédéric Laloux in his book *Reinventing Organisations*, we can characterise the twentieth-century union as 'Amber': formal, top-down, hierarchical, stable; the Houses in contrast are closer to 'Teal'; highly participatory, based on trust and rooted in organic everyday change.

167   *learning is a real promise:* It is important to note that twentieth-century

trade unions previously played a strong role in providing diverse forms of learning and its esteem.

167 *good green jobs:* Sebastian Payne, 'Grimsby's Green Revolution is a Model for Other Towns Post-Pandemic', *Financial Times*, 24 November 2020. In his book *Class Work*, Peter Rowley, a former Grimsby school teacher, looks at the challenges of linking the promised regional green energy revolution to local people; school leavers talk to him about the challenge of education but also of the social infrastructure that is missing and could provide routes from the East Marsh into new work.

167 *'Really learning':* In the United States the educationalist Jamie Merisotis uses the term 'wide learning', which I really like and is similar to the Imagineers phrase 'really learning'. Wide learning requires time, designs that include a wide range of people and new content. See Merisotis, *Human Work in the Age of Smart Machines*.

168 *the G.I. Bill:* The United States' Servicemen's Readjustment Act, 1944. James Plunkett tells the story of this bill in his book *End State*. In 1946 Harvard enrolment doubled as a result and by 1948 national college enrolments stood at over two million with veterans (6 per cent of the population) making up 40 per cent of admissions.

169 *'houses of the people':* The history is told in *Radical Space*, Margaret Kohn's fascinating study of the Italian houses of the people. Many of Kohn's ideas and discoveries reappear in Eric Klinenberg's *Palaces for the People*, although I am not sure if Klinenberg is aware of Kohn's earlier and brilliant work.

171 *'They thought, this was it':* The story of the Vickers workers and their remarkable plan is told in Beynon and Wainwright, *The Workers' Report on Vickers*.

172 *The ideas were taken up:* Mike Cooley, a design engineer and union leader at Lucas Aerospace, was inspired by the Workers' Report and led a participative process at Lucas which resulted in the Plan for Socially Useful Production – known as the Lucas Plan. This plan also re-purposed technology for social good with strong supporting business plans. Lucas's management and board saw Cooley as 'dangerous' and ejected him from the company in 1981. He moved to work for Ken Livingstone, the leader of the Greater London

Council, who effectively had a live laboratory within the city of alternative techno-industrial development (eventually closed down by Margaret Thatcher, for whom it was not politically expedient). Cooley tells his own fascinating story in his semi-autobiographical book *Architect or Bee?*. The London Industrial Strategy was published by the Greater London Council in 1985, setting out a worker-led vision for industrial transformation.

173 *Reuther proposed:* The story of the Reuther Plan is told by Nelson Lichtenstein in his biography of Walter Reuther, on which I have drawn.

174 *new coalitions with new tactics:* Sharon Graham, leader of Unite, the public sector workers' union, has made gains for members through a new strategy she calls 'leverage': a forensic examination of private sector contracts and shareholder payouts which enable her team to find the spaces in which she can argue for salary and other worker gains. Mick Lynch at the RMT (the transport union) has made himself into something of a folk hero through his ability to talk seriously about the social and economic challenges the nation is facing, in contrast to politicians alongside him, many of whom seem unable to answer a straight question. IWGB, started in 2012 by a group of Latin American cleaners fighting for better pay and conditions, has since expanded to include thousands of members, many of whom are in precarious gig work. IWGB is an example of a grassroots organising model with campaigns organised by members in response to specific challenges. In the United States, Amazon warehouse JFK8 on Staten Island made history in 2022 when, against all odds, including aggressive and intimidating tactics on the part of Amazon, over 2,500 workers came together to form a union. Not surprisingly, the path since has not been smooth, but their victory inspired workers at other big US companies, including McDonald's. In Britain almost a third of Imaginings participants were union members, above the national average of 22 per cent. In the United States fewer participants were union members.

179 *a new organisational path:* There is a new generation of organisers working in this way who include Ai-Jen Poo, founder of the National Domestic Workers Alliance mentioned in a previous

chapter, Hind El-Idrissi, the founder of WeMind in France, and Michelle Miller, the co-founder of Co-Worker, who use digital tools to organise locally around very specific locally driven agendas.

176 *close local networks:* Erica Smiley tells the story of her own journey and of this exciting new form of organising in a book she has co-authored with Sarita Gupta, titled *The Future We Need.* In the book, Smiley and Gupta argue that the idea of collective bargaining needs to be extended into all areas of social and economic life in order to allow workers to flourish but also to effectively design good work in the face of new economic contexts.

179 *a basic safety net:* Sidney Hillman, one of the most inspiring early union organisers, included these ideas in his organising at Amalgamated Clothing Workers of America. He set his sights high, not content simply to win protection for his workers; he wanted to know what else they needed, which led to support for housing, healthcare and education as well as loan schemes. Sara calls Sidney Hillman 'a gifted mutualist'; this was the model she wanted to build on. I am drawing on Sara's excellent book *Mutualism,* which is an immensely readable manual for anyone wanting to explore mutuals in more depth, and on more recent conversations and collaborations with Sara.

180 *characteristics that made them mutualist:* With the important exception of two participants in Mexicantown, Detroit, where I was hosted by a local church helping set up cooperatives. Dulce Detroit, a cooperative care business, was founded by four church members, one of whose sisters joined me at the Imagining. Primo worked for the Equitable Internet Initiative, a community owned business providing affordable internet to the local community.

181 *'Employers are the same':* Erica Smiley, 'The Great Awakening, and Workers' Fight to Stay Woke', *Nonprofit Quarterly Magazine* (summer 2023).

182 *Today power is more diffuse:* In 2018 two social entrepreneurs, Jeremy Heimans and Henry Timms, wrote a widely read book, *New Power.* Old power, they argued, works like a currency: it's held by a few and once owned is hoarded. New power, by contrast, operates like a current: it's made by many and is most forceful

when it surges (like school strikes against climate change), and is collaboratively channelled. It has become clear that old and new power are competing today; both are still shaping our future. At the Imaginings I perceived participants to be acutely aware of these two worlds and trying to feel a realistic way forward.

183 *A white core:* The flourishing economy of Baltimore's centre is commonly referred to as 'ed, meds and feds', a shorthand for the opportunities in education and medicine which centre on Johns Hopkins and professional work within federal agencies that have often relocated to Baltimore because of its lower real estate costs (for housing and offices) within proximity to Washington D.C. Resident author and journalist Alex MacGillis refers to this as the 'Baltimore bargain', the dividend that pays out to largely white middle-class professionals who can take advantage of opportunities in a city which are not open to its largely Black and poorer long term residents: 'My Baltimore Bargain', *Slate*, 4 May 2015.

183 *In the Black wings:* Baltimore scholar and urban futurist Lawrence T. Brown has described the city as a black butterfly: the majority Black population squeezed out to the city's wings, while an affluent minority white population occupy the centre ground. Greenmount Avenue, where Open Works is located, runs through the butterfly's thorax. East Side neighbourhoods have a life expectancy which averages ten years less that of their affluent white West Side neighbours.

184 *face a bitter choice:* Alec MacGillis has written a powerful book, *Fulfillment*, about Amazon and Amazon workers which spools out from his hometown of Baltimore to tell a global story.

185 *felt alien to her at first:* David Graeber called this 'interpretative labour' noting that the lower you are in any hierarchy of class or race, the more work you have to do to read and navigate your superiors; inequality heightens the work that has to be done (Graeber and Wengrow, *The Dawn of Everything*, p. 1095).

186 *his own space flight:* Rushkoff, *Survival of the Richest*, p. 175. Rushkoff calls this Silicon Valley escapism 'the Mindset'. Technology entrepreneurs with unprecedented and unimaginable wealth are, he argues, afraid of nature (and women). They assume the world will become unliveable and they are certain that they can somehow

develop a technology that will break with the laws of physics and offer them an individual means of escape.

187 *They colonise space:* The sociologist Mike Savage has argued that empire is capitalism's dominant form, and each time empire grows in new ways (*The Return of Inequality*). The escapist tendencies of today's figures such as Musk and Bezos can be understood within his historical frame as a logical extension of business as usual: if earth's own natural resources have already been ruthlessly colonised and extracted, it makes sense to look elsewhere. 'It's just mathematics,' as Bezos would say (quoted in MacGillis, *Fulfillment*, p. 315).

189 *Sara Breedlove:* Breedlove's story is now widely known through the Netflix biopic *Madam Walker* and her original products can be seen in the National Museum of African American History and Culture in Washington DC.

191 *servers parked in Arizona:* Microsoft, for example, own servers in Arizona that provide 174 jobs but whose power requirements are draining scarce water resources from the Sonoran Desert, where a drying Colorado River basin is already causing problems for the local populations, as reported by both the *Atlantic* and the *Daily Mail* in March 2024. Karen Hao, 'AI is Taking Water from the Desert', *Atlantic*, 1 March 2024; Isabelle Stanley, 'Huge Microsoft Plant is Draining Tiny Arizona Town of its Water Supply to Power AI and Cloud Development – With Locals Furious Tech Giant is Redacting its Figures in City's Records', *Daily Mail*, 17 March 2024. Workers for big corporates are of course aware of these stories and the dissonance (Microsoft claims it is committed to being carbon neutral despite its intense power and water demands) contributes to worker feelings that their work lacks meaning.

192 *the concept of* restanza: In Wales the idea of *restanza* has been explored by the Foundational Alliance with the residents of Blaenau Gwent, a place of nineteenth-century slate mining. Together these scholars and residents have created one of the most exciting worker-owned economies in Britain. Lowri Cunnington Wynn, Julie Froud and Karel Williams, 'A Way Ahead? Empowering Restanza in a Slate Valley', Foundational Economy Research Ltd, 1 March 2022.

192   *Staying behind:* These are ideas prominent in much feminist writ-
      ing, where the idea that the 'margins' are the place of creativity
      and productivity is frequently explored to important political
      effect, for example bell hooks's book *Feminist Theory from Margin
      to Center*, which proposes a transformation of society rooted in the
      experience of Black feminists whose experience has been left out
      of accounts of both feminism and capitalism, galvanised readers
      at the time of publication and has found a new audience in recent
      years.

Designing the Just Transition

199   *'I was constantly astonished':* Terkel, *Working.*
199   *'It's becoming harder':* Speaking at the British Academy on
      'Technology, Innovation and Long-Term Prosperity', Technology
      and the Future of Labour: Historical and Contemporary
      Perspectives conference, March 2022. The teams needed to get to
      innovation frontiers are bigger and graduate students are taking
      longer, he explained.
200   *Biologists and social psychologists:* I have already discussed (Principle
      Two) the important work of the biologist Dennis Noble who has
      shown that humans are not genetically determined machines, and
      the work of social psychologist Cecilia Heyes, who has shown how
      what we think is the product of the collective mind. The philos-
      opher Martha Nussbaum has long argued that social institutions
      shape our character and values, and it is clear that the 'houses' are
      designed with a different, collectively minded human at the centre.
201   *among many others:* Such is the current flourishing of heterodox
      economics there are many important scholars who could be in-
      cluded and this list is far from exhaustive, but other names include
      the Bristol-based Daniela Gabor; Stephanie Kelton, whose modern
      monetary theory argues that we can reconceive investment; Michel
      Bauwens, who has pioneered new thinking on the commons in his
      'peer to peer' work; Heather Boushey, who has re-shaped think-
      ing on the economy of care; and Sam Bowles and Wendy Carlin,
      whose CORE teaching tools are used worldwide to support the
      rethinking of economics teaching, as are the British economists

working for Rethinking Economics. It seems notable that women are at the forefront of a new economics but that the discipline still has a race problem, with scholars of post-colonialism, for example, more often choosing to make their critical arguments within the fields of cultural studies or sociology. Organisations such as The Black Economists Network in the UK work to champion Black economists and draw attention to the lack of diversity in the field. In the United States, influential Black economists working at the intersection of work and justice include Darrick Hamilton and the labour economists Valerie Wilson and Ellora Derenoncourt.

201 *developed the concept of Doughnut Economics:* Raworth, *Doughnut Economics.* DEAL (Doughnut Economics Action Lab) is helping cities put the principles into action.

202 *as measured by GDP:* GDP does not include the value of finite natural resources in its accounting and does include destructive activity such as war (see ibid.).

202 *a new economics of place:* Coyle, *GDP.* Many have experimented with alternative metrics to GDP. See, for example, the Social Progress Index and the Ethical Prosperity Index; the SAGE dashboard was developed by Dennis Snower and Katharina Lima de Miranda: Dennis Snower, 'Measuring Prosperity Ethically', *Global Solutions Journal,* 9 (November 2023). In the United States, the government has helped develop a seven 'healthy' signs framework (see 'Seven Vital Conditions for Health and Well-Being', Community Commons), and the governments of France and Canada, as well as the Catholic Church (through the Economy of Francesco), have advocated for alternative frameworks that centre human capabilities and flourishing. To date, no alternative framework has been able to dislodge GDP, which like *Homo economicus* is in need of an affectionate but timely burial.

202 *challenges our ideas:* Mazzucato, *The Value of Everything.*

204 *'Attachment is central':* See Jessica Prendergrast: 'Attachment Economics: Everyday Pioneers for the Next Economy', Medium, 10 May 2021; 'Liminal Economics: Swimming at the Edge of the Economy', Medium, 31 October 2023.

205 *Satya Nadella:* Nadella emigrated from India to the US at the age of twenty-one and joined Microsoft in 1992, which he describes as 'a

company filled with people who believed they were on a mission to change the world' (Nadella, *Hit Refresh*).

206 *I asked Nadella:* This conversation, which took place at the World Economic Forum meeting in Davos, included Satya Nadella and his former classmate Ajay Banga, who was at the time leading Mastercard.

208 *commonplace in other European countries:* Worker representation on boards is common in Germany and Scandinavia, and is widely understood as an important factor in innovation and business success. In Sweden, unions' strong, proactive and creative role on boards is credited as an important factor in the reversal of deep economic inequality, as documented by Piketty and discussed earlier in this book.

208 *Peter Drucker used to ask the CEOs:* Thank you to Stefan Stern for sharing this anecdote with me.

209 *'just talk':* Mazzucato, *The Value of Everything*.

209 *worker share of ownership:* Marjorie Kelly has written a fascinating study of the ownership revolution, *Owning Our Future*.

209 *'I asked a supermarket buyer':* Emma Weinbren, 'Guy Singh-Watson: Riverford's Veg Boxer Comes Out Swinging', *Grocer*, 25 February 2022.

210 *In the UK:* 'Would you Sell Your Business to Your Staff?', *Financial Times*, 16 February 2023. Employee Ownership Trusts established in 2014 incentivise owners by offering a write off of capital gains tax (currently taxed at 20 per cent in the UK) if a stake of at least 50 per cent is sold to workers. Businesses that have so far successfully transitioned to worker ownership range from commercial cleaning companies to nursery and after-school care providers.

210 *research shows employee-owned businesses:* Emma Bell and Charles Barthold, 'Managing Employee Ownership Transitions for Sustainability in Food and Farming Enterprises: Learning from Riverford', Open University, 2024. See also, for example, Storey and Salaman's evaluation of John Lewis, the employee-owned department store, in 'Employee Ownership and the Drive to Do Business Responsibly' and research on the productivity of employee-owned businesses: 'New Data Shows Employee Owned Businesses Deliver an 8–12% Productivity Boost', University of Stirling, 19 October 2023.

211 *'left behind':* My own view is that the portrait of the Basque region (Euskadi) as left behind is to misunderstand the region's complex political and economic history. Euskadi has an extremely strong fiscal base, with Spain's biggest energy provider Iberdrola and the multinational BBVA (Banco Bilbao Vizcaya Argentaria) domiciled in the region for tax purposes, and a strong settlement with the Madrid government which enables the region to retain approximately 70 per cent of taxes raised. Strong investment in business innovation and welfare has been critical to the region's success, which has included an emphasis on a fair economy with strong benefits to rural areas which it can justifiably be argued were previously economically 'left behind'. Mondragon, started in the 1960s by a local parish priest and a handful of workers who shared his vision of a differently designed future, has been a critical element in this success.

211 *One of the defining features of Mondragon:* To put this in context, companies registered on the Spanish IBEX market index average a 1:77 ratio between top- and bottom-income earners. A FTSE 100 chief executive in the UK earns 120 times the *average* earner, while in the US in 2022, it was estimated that the CEO-to-worker compensation ratio was 1:344 (www.statista.com).

211 *Funds have been used:* The distribution of profit is complex and included dividends to workers, the investment of 60 per cent net profit in research and investment, subventions to businesses in the group who may not have performed so well and a 10 per cent return to society, the latter governed by Basque law.

211 *The result is a capital market:* It's important here to draw a contrast with what is called social finance, which aims to leverage private capital to invest in social and environmental projects. In the social finance model the culture of private capital also transfers. Social finance enables some to attract investment who might otherwise struggle to find capital themselves in financial markets, but the terms of the loans are not dissimilar to those in private capital markets, which can make it difficult to grow new forms of work.

212 *'good business structures':* Christina Clamp and Michael Peck have published a collaborative handbook which looks at the global diffusion of Mondragon's ideas and similarly emphasises that

it is values married to sound business structures that make the difference.

213 *'Greed is dead':* Collier wrote a book of the same title with John Kay in 2020.

213 *a little previous:* It is estimated that billionaires added $5 trillion to their personal wealth during the pandemic alone.

213 *The production of billionaires:* Examples include the fortunes which have accrued to many technology titans in the US and UK figures, including Guy Hands, who has been a significant owner of the UK care system and who is a tax exile. Hands's companies are widely perceived to evade the payment of minimum wages to their staff. (See, for example, Mazzucato, *The Value of Everything*, p. 169.)

213 *consumption patterns:* According to research by Oxfam, 'the investments of just 125 billionaires emit 393 million tonnes of CO2 each year – the equivalent of France – at an individual annual average that is a million times higher than someone in the bottom 90 per cent of humanity'. 'Richest 1% Emit As Much Planet-Heating Pollution as Two-Thirds of Humanity – Oxfam', Oxfam GB Media Centre press release, 20 November 2023. Even among the extremely wealthy there is a growing pressure for change with groups such as the Patriotic Millionaires in the US lobbying for a more progressive tax regime.

213 *so called 'patriotic millionaires':* Patriotic Millionaires describe themselves as 'greedy for another country'.

214 *we see both forms of business growing:* For example, the Rockefellers, whose Standard Oil business was broken up by the US State into thirty-four separate companies in recognition of the unfair competition and practices the family monopoly represented.

214 *a dynamic state:* As Martin Wolf recognised in his book *The Crisis of Democratic Capitalism* (2017), a dynamic and democratic public policy should support the creation of work organisations.

214 *trust in government is at an all-time low:* Data, including UK data for Professor John Curtice, 'Trust and Confidence in Britain's System of Government at Record Low', National Centre for Social Research, 12 June 2024, and long-run data sets of the Edelman Trust Barometer in the UK and US.

215 *creating the forms of mission:* Mariana Mazzucato has led the field in

arguing for a mission approach to government and setting out what this means in terms of vision and structures: see *Mission Economy*.

215 *overly centralised bureaucratic model:* Britain is the most centralised state in modern Europe (see Collier, *Left Behind*). The Treasury Green Book drives all UK investment decisions and makes it almost impossible to invest outside the south-east of the country, much less in ways that communities and workers require, because the projected rates of return outside this region/model are not competitive according to the algorithm used.

216 *already offered clear analysis and advice:* Sam Bowles and Wendy Carlin, for example, have set out a compelling argument for the decline of current models of politics, suggesting a future model rooted in dignity, voice and the ethics of solidarity. In terms of reform of the mechanics, institutions and operating systems of government, see, for example, the work of Rainer Kattel and Rachel Coldicutt in the UK and in the US Jennifer Pahlka who, on the first page of her book *Re-Coding America,* implores public servants everywhere 'not to give up' in their quest to provide the public digital infrastructure on which so much else depends.

217 *force through an energy transition:* The influx of cheap North Sea oil, starting in the late 1970s, made possible a British energy transition and a Conservative government-in-waiting drew up plans for what was euphemistically called a 'national recovery'. National industries and no longer profitable coal mines were closed, bringing devastating mass unemployment.

217 *the Conservative government's own paper on levelling up: Levelling Up in the United Kingdom,* HM Government white paper, 2 February 2022.

218 *'leading humanitarians of their age':* Williams, *Capitalism and Slavery*.

218 *tracks the ambivalence and incoherence:* Williams is particularly scathing about William Wilberforce, who was 'addicted to compromise and delay'. Wilberforce was given to public oratory but personally conflicted in the way that many green campaigners, who for example take flights or use banks that invest in the oil economy, might find themselves today.

219 *The state also funded compensation:* In 1833 £20 million or 5 per cent of the UK national income at the time was paid to four thousand

slave holders (Piketty, *A Brief History of Equality*). Today, this would be a total bill of €120 billion, approximately €39 million to each slave holder (at the time, 0.5 per cent of the national income was spent on education).

219   *Today we are rightly outraged:* We may be seeing another parallel in our own times. Promised vast state investments in the so far unproven (and some argue unfeasible) technology of carbon capture and storage is in reality a further subsidy to the fossil fuel industry, but might perhaps be necessary realpolitik to forge an alliance and make the broader green economic pivot that human survival requires.

219   *Merkel brought billions of euros:* My colleague at IIPP, Damon Silvers, estimates a cost between €69 billion and €93 billion, the equivalent of 15 per cent of Germany's annual federal budget.

220   *develop new forms of work and economy:* 'Place-Based Regeneration: Shaping Structural Change in Germany's Coal Mining Regions', a lecture delivered by Thorsten Posselt, Director of Fraunhofer IIMW, at the Inaugural Summit on the Foundation of Values and Value in the 21st Century, Blavatnik School of Government, University of Oxford, 24 January 2023.

220   *a new mine was opened at Lutzerath:* In 2023 the world watched as more than ten thousand climate protesters, including Greta Thunberg, took part in violent clashes with police, next to machines carving a vast new open-cast coal mine at Lutzerath. It was a process of geo-engineering which necessitated not only the bulldozing of a village but the removal of a wind farm.

220   *Pacific nations on the front line:* In the Pacific, sea and land temperatures are rising at three times the global average. In Fiji, a nation made up of three hundred islands and home to a million people, the state has facilitated the first national blueprint for transition, 'Planned Relocation Guidelines: A Framework to Undertake Climate Change Related Relocation' (2018), published by the Ministry of the Economy. Six villages have been relocated to date, a complex and deeply participatory process that must take into account not only the movement of homes, but also of schools, burial grounds and livelihoods, all in a nation where land cannot be bought or sold.

221 *'emblematic policies':* Bowles and Carlin, 'Shrinking Capitalism'.

223 *Sandel writes about so scathingly:* Sandel, *The Tyranny of Merit.* In *Beyond Schooling,* David Hargreaves, a Cambridge professor, former teacher and government advisor, sets out a compelling idea of what he calls an anarchist education – because it draws on nineteenth-century anarchist beliefs in all human nature – which has many of the characteristics required. Hargreaves's vision is compelling because it is expansive, going beyond pedagogical methods and what should be on the curriculum.

225 *Piketty has modelled:* Piketty, *A Brief History of Equality.* See also Acemoglu and Johnson, *Power and Progress,* in which the authors argue that wealth taxes are an important strategic tool for government to redirect technology investment. Mazzucato has argued repeatedly that the state must direct investment away from what she calls the FIRE economy (financial products, insurance, real estate and other forms of speculation) towards productive sectors including health and education which will grow work and household wealth: see *The Value of Everything.*

225 *along with world leaders of the G20:* In 2021, for example, the G20 agreed to a common tax framework for multinational corporations which was agreed by 130 nations. Like recent moves on wealth taxes, these are steps that many predicted would be impossible to negotiate, but they are happening.

Twenty-First-Century Work: A Radical Re-Conception

228 *'I want a profession':* I wrote about Earl in *Radical Help,* exploring how welfare services designed to support people into work rarely see us as whole humans who want to progress and flourish, but instead as a set of parts – hands or brains, whatever can be best described on a CV, enabling us to take 'any job'.

229 *'being ready':* Levi and Ugolnik, 'Mobilizing in the Interest of Others'. Margaret Levi describes being ready, as the 'Frances Perkins theory of change', in homage to the US union organiser who understood the importance of being sufficiently alert to seize the moment and the spaces for collaborative action. Levi has led an expansive and interdisciplinary research programme looking at

how we could grow a new moral political economy at the Stanford University Center for Advanced Study in the Behavioural Sciences (CASBS). In earlier research Levi, with John Ahlquist (*In the Interest of Others*) looked at the ways in which labour union members frequently take decisions which are in the interests of global labour, but not always in their own personal interests, to develop her idea of a common fate, which I use here. Levi has expanded on the principles in *A Moral Political Economy*, her book jointly authored with Frederica Carugati.

235   *'All reality is made up'*: Taussig, *The Magic of the State*.

Bibliography

Abrams, Rebecca, *The Playful Self: Why Women Need Play in Their Lives* (London: 4th Estate, 1997)

Acemoglu, Daron and Simon Johnson, *Power and Progress* (New York: Basic Books, 2023)

Alqhuist, John S. and Margaret Levi, *In the Interest of Others: Organizations and Social Activism* (Princeton: Princeton University Press, 2013)

Anderson, Benedict, *Imagined Communities: Reflections on the Origin and Spread of Nationalism* (1983; London: Verso, 1991)

Arendt, Hannah, *On Revolution* (1963; London: Penguin, 1973)

Armstrong, Stephen, *The New Poverty* (London: Verso, 2017)

Autor, David, 'Why Are There Still So Many Jobs? The History and Future of Workplace Automation', *Journal of Economic Perspectives*, 29:3 (summer 2015)

——, Caroline Chin, Anna Salomons and Bryan Seegmiller, *New Frontiers: The Origins and Content of New Work, 1940–2018*, National Bureau of Economic Research Working Paper 30389 (2022)

——, David Dorn, Lawrence F. Katz, Christina Patterson and John Van Reenen, 'The Fall of the Labour Share and the Rise of Superstar Firms', *Quarterly Journal of Economics*, 135:2 (May 2020)

Bauluz, Luis et al., *Spatial Wage Inequality in North America and Western Europe: Changes Between and Within Local Labour Markets 1975–2019*, LSE International Inequalities Institute Working Paper 98 (2023)

Beveridge, William, *Unemployment: A Problem of Industry* (London: Longmans, Green, 1909)

Beynon, Huw and Hilary Wainwright, *The Workers' Report on Vickers: The Vickers Shop Stewards Combine Committee Report on Work, Wages, Rationalisation, Closure and Rank-and-File Organisation in a Multinational Company* (London: Pluto Press, 1979)

—— and Ray Hudson, *The Shadow of the Mine: Coal and the End of Industrial Britain* (London: Verso, 2021)

Bloodworth, James, *Hired: Undercover in Low-Wage Britain* (London: Atlantic, 2019)

Boggs Centre, *New Work New Culture Reader*, produced in preparation for Reimagining Work and Culture conference, October 2014 (mimeo)

Boggs, Grace Lee, *New Cultural Reader* (mimeo)

Boggs, James and Grace Lee, *Revolution and Evolution in the Twentieth Century* (New York: Monthly Review Press, 1974)

Bourdieu, Pierre (trans. Richard Nice), *Outline of a Theory of Practice* (Cambridge: Cambridge University Press, 1977)

Boushey, Heather, *Finding Time: The Economics of Work–Life Conflict* (Cambridge, MA: Harvard University Press, 2016)

Bowles, Samuel and Wendy Carlin, 'Shrinking Capitalism: Components of a New Political Economy Paradigm', *Oxford Review of Economic Policy*, 37:4 (2021)

Brown, Lawrence T., *The Black Butterfly: The Harmful Politics of Race and Space in America* (Baltimore: Johns Hopkins University Press, 2021)

Brown, Stuart, *Play: How it Shapes the Brain, Opens the Imagination and Invigorates the Soul* (New York: Penguin, 2010)

Bunting, Madeleine, *Labours of Love: The Crisis of Care* (London: Granta, 2020)

Butler, Lise, *Michael Young, Social Science, and the British Left, 1945–1970* (Oxford: Oxford University Press, 2020)

Butler, Octavia E., *Kindred* (1979; London: Headline, 2018)

Calafati, Luca, Julie Froud, Colin Haslam, Sukhdev Johal and Karel Williams, *When Nothing Works: From Cost of Living to Foundational Liveability* (Manchester: Manchester University Press, 2023)

Carugati, Frederica and Margaret Levi, *A Moral Political Economy: Present, Past and Future* (Cambridge: Cambridge University Press, 2021)

Case, Anne and Angus Deaton, *Deaths of Despair and the Future of Capitalism* (Princeton: Princeton University Press, 2020)

Chang, Ruth, 'Hard Choices', *Journal of American Philosophical Association*, 3:1 (2017)

Clamp, Christina A. and Michael A. Peck (eds), *Humanity @ Work & Life: Global Diffusion of the Mondragon Cooperative Ecosystem Experience* (Cork: Oak Tree Press, 2023)

Cohen, Elizabeth, *The Political Value of Time: Citizenship, Duration and Democratic Justice* (Cambridge: Cambridge University Press, 2018)

Collier, Paul, *Left Behind: A New Economics for Neglected Places* (London: Allen Lane, 2024)

—— and John Kay, *Greed is Dead: Politics after Individualism* (London: Penguin, 2020)

Cooley, Mike, *Architect or Bee? The Human Price of Technology* (1980; London: Hogarth Press, 1987)

Coote, Anna, 'Universal Basic Services and Sustainable Consumption', *Sustainability: Science, Practice and Policy*, 17:1 (2020)

Cottam, Hilary, *Radical Help* (London: Virago, 2018)

——, *Welfare 5.0: Why We Need a Social Revolution and How to Make it Happen*, UCL Institute for Innovation and Public Purpose, Policy Report (IIPP WP 2020-10) (2020)

Coyle, Diane, *GDP: A Brief but Affectionate History* (Princeton: Princeton University Press, 2014)

——, *Markets, State and People: Economics for Public Policy* (Princeton: Princeton University Press, 2020)

Crafts, Nicholas, 'The 15-Hour Week: Keynes's Prediction Revisited', *Economica*, 89:356 (2022)

Crenshaw, Kimberlé, 'Demarginalizing the Intersection of Race and Sex: A Black Feminist Critique of Antidiscrimination Doctrine, Feminist Theory and Antiracist Politics', *University of Chicago Legal Forum*, 1989:1 (1989)

Cunnington Wynn, Lowri, Julie Froud and Karel Williams, *A Way Ahead? Empowering Restanza in a Slate Valley*, Foundational Economy Research Limited report (2022)

Curran, Kevin B., *Organising to Win: A Programme for Trade Union Renewal*, Compass report (2006)

Curtis, Polly, *Behind Closed Doors: Why We Break Up Families and How to Mend Them* (London: Virago, 2022)

Davis, Angela Y., *Women, Race & Class* (1981; London: Penguin, 2021)

Donzelot, Jaques, 'Pleasure in Work', in Graham Burchell, Colin Gordon and Peter Miller (eds), *The Foucault Effect: Studies in Governmentality* (Chicago: University of Chicago Press, 1991)

Dorling, Danny, *Seven Children: Inequality and Britain's Next Generation* (Oxford: Oxford University Press, 2024)

Elf, P., A. Isham and T. Jackson, *Self-Transcendent Experiences and Sustainable Prosperity*, Centre for the Understanding of Sustainable Prosperity Working Paper 32 (2022)

Federici, Silvia, *Caliban and the Witch: Women, the Body and Primitive Accumulation* (2004; London: Penguin, 2021)

——, *Revolution at Point Zero: Housework, Reproduction and Feminist Struggle* (Oakland: PM Press, 2021)

Folbre, Nancy, *The Invisible Heart: Economics and Family Values* (New York: New Press, 2001)

Foucault, Michel (trans. Alan Sheridan), *The Archaeology of Knowledge* (London: Routledge, 1989)

Frankl, Victor E., *The Unheard Cry for Meaning* (New York: Simon & Schuster, 1978)

Fraser, Nancy, *Cannibal Capitalism* (London: Verso, 2022)

Freeman, Joshua, *Behemoth: A History of the Factory and the Making of the Modern World* (New York: W. W. Norton, 2018)

Garlow, Elizabeth and Anne-Marie Slaughter, 'A Worldview of Care and a New Economics', *Daedalus* (winter 2025)

Ghosh, Amitav, *The Nutmeg's Curse: Parables for a Planet in Crisis* (London: John Murray, 2021)

Goldin, Claudia, *Career and Family: Women's Century-Long Journey Towards Equity* (Princeton: Princeton University Press, 2021)

Goodhart, David, *Head Hand Heart: The Struggle for Dignity and Status in the 21st Century* (London: Penguin, 2020)

Gorz, André (trans. Chris Turner), *Reclaiming Work: Beyond the Wage-Based Society* (Cambridge: Polity, 1999)

Graeber, David, 'On the Phenomenon of Bullshit Jobs: A Work Rant', *Strike!*, 3 (August 2013)

—— and David Wengrow, *The Dawn of Everything: A New History of Humanity* (London: Penguin, 2021)

Gramsci, Antonio, *Selections from the Prison Notebooks* (London: Lawrence &Wishart, 1996)

Gratton, Lynda and Andrew Scott, *The 100-Year Life: Living and Working in an Age of Longevity* (London: Bloomsbury, 2016)

Haraway, Donna, *Staying with the Trouble: Making Kin in the Chthulucene* (Durham, NC: Duke University Press, 2016)

Hargreaves, David H., *Beyond Schooling: An Anarchist Challenge* (London: Routledge, 2019)

Harris, Jose, *Beveridge, A Biography* (1977; Oxford: Clarendon Press, 2003)

Hayden, Dolores, *The Grand Domestic Revolution* (Cambridge, MA: MIT Press, 1981)

Hecht, K., M. Savage and K. Summers, 'Why Isn't There More Support for Progressive Taxation of Wealth? A Sociological Contribution to the Wider Debate', *LSE Public Policy Review*, 2:4 (2022)

Heimans, Jeremy and Henry Timms, *New Power: How It's Changing the 21st Century – and Why You Need to Know* (London: Pan Macmillan, 2018)

Heyes, Cecilia, *Cognitive Gadgets: The Cultural Evolution of Thinking* (Cambridge, MA: The Belknap Press of Harvard University Press, 2018)

Higham, Dave, *Rat Hell to Rat Park: The Core Conditions for Recovery. A Manifesto for Change* (Morecambe: Dave Higham Ltd, 2022)

Hochschild, Arlie Russell, *The Managed Heart: Commercialization of Human Feeling* (Berkeley and Los Angeles: University of California Press, 1983)

hooks, bell, *Feminist Theory: From Margin to Centre* (Boston: South End Press, 1984)

Hopkins, Rob, *From What Is to What If: Unleashing the Power of Imagination to Create the Future We Want* (White River Junction: Chelsea Green, 2019)

Horgan, Amelia, *Lost in Work: Escaping Capitalism* (London: Pluto Press, 2021)

Horowitz, Sara, *Mutualism: Building the Next Economy from the Ground Up* (New York: Random House, 2021)

Hunnicutt, Benjamin Kline, *Kellogg's Six-Hour Day* (Philadelphia: Temple University Press, 1996)

Jager, Anton and Daniel Zamora Vargas, *Welfare for Markets: A Global History of Basic Income* (Chicago: University of Chicago Press, 2023)

Kattel, Rainer, Wolfgang Drechsler and Erkki Karo, *How to Make an Entrepreneurial State: Why Innovation Needs Bureaucracy* (New Haven: Yale University Press, 2022)

Kelly, Marjorie, *Owning Our Future: The Emerging Ownership Revolution* (San Francisco: Berrett-Koehler, 2012)

Kenway, Emily, *Who Cares: The Hidden Crisis of Caregiving, and How We Solve It* (London: Wildfire, 2023)

Kimmerer, Robin Wall, *Braiding Sweetgrass* (Minneapolis: Milkweed Editions, 2013)

Klinenberg, Eric, *Palaces for the People: How to Build a More Equal and United Society* (London: Vintage, 2018)

Kohn, Margaret, *Radical Space: Building the House of the People* (Ithaca: Cornell University Press, 2003)

Laloux, Frédéric, *Reinventing Organizations: A Guide to Creating Organizations Inspired by the Next Stage of Human Consciousness* (Brussels: Nelson Parker, 2014)

Lambert, Craig, *Shadow Work: The Unpaid, Unseen Jobs That Fill Your Day* (Berkeley: Counterpoint, 2016)

Lefebvre, Henri (trans. Donald Nicholson-Smith), *The Production of Space* (Oxford: Blackwell, 1991)

Levi, Margaret and Zachary Ugolnik, 'Mobilizing in the Interest of Others', *Daedalus* (winter 2023)

Lichtenstein, Nelson, *Walther Reuther: The Most Dangerous Man in Detroit* (Urbana: University of Illinois Press, 1997)

López Gil, Silvia, 'Las Lógicas del Cuidado', *Diagonal*, 50 (2007)

Lowrey, Annie, *Give People Money: The Simple Idea to Solve Inequality and Revolutionise Our Lives* (London: W. H. Allen, 2018)

MacGillis, Alec, *Fulfillment: Winning and Losing in One-Click America* (London: Scribe, 2021)

Machado de Oliveira, Vanessa, *Hospicing Modernity: Facing Humanity's Wrongs and the Implications for Social Activism* (Berkeley: North Atlantic Books, 2021)

Manzini, Ezio, *Politics of the Everyday* (London: Bloomsbury Visual Arts, 2019)

Marmot, Michael, *The Health Gap: The Challenge of an Unequal World* (London: Bloomsbury, 2015)

——, Jessica Allen, Tammy Boyce, Peter Goldblatt and Joana Morrison, *Health Equity in England: The Marmot Review 10 Years On* (London: Institute of Health Equity, 2020)

Marris, Peter, *Loss and Change* (New York: Pantheon, 1974)

Marx, Karl, *Capital: A Critique of Political Economy* (1867)

Mason, Sarah, 'Chasing the Pink: A Report from our Gamified Future', *Logic(s)*, 6 (2019)

Mayer, Colin, *Prosperity: Better Business Makes the Greater Good* (Oxford: Oxford University Press, 2018)

Mazzucato, Mariana, *The Value of Everything: Making and Taking in the Global Economy* (London: Allen Lane, 2018)

——, *Mission Economy: A Moonshot Guide to Changing Capitalism* (London: Allen Lane, 2021)

Merisotis, Jamie, *Human Work: In the Age of Smart Machines* (New York: Rosetta Books, 2020)

Moore, L. Henrietta and Hannah Collins, *Towards Prosperity: Reinvigorating Local Economies Through Universal Basic Services*, Institute of Global Prosperity Working Paper 01_2020 (2020)

Nadella, Satya, *Hit Refresh* (London: William Collins, 2017)

Neal, Lucy, *Playing for Time: Making Art as if the World Mattered* (2015; Axminster: Triarchy Press, 2023)

Noble, Denis, 'It's Time to Admit that Genes are Not the Blueprint for Life', *Nature*, 626:7998 (8 February 2024)

Noble, Raymond and Denis Noble, *Understanding Living Systems* (Cambridge: Cambridge University Press, 2023)

Nussbaum, Martha C., *Political Emotions: Why Love Matters for Justice* (Cambridge, MA: Harvard University Press, 2013)

Offer, Avner, *The Challenge of Affluence: Self-Control and Well-Being in the United States and Britain since 1950* (Oxford: Oxford University Press, 2006)

O'Mara, Margaret, *The Code: Silicon Valley and the Remaking of America* (New York: Penguin, 2019)

O'Reilly, Tim, *WTF: What's the Future and Why It's Up to Us* (London: Harper Business, 2017)

Ostrom, Elinor, *Governing the Commons: The Evolution of Institutions for Collective Action* (Cambridge: Cambridge University Press, 1990)

——, 'Beyond Markets and States: Polycentric Governance of Complex Economic Systems', *American Economic Review*, 100:3 (June 2010)

Pahlka, Jennifer, *Recoding America: Why Government is Failing in the Digital Age and How We Can Do Better* (New York: Macmillan, 2023)

Perez, Carlota, *Technological Revolutions and Financial Capital: The Dynamics of Bubbles and Golden Ages* (Cheltenham: Edward Elgar, 2002)

——, 'Technological Revolutions and Techno-Economic Paradigms', *Cambridge Journal of Economics*, 34:1 (2010), pp. 185–202.

——, 'Capitalism, Technology and a Green Global Golden Age: The Role of History in Helping to Shape the Future', in Michael Jacobs and Mariana Mazzucato (eds), *Rethinking Capitalism: Economics and Policy for Sustainable Inclusive Growth* (Hoboken: Wiley-Blackwell, 2016)

——, *The Social Shaping of Technological Revolutions* (forthcoming, 2025)

Petersen, Anne Helen, *Can't Even: How Millennials Became the Burnout Generation* (London: Chatto & Windus, 2021)

Pieper, Josef, *Leisure: The Basis of Culture* (1952; London: Faber, 1965)

Piketty, Thomas (trans. Arthur Goldhammer), *Capital in the Twenty-First Century* (Cambridge, MA: The Belknap Press of Harvard University Press, 2014)

—— (trans. Steven Rendall), *A Brief History of Equality* (Cambridge, MA: Harvard University Press, 2024)

Plunkett, James, *End State: 9 Ways Society is Broken and How We Fix It* (London: Trapeze, 2021)

Poo, Ai-Jen, *The Age of Dignity: Preparing for the Elder Boom in a Changing America* (New York: New Press, 2015)

Puig de la Bellacasa, Maria, *Matters of Care: Speculative Ethics in More than Human Worlds* (Minneapolis: University of Minnesota Press, 2017)

Raghuran, Rajan, *The Third Pillar: The Revival of Community in a Polarised World* (London: William Collins, 2019)

Ravn, Olga (trans. Martin Aitken), *The Employees: A Workplace Novel of the 22nd Century* (London: Lolli Editions, 2018)

Raworth, Kate, *Doughnut Economics: Seven Ways to think like a 21st-Century Economist* (London: Random House Business, 2017)

Reid, Alastair J., *United We Stand: A History of Britain's Trade Unions* (London: Allen Lane, 2004)

Rodrik, Dani, *An Industrial Policy for Good Jobs*, The Hamilton Project policy proposal, Brookings (2022)

—— and Stefanie Stantcheva, 'Fixing Capitalism's Good Jobs Problem', *Oxford Review of Economic Policy*, 37:4 (2021)

Rose, Hilary, 'Hand, Brain, and Heart: A Feminist Epistemology for the Natural Sciences', *Women and Religion*, 9:1 (autumn 1983)

Rosenblat, Alex, *Uberland: How Algorithms are Rewriting the Rules of Work* (Oakland: University of California Press, 2018)

Rovelli, Carlo (trans. Erica Segre), *The Order of Time* (London: Penguin, 2018)

Rowley, Peter, *Class Work* (independently published, 2017)

Rushkoff, Douglas, *Survival of the Richest: Escape Fantasies of the Tech Billionaires* (Melbourne: Scribe, 2022)

Saltzman, Amy, *Downshifting: Reinventing Success on a Slower Track* (London: HarperCollins, 1991)

Sandel, Michael J., *The Tyranny of Merit: What's Become of the Common Good?* (New York: Farrar, Straus and Giroux, 2020)

Savage, Mike, *The Return of Inequality: Social Change and the Weight of the Past* (Cambridge, MA: Harvard University Press, 2021)

Schor, Juliet B., *Plenitude: The New Economics of True Wealth* (London: Penguin, 2011)

Schulte, Brigid, *Overwhelmed: How to Work, Love and Play When No One Has the Time* (London: Bloomsbury, 2014)

Schwab, Klaus with Nicholas Davis, *Shaping the Future of the Fourth Industrial Revolution* (London: Penguin, 2018)

Sen, Amartya, 'Equality of What?', in Sterling M. McMurrin (ed.), *The Tanner Lectures on Human Values* (1979; Cambridge: Cambridge University Press, 2010)

——, 'Poor, Relatively Speaking', *Oxford Economic Papers*, 35:2 (July 1983)

Sennett, Richard, *The Craftsman* (London: Penguin, 2009)

Shaheen, Faiza, *Know Your Place* (London: Simon & Schuster, 2024)

Shaiken, Harley, 'Craftsman into Babysitter', in Ivan Illich et al., *Disabling Professions* (1977; New York: Marion Boyars, 2005)

Slaughter, Anne-Marie, *Unfinished Business: Women, Men, Work, Family* (London: Oneworld, 2015)

——, *Renewal: From Crisis to Transformation in Our Lives, Work, and Politics* (Princeton: Princeton University Press, 2021)

—— and Hilary Cottam, 'We Need a New Economic Category', *Atlantic* (September 2021)

Smiley, Erica and Sarita Gupta, *The Future We Need: Organising for a Better Democracy in the 21st Century* (Ithaca: Cornell University Press, 2022)

Smith, Bren, *Eat Like a Fish: My Adventures as a Fisherman Turned Restorative Ocean Farmer* (New York: Vintage, 2019)

Solnit, Rebecca, *A Paradise Built in Hell: The Extraordinary Communities that Arise in Disaster* (New York: Penguin, 2009)

Soni, Saket, *The Great Escape: A True Story of Forced Labor and Immigrant Dreams in America* (Chapel Hill: Algonquin Books, 2023)

Standing, Guy, *Basic Income: And How We Can Make It Happen* (London: Pelican, 2017)

Stockwood, Jason, *Reboot: A Blueprint for Happy, Human Business in the Digital Age* (London: Virgin Books, 2018)

Storey, John and Graeme Salaman, 'Employee Ownership and the Drive to do Business Responsibly: A Study of the John Lewis Partnership', *Oxford Review of Economic Policy*, 33:2 (2017)

Susskind, Daniel, *A World Without Work: Technology, Automation and How We Should Respond* (London: Penguin, 2021)

Susskind, Richard and Daniel Susskind, *The Future of the Professions: How*

Technology Will Transform the Work of Human Experts (Oxford: Oxford University Press, 2022)

Taussig, Michael, *The Magic of the State* (London: Routledge, 1997)

Taylor, Astra, 'The Automation Charade', *Logic(s)*, 5 (2018)

Terkel, Studs, *Working: People Talk About What They Do All Day and How They Feel About What They Do* (Harmondsworth: Penguin, 1974)

Thomas, Keith, *The Ends of Life: Roads to Fulfilment in Early Modern England* (Oxford: Oxford University Press, 2009)

Thompson, E. P., 'Time, Work-Discipline, and Industrial Capitalism', *Past & Present*, 38 (December 1967)

Toynbee, Polly, *Hard Work: Life in Low-Pay Britain* (London: Bloomsbury, 2003)

Tristan, Flora, *The Workers' Union* (1843)

—— (trans. Jean Hawkes), *The London Journal of Flora Tristan* (1842; London: Virago, 1982)

Turner, Victor, *Dramas, Fields, and Metaphors: Symbolic Action in Human Society* (Ithaca: Cornell University Press, 1974)

Twilley, Nicola, *Frostbite: How Refrigeration Changed Our Food, Our Planet and Ourselves* (London: Penguin, 2024)

Tyler, Imogen, *Stigma: The Machinery of Inequality* (London: Zed Books, 2020)

Unger, Roberto Mangabeira, *The Knowledge Economy* (London: Verso, 2019)

Vince, Gaia, *Nomad Century: How to Survive the Climate Upheaval* (London: Allen Lane, 2022)

Walker C., V. Kotecha, A. Druckman and T. Jackson, *Held to Ransom: What Happens When Investment Firms Take Over UK Care Homes*, Centre for the Understanding of Sustainable Prosperity Working Paper 35 (2022)

Warzel, Charlie and Anne Helen Peterson, *Out of Office: The Big Problem and Bigger Promise of Working from Home* (London: Knopf, 2021)

Weheliye, Alexander G., *Habeus Viscus: Racializing Assemblages, Biopolitics, and Black Feminist Theories of the Human* (Durham, NC: Duke University Press, 2014)

Wilkinson, Richard and Kate Pickett, *The Spirit Level: Why Equality is Better for Everyone* (London: Penguin, 2010)

Williams, Eric, *Capitalism and Slavery* (1944; London: Penguin, 2022)

Williams, Fiona, 'A Good-Enough Life: Developing the Grounds for a Political Ethic of Care', *Soundings*, 30 (2005)

Wingfield, Adia Harvey, *Flatlining: Race, Work, and Health Care in the New Economy* (Oakland: University of California Press, 2019)

Winnicott, D. W., *Playing and Reality* (London: Tavistock, 1971)

Wolf, Martin, *The Crisis of Democratic Capitalism* (London: Allen Lane, 2017)

Zuboff, Shoshana, *The Age of Surveillance Capitalism: The Fight for the Future at the New Frontier of Power* (London: Profile, 2019)

Acknowledgements

The experience and ideas of hundreds of people have shaped this book. I'm immensely grateful to every person who joined me at the Imaginings and I feel privileged to have spent time with you. While each individual story and encounter cannot be recounted within the pages of this book, every Imagining has formed a part of the whole. Because I promised to change all names in the event that I would talk or write about the Imaginings, I want to acknowledge the resulting uncomfortable imbalance where those who contributed to some of the most important ideas in the book do not always appear with their real names.

My thanks also go to those who funded the Imaginings and made the work possible. In 2019 the Open Society Foundations awarded me a fellowship from the Economic Justice Program; this funding, combined with the philanthropic support of James Anderson, enabled me to make my UK journeys. I am also grateful to Laudes Foundation and Lumina Foundation for grants which later supported archival research and writing.

My work in the US was made possible by the invitation and fellowship offered by the New Practice Lab at New America. I would particularly like to thank Anne-Marie Slaughter for her invaluable friendship and for the joy of developing ideas

298 The Work We Need

together, and Tara Dawson McGuiness and Elizabeth Garlow, who not only made the work possible but accompanied me as I travelled, offering inspiration and solidarity. It has been so enriching to work with you. Thank you too to Vontisha Fludd and Molly Martin for your support.

The creativity of the Imaginings was enabled by a design process. I would like to thank Jenni Parker and her colleagues at Humanly for collaborating with me on the design of the tools I carried with me. Thank you to Sheri Trevedi for later helping me tweak the tools for a US context.

Pilgrimages rely on the kindness of fellow travellers and from strangers, and as I have noted in the book, I received this in abundance. In the UK I am grateful to Joada Allen, Tessy Britton, Hannah Brooks, Jordan Brompton, Suzanne Clark, Billy Dashien, Will Douglas, Andrea Fitzgerald, Janet Garner, Mark Hodson, Tracey Johnson, Kathlynne Hewitson, Andy Knox, Laura Lake, Winter Lappin, Fiona Lees, Kathy McArdle, Sarah Norman, Sue and Roger Mitchell, Sam Plum, Alec Proffitt, Rebecca Robson, Trina Robson, Peter Rowley, Jason Stockwood, Lisa Smith, Claire Thompson and Rob Walsh.

In the United States I would like to extend my thanks to Genevieve and Matthew Anderson, Aishah Alfadhalah and Emily Lerner at Mera's Kitchen Collective, Michael Brennan and colleagues at Civilla, Regina Campbell, Anmol Chaddha, Shelley Danner, Richard Feldman for the walk of a lifetime, Dr Rita Fields, Michelle Geiss, Jen Guarino, Ritchie Harrison of Everyday Sacred, My-Azia Johnson, Nicole Jordan, Shel Kimen, April Lewis, Brian Lyght, Alec MacGillis, Ben Seigel and Antwuan Wallace.

Returning home, I have been grateful to many people who have offered insight, critique and the generous space of conversation, helping me shape this book in tangible and intangible ways. Thank you: Tom Adeyoola, Iris Andrews, Taufiq Bakiranze, Matthew Bishop, Colin Burns, Rachel Coldicutt, Paul Collier, David Crichton-Miller, Kevin Curran, Hadeel Elshak, Bruno Giussani, Sarita Gupta, Julia Hobsbawm, Sara Horowitz, Terry Irwin, Sven Kimenai, Brendan Martin, Philip McCann, Jamie Merisotis, Gemma Mortensen, Lucy Neal, Michael Peck, Lily Piachaud, Ruth Potts, Kevin Rowan, Jonathan Rutherford, Daniel Sachs, Brigid Schulte, Stefan Stern, David Tuckett, Mabel van Oranje, Laetitia Vitaud, Karel Williams and Haeyoung Yoon.

My thanks to Frederic Laloux for reading an early draft, to Matthew Lockwood for his equally critical eye, and to the much-missed Philippa Brewster, who offered invaluable advice in the middle stages and whose wisdom on writing helped me beyond measure.

I would also like to thank my colleagues at the UCL Institute for Innovation and Public Purpose, who generously took time to discuss emerging ideas; thank you Mariana Mazzucato, Rainer Kattel, Rowan Conway, Iacopo Gronchi, Nai Kalema and Kate Roll. During the writing of the book, I have been honoured to take part in a series of unique interdisciplinary conversations on the role of values in public policy at the Blavatnik School at the University of Oxford and I would like to thank Cecilia Heyes, Colin Mayer and Dennis Snower in particular for taking the time to discuss some of the knottier issues of this book with me. I am also immensely grateful to Margaret Levi and colleagues at CASBS at Stanford University for intellectual friendship and a series of critical conversations on care, and for Margaret Levi's scholarship on communities of fate, which has informed my thinking and writing.

A particular and very special thank you to Carlota Perez, who in addition to inspiring me with her scholarship has been an anchor, a constant source of encouragement and friendship throughout.

Thank you to my agent Georgina Capel for her unfailing support, and to Irene Baldoni and the team at Georgina Capel Associates; to my mighty editor Lennie Goodings and to Susan de Soissons, Zoe Gullen and the team at Virago, with whom I have been so lucky to work again.

Gratitude to Andre Williams at Trifle Studio for my beautiful cover and to Into Art for making the collaboration possible.

And lastly, but with boundless love, thank you Nigel and Mabel.

Index